DOMINATION AND
CULTURAL RESISTANCE

Authority and Power

among an Andean People

Roger Neil Rasnake

Duke University Press

Durham and London   1988

© Duke University Press
All rights reserved
Printed in the United States of America
on acid-free paper ∞

Library of Congress Cataloging-in-Publication Data
Rasnake, Roger Neil, 1951–
Domination and cultural resistance.
Bibliography: p.
Includes index.
1. Quechua Indians—Social life and customs.   2. Quechua
Indians—Ethnic identity.   3. Quechua Indians—Government
relations.   4. Indians of South America—Bolivia—Yura—
Social life and customs.   5. Indians of South America—
Bolivia—Yura—Ethnic identity.   6. Indians of South
America—Bolivia—Government relations.   7. Yura
(Bolivia)—Social life and customs.   1. Title.
F2230.2.K4R37   1988   984'.14   87-35834
ISBN 0-8223-0809-6

for Inge

CONTENTS

ILLUSTRATIONS

Photographs

ACKNOWLEDGMENTS

No work in anthropology is ever an individual undertaking, in spite of the sometimes solitary life experienced in the field or at the writing table. Many people have generously contributed their time and support to make this study a reality; it is thus, in a very real sense, the result of the efforts of all those whose goodwill made it possible to bring the project to fruition.

This study might never have been written without the help, encouragement, intellectual stimulation, and scholarly example of Professor John V. Murra. For fifteen years John Murra has been a good critic and a good friend, and in the course of that time he has taught me many things. First and foremost, he introduced me to a new view of Andean society which is positive and exciting. He argued that we can look underneath the poverty and oppression of present-day rural peoples in the Andes to find the sociocultural continuities which still serve as a source of meaning and purpose for them. He also taught me a great deal about the concept "commitment." His dedication to anthropology as a profession and his demand that we consider the implication of research for the people studied and for the host country are models that we should all follow.

I also would like to thank the other members of my doctoral committee at Cornell, Professors Donald Solá and Thomas Kirsch.

Both were gracious and generous with their time and guidance. Jeff Cole, Marilyn Cole, and Thomas Abercrombie all provided inestimable help in obtaining documents from the Archivo General de la Nación in Buenos Aires and in our discussions about Yura and the study. Other friends and colleagues in the northern hemisphere provided moral support, good ideas and suggestions, and hours of challenging conversation. I cannot refer to all of them here, but I would like to mention Martha Anders, Deborah Caro, Valerie Estes, Olivia Harris, Kevin Healy, Jim Jones, Brook Larson, Mary Ann Medlin, Tristan Platt, and Frank Salomon. Many students in my classes at Goucher College also stimulated me to rethink certain aspects of the study. I especially thank Lisa deLeonardis for her work on the maps and diagrams. Madeline Kotowski patiently retyped much of the manuscript.

In Bolivia, Dr. Gunnar Mendoza, director of the National Archive of Bolivia in Sucre, greatly facilitated my access to litigation and census records from the Yura area. The *padrecitos* Jesús Bello, Luis Alfredo Díaz, Paco Dubert, and especially my good friend Ricardo Senande were always ready to assist in any way they could. Daniel Acebey generously loaned us living quarters when we were in the town of Yura. Luis Morató and Haydée Lara de Morató deserve a special thanks for all their years of friendship.

In Yura there are so many people to whom I should express gratitude that I hardly know where to begin. The Yuras were kind and generous hosts; I still marvel at the warmth with which they received us. Let me at least mention Alejandra Herrera and Justo Quiroga; Julia Puma and Francisco Quiroga; and the Chiquchi alcalde troupe of 1979. Many others, who will go unnamed, were of great assistance during the stay in Yura.

The original research was carried out under the auspices of a Fellowship on Social Change from the Inter-American Foundation. A return trip in 1984 was partially financed by a grant from Goucher College and the stay in 1987 by a Fulbright fellowship.

Above all, I owe the deepest gratitude to Inge Maria Harman, my wife, fellow anthropologist, and companion in the field. As we carried out our two fieldwork projects together, Inge was a constant adviser, colleague, and supporter. Her sensitivity to others is unparalleled. Her editorial hand has been a great help in preparing the present study. Words cannot begin to express my thanks. It is to Inge that this work is dedicated.

INTRODUCTION

Travelers from the Northern Hemisphere who arrive on the Pacific coast of South America encounter, looming before them, the Andes. One of the most impressive and starkly beautiful landscapes on earth, this broken terrain stretches five thousand miles from the mists of Tierra del Fuego and the Antarctic Sea to precipitous peaks in northern Colombia and Venezuela that plunge into the Caribbean. The Andes straddle the equator and sit squarely in the world's tropical zone. Yet due to the great height of this land mass (surpassed only by the Himalayas), the Andean mountain chain creates the conditions for an amazing diversity of climates. Along the mountains' western edge stretch the barren deserts of the Pacific coast; on the eastern slopes lie verdant rain forests; within the rugged, rocky uplands of the central massif are found moist alpine meadows, high, arid steppes, and temperate, lightly forested valleys.

Due in part to this ecological diversity, the Andean region has been the scene of one of the most fascinating successful attempts at creating the level of social complexity that we distinguish with the label "civilization." In all of human history only a few cases of independent civilizational development have occurred. Andean civilization, which evolved largely unaffected by currents from other centers of complex culture, is in that select group. The process stretched over more than four thousand years, with its early beginnings in coastal fishing villages and the highland ceremonial centers of migrating hunters and incipient farmers.[1] Population movements, religious proselytization, economic exchange, warfare, and political expansion all apparently contributed to the emergence of such celebrated Andean cultural traditions as Chavín, Nazca, Moche, Chimú, and Tiwanaku. Over this long period of contact and communication, involving moments both of expansion and contraction and of greater and lesser unity, Andean peoples came to share widespread patterns of cultural practice and expression whose common themes spread from one area to another and underwent continual restructuring. Especially in the core of the central Andes, the area from what is today Ecuador through northern Argentina, we find a coherent culture area that has retained considerable unity into the contemporary period.

Political evolution in the Andes a thousand years ago led to the creation of Wari, an expansive, all-inclusive state which united scores, perhaps hundreds, of local ethnic groups. Processes of independent political growth and dissolution finally reached their zenith in the great state of Tawantinsuyu, the Inka Empire. This Andean experiment in civilization was abruptly cut short by the military incursion of another rather hybrid empire—Spain. Spawned by the centuries-long struggle against Islam, which spread into Spain from North Africa, fiercely Catholic in a puritanical way, and a major entrepôt for expanding mercantile capitalism, Spain came to the Andes. Or, rather, Spaniards came, drawn from various social classes and accompanied by their slaves, wives, priests, and concubines, and, naturally, their horses. They descended upon the ancient cities and shrines of the Peruvian coast. They climbed to the villages and *estancias* of the high Andean valleys and on to the cold and windswept Altiplano, the high intermontane plateau. They came for gold and silver, which they found—especially the latter. They came to convert the heathen to the Catholic faith. They came to rule; and rule they did, and in some ways, still do, in spite of the fact that the Andean republics have all been independent from their former colonial masters for well over a century and a half.

Change—and the conflicts and struggles that precede, accompany, and follow it—is the essence of the human condition. Change has certainly not been lacking in the Andes. But what of the great Andean civilizational experiment? Has it been erased by subsequent events? As we shall see in the coming pages, the answer to that question is quite clearly "no."

Andean history did not come to an end with the Spanish invasion and conquest. It continues today in the lives of the protagonists of this book, the Yura of central Bolivia. The Yuras' way of life represents one manifestation of an Andean solution to the human condition. As a people the Yura have retained and reformulated many aspects of the original Andean worldview. Yet this retention is not an anachronistic throwback to bygone days, a result of lack of contact with the wider world. It is, I will argue, a cultural strategy, one that is perhaps not consciously chosen, or even verbally articulated, but a strategy nonetheless.

As we shall see, the Yura appear to be culturally conservative; they cultivate with care an identity and a pattern of social life that draws heavily on their Andean past. This strategy has united them for centuries as they faced, first, Spanish colonial domination and, subsequently, the ruling hispanicized national elite which at present controls the Bolivian economy and the structures of the republican state. For centuries the Yura have confronted (as have other Andean peasants) a dominant class which denigrates them and decries their "ignorance"; it has exploited their labor, expropriated their agricultural products and animals, and stolen their lands—not to mention taken their lives. The Andean world which the peasants of Yura have constructed in the late twentieth century must be seen in terms of the reality of the domination they face. Their efforts to maintain autonomy and a unique identity are for them a form of cultural resistance.

I

THE CULTURAL TRADITIONALISM OF THE ANDEAN WORLD

The Reality of Foreign Domination and "Cultural Resistance"

The people of the rural Andes present a seeming paradox. For over four hundred and fifty years they have been subjected to control by a succession of external rulers: European invaders, then European-oriented, colonial elite classes, and finally hispanicized national dominant classes. All of these have attempted to impose on the rural peoples of the Andes their own cultures and institutions, first those of Spain and then later those of the nascent republics of Ecuador, Peru, and Bolivia. Yet today, in spite of centuries of pressure from above, many Andean ethnic groups have maintained a way of life—or more specifically, symbolic configurations and complex modes of organization—which is derived from their Andean past and which distinguishes them from the hispanicized world of the "modern" classes inhabiting the towns and cities of the three countries. The continuities that characterize Andean rural life are not due simply to a lack of awareness of alternatives or to isolation from the national elites and the mechanisms of the state. Peasant populations of the Andes, unlike the neighboring lowland tribal peoples of the Amazonian rain forest, have long experience in dealing with larger and more encompassing political entities. As a case in point, the Yura, the peasant group of the southern Bolivian Andes who form the focus of this study, have confronted state impositions at least from the time of the Inka Empire. Historical evidence points to the prior creation of state-level institutions even before the Inkas appeared on the scene.[1]

When the Spanish expeditionary force invaded the Andes after 1532, its military successes therefore did not lead to the creation of new, complex civilizational forms where none had previously existed. Rather, the Spanish conquest brought about the destruction and replacement of the overarching Inkan and regional state structures which the invaders found in place at their arrival. As sensitive as some of them were to the complexities of the Andean civilization they found,[2] the new colonial regime was not in the business of upholding what many of the administrators and ecclesiastics saw as an alien and barbaric political structure.

Furthermore, their goal was to create a new colonial order to provide economic support for the motherland and permit those who came to make their fortune. Given the dense populations of the Andean highlands, that goal could best be accomplished by creating ways to control the labor of Andean agriculturalists and herders and to appropriate their wealth. The new Spanish rulers soon established the institutional means by which the defeated populations were forced to provide their resources and their work in fields and mines for the benefit of colonists and Crown. At the same time Spanish policy imposed a continually more severe and rigid proselytization in the Catholic faith, apparently based on the assumption that Andean peoples would, as they accepted Christianity, also come to know and accept, part and parcel, the hispanic worldview and its fundamental values.

The Spaniards and their successors were able to establish efficient means of economic extraction, even at the cost of drastic depopulation and the massive flight of groups to areas beyond colonial control. Although native Andean groups fought the worst abuses of the new exploitative institutions in the Crown's courts and even, from time to time, on the battlefield and in millenarian movements, they generally acquiesced in paying the head tax and working in the mines; it was for them the simplest strategy in the struggle to maintain a bare existence for themselves and their families.

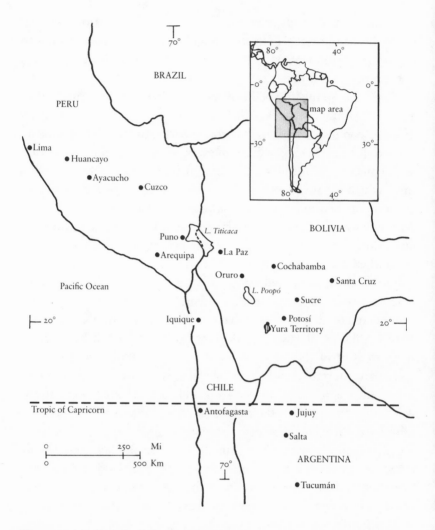

Figure 1.1 Bolivia and the Central Andes

However, the Spaniards failed in the attempt to convince Andean groups to abandon their cultural heritage. The rural peoples did not easily give up their ethnic identities in those early decades. Indeed, even now many groups retain an ethnic identification which is distinctly Andean, not European. In terms of their social order such peoples organize themselves according to models foreign to hispanic patterns, in ways that historical investigation shows are contemporary versions of forms already in place from the earliest years of European rule. The same is true of other aspects of Andean life in the late twentieth century. For example, the agricultural and herding practices found in many areas today are clearly the result of adaptations over millennia to the special Andean environment. In the symbolic realm the ritual life of these groups creates a symbolic context which refers to their indigenous internal organization and to the physical world around them in an idiom alien to the European elites.

The paradox, then, lies in the fact that Andean peoples have accepted the burdens of the state, rarely directly challenging its legitimacy and impositions, yet, on the other hand, they have not accepted the "symbolic universe" (including both systems of values and common conceptions) that the urban, nationally oriented population would have them adopt. Nor do they accept the concomitant social identity that these latter find more amenable.

There is no simple explanation for such cultural continuities in the Andes. Rural people's integration into the wider economy (Caballero 1983; Figueroa 1983), the historical patterns of social relations reproduced from colonial times (Service 1955; Kleymeyer 1982), and the way these are related to present-day structures of power and control (Bourricaud 1967) have all been advanced to account for the continuing retention and coherence of Andean cultural patterns. The research described in the following pages argues that many of these factors can be more adequately highlighted and integrated into a wider pattern of analysis by examining one central institution—the indigenous authorities found in local rural groups throughout the Andean republics. Indeed, the authorities provide real insight into the patterns of resistance, passive and active, that Andean peasants have shown for centuries to the impositions of the national society. Through the study of the indigenous authority and service roles that are still retained today, we can examine the complex and ambiguous links between Andean social groups and the states that now incorporate them. Furthermore, our understanding of the process by which ethnic groups are able to maintain their autonomy can be broadened by adopting a diachronic view of the authorities, by delving into their long history, since it is now quite clear that for centuries the indigenous leaders have served as the primary mediators between the "top" and the "bottom"—in the past between the component ethnic groups and the rulers of the various colonial regimes, and today between the peasants and the modernizing governments of the Andean nations.

The present state of our knowledge of historical processes and of varying patterns of symbolic resistance is not complete enough, unfortunately, to undertake a general study of indigenous authorities throughout the Andes. These pages are therefore devoted to the examination of a single case, the Yura of the department of Potosí in south-central Bolivia. The Yura have nurtured their authority roles with care up to the present; even today these posts are a major focus of activity in social and ritual life. For the Yura, the authorities—whom they call *kuraqkuna,* or "elders"—mediate structurally as a direct social link between the Bolivian state and the ethnic group members. For example, the kuraqkuna are responsible for collecting the land taxes that have for centuries been paid to the colonial and republican governments; and they continue to serve as constables for the state's local magistrates.

As we shall see, they also act as *symbolic* mediators, and it is clear that this is the more important aspect of the roles today. In the context of ritual the kuraqkuna create models of Yura social organization which tie them to a sacred vision of the world. In rituals —and especially in festivals—the actions of the elders serve to construct a symbolic formulation of the Yura ethnic group's internal organization which is then intertwined with a broader set of meanings referring to Yura relations with other social groupings within Bolivia as well as with the state. The elders' ritual actions provide for themselves and their fellow Yura (who participate wholeheartedly with them in these symbolic performances) a coherent vision of their world and their place in it. Ritual thus reproduces the meanings and values that orient the Yura understanding of their placement within their own territory and in the larger social world. But, as we shall see, rituals can also serve as a basis for change, for reformulating those concepts and values.

Before we turn to the specific case of Yura, though, let us briefly review several ethnological studies that have looked at Andean local-level authorities.

The Warayuq: Studies of Andean Authorities

As early as 1919 Pastor Ordóñez stressed the ritual and traditional elements of the indigenous Andean authorities, what he termed the *varayocc* (or, to use a more modern spelling, the *warayuq*, or "staff bearers"). He viewed the peasant leaders around Cuzco as an institution that surely had its origins among the Inkas. The alcaldes, regidores, and campos he saw in native Andean villages were, for him, the modern descendants of the Inka *tukuy rikuq* (inspector) and *llaqta kamayuq* (town leader) described in the early Spanish sources. Basing his description of the contemporary offices largely on what he observed in the single Cuzco community of Acomayo, he urged the national government to reconsider its disdain and neglect of these roles. According to Ordóñez, the warayuq "would offer better and more efficient services if they were officially recognized as authorities which serve as a link that unites the *misti* [the mestizo, or hispanicized] classes with the indigenous groupings in the perfect, harmonic and progressive march of the nation" (1920:42).[3]

More than twenty years later Bernard Mishkin described the set of Quechua authorities he had encountered in the late 1930s in a community near Urcos in southern Peru. In contrast to Ordóñez, he stressed the Spanish characteristics of the warayuq there, emphasizing the facts that, as in Acomayo, all the names of the posts were in Spanish and "the functions of the Quechua officers parallel those of the Spanish village officialdom in the 16th and 17th centuries" (1946:443). He recognized that the *varas*, the staffs that the authorities carry, "possess some religious significance, but precisely what is unclear" (1946:444).[4] Mishkin also observed that there was considerable variation in the political organization of different villages. Although his own experience in Kauri led him to doubt the continued vitality of the warayuq system, he was nevertheless impressed by a description of the strength of similar authorities in

Q'iru. It was his general conclusion, however, that the indigenous authorities, a syncretic phenomenon to begin with, were gradually breaking down in southern Peru except in extremely isolated areas.

An examination of the warayuq in the north of Peru was carried out by William Stein in Hualcan, not far from the hacienda of Vicos. A nominally free community when it was studied in 1952, Hualcan was the home of Andean peasants who maintained a set of authorities like those in Acomayo and Kauri. Here, too, the names are Spanish, and the chief official, called a *comisario*, is described as being nothing more than an errand boy for the mestizo authorities in nearby Carhuáz (Stein 1961:182–91). The warayuq, however, are said to have important roles in the festive life of the community, roles which structure ritual action (1961:262–63). Following the pattern of the day, Stein also describes the warayuq of Hualcan as if they formed an institution solely at the level of the community. Yet there are indications that this organization may be integrated into a much more encompassing system. For example, at one point he mentions an official at a higher level than the comisario of Hualcan, one who ruled over "a division of the District of Carhuáz, a leader of another varayuh organization which is separate from that of Hualcan" (1961:186). He then states that the two high-level officials of this larger warayuq system share their authority in the numerous communities of a large section of the Santa River valley—one official governed the villages on the east bank of the river, and the other those on the west. Indeed, the highest authority for the west bank is chosen in alternate years from Hualcan itself (1961:195). Unfortunately, the warayuq system is not a main focus of Stein's study, so these loose ends are not tied. The psychologistic tone of the study (which Stein later regretted) took the author's attention elsewhere, and the indigenous organization was not examined further.

One researcher who focused primarily on indigenous authorities was Gabriel Escobar. His study (1961) makes several advances over Stein's, going above the community level to look at indigenous leaders in an entire zone. It struggles with the ambiguities of the relationship between indigenous and local-level mestizo state officials. It is more dynamic in examining the creation of state-mandated authorities and their links to the traditional warayuq. Yet Escobar encountered the same situation as Mishkin and Ordóñez: although village authorities are frequently strong in Peru, the higher levels of indigenous authority (those roles that Stein saw but did not pursue) are either greatly weakened or have apparently largely disappeared.

In the sixties and seventies the studies of Andean communities and groups multiplied, giving a wider base for comparison. Each community study—and most of them have been community studies —addresses the question of indigenous authorities more or less directly. On one hand, some confirm that in a few areas of Peru the indigenous political organization has been lost completely. Brush, for example, found no remnant of it in Spanish-speaking Uchuc-marca in the northern part of the country (1977:51). In other areas, especially in the south, the community-level authorities have been beaten down and fragmented. Núñez del Prado writes that the indigenous leaders of Kuyo Chico and surrounding villages close to Pisac are "absolutely subordinate to the Mestizo authorities" (1973:16). Yet in still other areas of Peru the warayuq have re-tained a certain freedom of action and function in the community which suggests that they are more than mere puppets of the national society.

Perhaps most notable in this respect is Isbell's description, from the department of Ayacucho, of the three systems of warayuq she found in Chuschi. One set of warayuq worked under national gov-ernmental authorities; another group supervised herding in the high pastures; while a third, which was organized according to the moi-eties of the town of Chuschi, oversaw affairs in the population cen-ter and in the surrounding cultivated fields. The latter authorities had a very important ritual role in the annual cleaning of the irri-gation canals that bring water from highland lakes to the villagers' fields (1978:83–93, 138–45). Mitchell (1972) has described a simi-lar, if somewhat more reduced, warayuq system in the Ayacucho district of Quinua.

The list of Peruvian studies could be expanded with further examples of the local-level authorities. All could be placed on the same continuum, however, from the relative complexity and inde-pendence of the system in Chuschi to the subordination of Kuyo

Chico and Kauri, and even to its loss, as in Uchucmarca. None of these shed much more light on the nature of the system or its history than we have already seen.

Moving south into Bolivia, we find a contrast between the former hacienda areas and those zones where Andean peoples historically retained control of their lands. In studies of ex-haciendas, such as Compi on the Altiplano and Charazani in the high steppes and mountain valleys north of Lake Titicaca, most peasant groups accepted a new sindicato (or labor union) structure after the agrarian reform promulgated in 1953 by the government of the Movimiento Nacionalista Revolucionario. The sindicatos of the ex-haciendas were to be ruled each by a committee of twelve secretaries led by a secretary general. In the case of Compi the sections of the community soon split apart and the secretary system withered (Buechler and Buechler 1971:53–54). In Charazani, where an ethnic identity and traditional social groupings unite settlements over a large area, the system of secretaries seems to have been molded by the people in a way that parallels the former indigenous authorities, where ritual responsibilities were as important as political ones (Bastien 1978:62).

Recent research in the non-hacienda areas is perhaps more intriguing in this light. Although no study in Bolivia has yet focused exclusively on indigenous political organization in either type of peasant community, a significant change is evident, especially among those who have studied independent, non-hacienda areas. The perspective has shifted from the single, delimited small-scale community as the unit of investigation to one which attempts to see the relationships linking many communities dispersed over large areas.

There are two principal reasons for this shift. One lies in the nature of the social groups themselves while the other is related to a change in the way anthropology is being done. In many parts of what is today Bolivia the *ayllu*, an Andean organizational form with its roots in the prehispanic past, continues to exist as a more inclusive principle of social order than one finds in Peru. After 1928 the Peruvian central government imposed the concept of *comunidad indígena* (native community) on the rural population. This obliged peasants to adopt a mode of local organization which specifically did not recognize intercommunity alliances and a wider ethnic sense (Escobar 1967:42; Murra 1984:128–30).

Andean villages in Peru could thus protect access to lands at least in their immediate vicinity by incorporating as separate legal entities. The resulting insularity gave many investigators the impression, however false, that the atomism of community and group deriving from this legal maneuver was an Andean cultural trait, rather than a relatively recent strategy (consistent with Peruvian national legislation) to maintain a certain degree of control over their subsistence base.

When field-workers began research in the Peruvian Andes, many apparently assumed that what they found were examples of what Eric Wolf termed the "closed corporate community" (1957). Many of his postulates seem appropriate for the Andean rural community. However the model, as Wolf has recently recognized (1986), seems "overly schematic" for describing patterns of community boundedness which subsequent historical research shows to be derived from forces related to the experience of colonialism and (one might add) neocolonialism. In the Andes, where far-reaching ties have traditionally been maintained among both ecological levels and ethnic groups, the "closed corporate" nature of peasant villages would have been highly suspect, even if such villagers have attempted to restrict outside control and access by the dominant classes. If researchers had included a historical dimension to buttress assumptions about the lack of openness of Andean communities, they would have taken into account the impact of the particular political history of twentieth-century Peru.

The situation has been rather different in Bolivia. In spite of the very real pressures on indigenous lands and social autonomy in this century, ayllu organization continues, in many areas, to incorporate hundreds, even thousands, of households. While one cannot utterly disagree with Orlove and Custred's focus (1980) on the importance of the household as a fundamental unit of production and socialization, it is nevertheless true that the ayllu order as it exists today places a different perspective on any attempt to define community. Bastien's Charazani, as well as research by Olivia Harris among the Laymis (1978a, 1982a, 1985), Platt among the Machas (1976, 1981, 1982), and Godoy among the Jukumanis (1983, 1985) have all demonstrated the continuity and vigor of these large-scale groupings; and Yura, the subject of this study, comprises an ethnic group on such a scale. The continuing existence of the ayllu in Bolivia has thus helped to show by comparison that the fragmentation of ethnic groupings in Peru is not an ancient characteristic but is rather due to recent changes in the rural social order. The ongoing reality of the ayllu also has its methodological implications, leading to a shift away from the traditional community study. The present study, then, joins those cited above in its rejection of the restricted community-level view in order to examine an entire ethnic region.

The ability to "see" social entities such as these large-scale ayllus is also due to a reformulation of the questions that are asked, or, as I have said, in the way anthropology is done. This refocusing has come about in recent years as ethnographers have begun to absorb the implications of historical studies of both prehispanic states and of indigenous polities that retained much of their coherence during the colonial period.

John Murra (1964, 1975, 1980) has led the way in this, accompanied by Tom Zuidema (1964, 1977, 1978) and John Rowe (1946, 1982). They have been joined by Larson (1984), Pease (1978, 1980), Platt (1981), Rostworowski (1977, 1978, 1983), Salomon (1980), Stern (1983), Spalding (1974, 1984), and Wachtel (1973, 1977), among others. One result of these studies has been to reorient our investigations away from the atemporal analysis of Andean peoples that treated them as just another case of Third World peasants without a past. Rather, there is a new emphasis on cultural and structural continuities, so that tradition is not understood as mere sterile custom, but rather as a resource that defines a group's internal and external relations in a changing context of power relations.[5] These historical studies, combined with the real differences of social groupings in the southern Andes, have led to real advances in our understanding of contemporary Andean society.

The present study is very much rooted in these developments. By examining Yura in the light of the past, many questions can be clarified—in this one case—that seemed unresolvable before. Archival documents show, for example, that the authorities of Yura, the kuraqkuna, are indeed linked historically to the ethnic lords who ruled at the time of the Spanish invasion. We no longer have to say, as Pastor Ordóñez did, that they were "surely" instituted by the Inkas or that they were, as Mishkin thought, entirely Spanish creations. But this historical descent was no simple thing. Rather, we see that the indigenous authorities of the area underwent a gradual but fundamental transformation through the centuries in an ongoing struggle to respond to the exploitative mechanisms of the state. At some moments this was a very dramatic process, while at others it was a subtle reorganization that came about as the Yura reflected on changing conditions and opportunities. For other periods, unfortunately, we still know nothing at all.

It also becomes clear that as large as the ayllu ethnic group is today, it too has suffered from the fragmentation of Andean structures so common in other areas. This came about from the continuing attempts of the state to strengthen its control of the peasant population on the one hand, and from the rejection by ethnic leaders of the onerous extractive duties that the Spanish regime attempted to force on them on the other. Yura itself is an example of a kind of ethnogenesis, to use a term coined by Soviet ethnographers, in that the contemporary ethnic identification of "being a Yura" was created by ayllu members from the breakup of larger, more inclusive groupings.

History, both that reconstructed from archival sources and that based on a people's own understanding of their past, is therefore important in both theory and method to what transpires in these pages. However, while the research this book describes was carried out with the past as a point of reference, it is an ethnological—not a historical—study, and it attempts to enlarge our understanding of the way of life of a living human group. One of its specific goals is to fill a lacuna that exists in the ethnographic record of Andean peoples; that is, no other research has undertaken the detailed study of the indigenous political leadership of one of the large ayllus of Bolivia. With that end we shall examine how the kuraqkuna of Yura reflect the group's social organization and social categories, as well as the ways in which they participate in ritual life and thereby address, in the context of the festivals they sponsor, the most basic concepts and values the Yura hold concerning how the world is ordered.

As we examine each of these topics in turn, two things will gradually become clear. First, although the nature of the power exercised by the kuraqkuna is no simple affair of the imposition of will or of domination, its characteristics lead us to emphasize the importance of symbolic action for the creation of consensus and the acceptance of authority, a theoretical consideration to which we shall return. Second, it will become apparent that the Yura do not retain the kuraqkuna out of a blind, unwavering conformity to a mythic Andean tradition, divorced from the awareness of their real position as participants in a state structure in which they find themselves at the bottom. Here I would like to draw a clear line of demarcation between this study and those which look for some species of "pure" Andean society unaffected by the realities of four centuries of colonial subjugation. The kuraqkuna of Yura are not of interest to us simply as a case of supposed cultural conservatism. Rather, we shall establish that the systems of meanings and actions surrounding these roles respond to the Yuras' acute perception of their place in the broader society. The Yura retain and support the kuraqkuna not from inertia, but through an implicit awareness of their unifying power for the group as a whole.

A further goal is a more theoretical one: to advance our understanding, through the study of the particular, of the relationship through time between symbolic structures and social relationships. The perspective taken here assumes that members of human groups produce and reproduce a shared understanding of the world, embodied in language and in a shared symbolic framework. While we say that such a symbolic framework is shared, it is necessary to recognize that such sharing is always only approximate; and it is internally never fully coherent or systematic (for it to be so would require a rigidity in thought and action that the flux of social life never permits). These shared sets of meanings are constantly challenged by competing definitions, values, concepts, and demands, which may exist alongside the more inclusive symbolic frameworks and which are brought to the fore in specific social contexts. Other, competing, symbol systems are also newly formulated through human creativity in the course of lived history. Nevertheless, we can point to these widely shared symbolic frameworks, which anchor and orient social groups, as a central aspect of what is commonly termed culture. Such shared understandings, developed in social action, are grounded in the realities of relationships of political and economic control; but they are never simply mirror images of these. Rather, I argue that such sets of meanings are in a dialectical relationship with structures of power and domination. The symbolic framework serves, often enough, to reproduce and legitimate these relationships; but within these shared sets of meanings there always exist the seeds to challenge them and to initiate change. To illuminate this dialectical relationship between structures of power and systems of meaning we need to adopt a diachronic perspective, that is, one that is essentially concerned with examining change through time.

Within the dual goals of, on one hand, studying a specific Andean group and, on the other, advancing somewhat the understanding of the relationship between shared symbolic systems and a changing social order, we will spin out the story of the Yura: their authorities, their evolving role in what is today Bolivian society, and their view of themselves and the world around them, including the supernatural forces that they conceive to guide their destiny.

Fieldwork in Yura

It is the nature of anthropology that one accomplishes such general ends as those outlined above only by the very concrete method and experience of fieldwork. Since the following pages focus on a particular place and provide a great deal of information about the people who inhabit it, it seems appropriate, before we turn to a brief preview of the chapters to come, to describe how the *cantón* of Yura came to be chosen and how the research was carried out.

As is frequently the case with those momentous events and occurrences that change one's life, the very existence of the people of Yura first came to the attention of Inge Harman (my fellow anthropologist and wife) and myself by chance. The year was 1975, and Inge and I were studying Quechua at the Instituto de Idiomas de los Padres de Maryknoll in Cochabamba, Bolivia, after having taken a year off from our graduate studies. A fellow student, a Galician priest named Ricardo Senande, had recently been assigned to the Yura area as part of his pastoral domain and had become fascinated with the people and their way of life. He communicated that excitement to us, and we resolved to learn more about the region and to place it on our growing list of possible sites for anthropological fieldwork. On a visit to Potosí later that year we were disappointed when we were unable to visit Yura due to difficulties in scheduling transportation; but in compensation we did manage to interview a number of persons familiar with the zone. We went back to the United States to resume our studies, greatly excited by the prospect of returning to Yura to carry out our research.

The decision to choose a specific field site is never an easy one, and the reasons that lead to the selection of one area over another are not always based on research interests alone. Yet as Inge and I discussed the possibility of choosing Yura for our two fieldwork projects, a number of factors led us to place it high on the list. One was the fact that it is an area in which the indigenous folk largely control their own lands, a characteristic of large parts of southern Bolivia which had, due to an earlier focus of many studies on haciendas or ex-haciendas, received little attention. Second, the apparent strength of Andean organizational principles—especially the facility with which our interviewees spoke about the ayllus—reinforced the choice. Third, we wanted not to carry out yet another community study but rather to focus on an entire region. We had learned that the ethnic region of Yura covered a large territory and, in spite of its arid environment, was still today the home of over a hundred small communities and thousands of people. A regional study, then, was both possible and necessary in Yura. The fact that Yura was representative of a major, but previously unstudied, geographic section of the department of Potosí (that is, someplace besides the Norte de Potosí) was an additional element in the decision. A quick review of archival sources in Sucre had also revealed a number of what looked to be important colonial and republican documents about the area, so that we could be sure of placing the contemporary situation into a larger historical context.

Furthermore, it was clear that in spite of the evident traditionalism of the Yura, they still had been in long-term contact with the national society around them, due primarily to their proximity to Potosí and the mines there. That is, these people were no Andean "fossils," but a living, vibrant people who had adapted their way of life to the currents and vicissitudes of history. The reports of a relatively benign climate and magnificent views of mountain and valley, as well as the reputation of the Yura as open, amiable people, only served to confirm our decision.

As it turned out, the choice of Yura could not have been better. When we arrived in October 1977 to begin the fieldwork, we were received with interest and goodwill. I soon saw that the topic I wished to research, the indigenous leadership system, was a suitable one, since the Yura maintained an elaborate and cohesive set of authority posts. Inge also found that Yura was an excellent place to investigate her research problem, the organization of mutual aid in labor relations (see Harman 1987). We soon had many Yura friends who, in the main, were pleased that two *gringuitos* (as we are still called, in spite of our towering over them) were interested in their institutions and their lives. They were intrigued by our growing command of Quechua and amused by our insistence on writing everything down.

We made our base location in a house loaned to us by some ex-residents who now lived in Potosí; it was located in a *rancho,* or hamlet, on the edge of the central village of Yura. We also spent time in settlements in other valleys, especially in the planting season and during local festivals, in order to participate in daily life in a range of communities. During the two years we spent in Yura we came to know most of the territory at first hand. Depending on where we were, we cooked for ourselves (necessarily a simple affair) or we arranged to eat with families. And, as food sharing and exchange is a major form of Yura sociability, we were soon involved in a network of mutual giving and receiving of staples and other items.

Much of the descriptive ethnographic data utilized in the following pages came from participant observation: watching what others did and taking part in the activities ourselves. A great deal of the information to be found here came from nonstructured interviews, mostly carried out in Quechua. In addition, during the course of the study I also conducted formal interviews on a number of topics, including fiesta sponsorship, labor migration, and social organization, following a written schedule of questions in Quechua. Most interviews concerning the kuraqkuna, the indigenous authorities, were accomplished in this way. Nevertheless, as is often true in anthropological research, some of the interpretations of events and practices in Yura which I found most fruitful were first mentioned, often in passing, in informal conversations over a bowl of corn beer or as we worked in the field or rested in the patios in the evenings.

Some Yuras were especially good informants on a wide range of topics and took an interest in the work themselves; I have mentioned a few of them in the acknowledgments. As the months passed I tended to turn to these ten or twelve closest friends as key informants. However, we worked to maintain a broad range of contacts with Yuras throughout the region during the course of the research, so that this study represents the contributions of hundreds of Yuras.

We remained in Yura until October 1979, leaving for two months during the second year to carry out archival research in Sucre and Potosí (the result of which, combined with other sources obtained after returning to the United States, forms the basis for chapters 5 and 6). I have since been fortunate enough to return to Yura three times for shorter periods, for several weeks in June 1981, for a good part of the (northern) summer of 1984, and off and on during 1987. In those times I have been able to renew friendships and be brought up to date on important events. The area continues to be a focus of research interest as Yuras develop new institutions, such as the recently formed (and now faltering) peasant unions, which have been the most recent topic of investigation.

The Study Described: A Preview

In the previous pages we have presented the overall goals of the study and placed them in the context both of previous studies

carried out among Andean peoples and of a general theoretical perspective related to symbolism, power, and history. This serves as a
way to think about the overall concept of the story about to begin.
To set the stage, we also described something of the experience of
living among the Yura and of the way the research was carried out.
But before asking the actors to find their marks so the curtain can
rise, let us quickly look at the program.

The study is organized into three parts, all of which highlight
different aspects of the lives of the Yura. The first section, chapters 2 through 4, is largely an ethnographic presentation of Yura.
We look at the social group and their world today, the physical
environment they inhabit, the relations they maintain with others
in their midst, and their own ways of organizing themselves. The
kuraqkuna are also described in some detail. Part two is devoted
to a sketch of the history of the Yura and their indigenous leaders.
In chapter 5 we begin with a brief recounting of the large Andean
polity to which the predecessors of the Yura apparently owed their
allegiance; their incorporation into the Inka Empire and their response to the heavy impositions and reorganizations of the Spanish
colonial regime are then described. In the colonial period one constant pressure they faced from above was that of a progressive fragmentation of the group and a "leveling" of indigenous authority.
This continued through the centuries, a process in which the populations of the Andean polities, each with their own ethnic identity
and pattern of organization, were gradually turned into "Indians"
(at least as far as the Spanish elites were concerned). In chapter 6
we see a culmination of this process in the insurrection of 1781,
when the hereditary principle of succession was replaced by a rotational sharing of the roles. The policies and exactions of the central
government toward indigenous peoples during the republican era
(after Bolivia gained its independence from Spain in 1825)—and
the concomitant experience of the Yura—are also briefly reviewed.

In part three we return to the present in order to focus once
again on the kuraqkuna and their central role in social life today
—their festival sponsorship. It is the goal of this section to enter
into the "meaning-world" of the Yura native authorities in order to
examine how they relate in ritual to their fellows as well as how they

conceive of the supernatural world, for which they act as important mediators. Chapter 7 is devoted to a discussion of festival forms, for festival sponsorship currently involves a considerable investment of energy and resources, not only on the part of the kuraqkuna, but for other kinds of fiesta hosts as well. In this chapter we clarify the categories of festivals and recount the festival cycle of the group. Chapter 8 goes on to a detailed description and analysis of one such kuraqkuna festival, Reyes (Epiphany). In the context of Reyes we examine the social symbolism that forms the core of these ritual performances.

Chapter 9 looks at the symbolic world of the kuraqkuna more closely by focusing on a key symbol closely associated with the kuraqkuna's activities, the *kinsa rey,* or wooden staff of authority, that is kept with them during their term of office. By investigating the ideas and rituals which surround this sacred object—and through an analysis in chapter 10 both of various Yura divinities and of yet another festival, Carnaval—we are able to delve more deeply into the complex sets of meanings that the kuraqkuna create in ritual. The study concludes in chapter 11 with a consideration of the significance of these meanings for our understanding of authority in Yura. The prospects for the future are considered, as are recent developments in the political organization in Yura since the original fieldwork was completed.

PART I

THE YURA
SOCIAL ORDER AND
THE KURAQKUNA

The canton of Yura, in spite of its relatively small population, supports a complex social organization. The Yura social order is stratified ethnically and boasts an intricate structure of vital indigenous social groupings. Our description of the Yura region begins with an examination in chapter 2 of the special conditions of the physical environment—the arid, high valleys which these peasant farmers have adapted to a regime of intensive small farming. The territory and the ecology of the area are discussed here as well as the settlement patterns of the Yura, their agriculture, and briefly, their economic arrangements. We then turn to an analysis of the social relationships and social groups to be found in Yura. Focusing on the contrast between the *vecinos,* the urban-oriented, hispanicized dominant class, and the Yura, the Quechua-speaking Andean peasants, we construct an "ideal typical" model for each of the two categories and point to the very different expectations and values that guide them in social interactions and in life goals.

In comparing these two social identities, we see that one of the factors most essential to the Yura identity, which the vecinos do not share, is membership and participation in the indigenous social groups called ayllus. In chapter 3 the ayllu becomes the center of our attention. Widespread throughout the Andes, the ayllu concept shapes Yura social life in distinctive ways. The range of meanings given to the term elsewhere in the Andes and the particular characteristics of the ayllu in Yura are discussed in this section.

One of the principal ways the system of ayllus is made manifest in social life in Yura is through the actions of the kuraqkuna, the indigenous authorities. Chapter 4 continues the ethnographic emphasis with a detailed exposition of the kuraqkuna posts, highlighting especially what we might call the civil aspects of the authority roles. The continuing strength both of the kuraqkuna and of the ayllus they support becomes apparent in this context. Part one concludes with a brief description of the political positions held by members of the vecino elite, which contrast strikingly with the activities and values of the kuraqkuna.

2

YURA
Environment and People

The Yura have chosen to inhabit a region of striking physical beauty, with deep valleys, barren slopes, and precipitous peaks. They have created an inviting and attractive environment within the valleys, in spite of the harshness of the climate and the landscape. By carefully managing the limited water available to them, they cultivate cornfields and orchards, plant willows and poplars, and pasture their flocks. Before beginning our inquiry into Yura social organization and the indigenous authorities, let us look at the world in which the Yura live, and at the ways they have adapted that physical world through agriculture and herding to gain a livelihood. We then turn our attention to the social classes and ethnic categories in Yura, with an eye to the typical characteristics that distinguish them.

Geography and Climate

The territory of the Yura, in the heart of the Bolivian department of Potosí, is located in the high valleys which lead south from the Cordillera de los Frailes, itself an extension of the central chain of the Andes. As in all of Potosí department, the central Cordillera is at its widest here, stretching 350 kilometers from the Salar de Uyuni in the west to the rolling hills approaching sea level east of the Pillcomayo River. The mountain peaks of this region are not, however, the spectacular snowcapped massifs of the western Cordillera bordering Chile. They average under 4,500 meters, and only a few, such as Chorolque (5,597 meters above sea level) and Mundo (5,437 meters) project notably above their neighbors. The valleys tend to be deep and narrow, with fast-moving, crystalline streams running through them above 4,000 meters, and wider, meandering rivers of more turbid waters below that.

As one moves south in Bolivia, and especially from the Cordillera de los Frailes toward the Argentinian border, the countryside is characterized by an increasing aridity. The Yura region and the area around it are, by most measures, high-altitude deserts. In the Holdridge life zone system this area of central Potosí is classified as "desert underbrush" (Bolivia, MACA 1975:238). Ground cover on the slopes is sparse and consists mainly of low bushes (*t'ula, muña, q'uwa,* and *chachaquma*), wild grasses, and a bewildering array of cactuses. Great expanses of the mountainsides may be completely bare. Only in the irrigated valleys is agriculture possible.

The present boundaries of the Yura region were established by 1590 and have remained unchanged since that time; the territory included within them comprises an area of some 2,000 square kilometers. As the map of Yura territory shows (figure 2.1), the region is made up of the valleys of several rivers and their tributaries (the courses of which flow generally from the northwest and west to the southeast) and includes the intervening peaks and arid ravines. A cantón within the Bolivian government's administrative categories, Yura thus embraces dry, broken terrain in which the patches of green provided by the rivers bring the only relief to what the unaccustomed eye sees as an unchanging vista of arid slopes and ravines.

The word rivers, however, may be a term too grand to describe the reality. Except for the Río Yura, which at its smallest is at least two feet deep and twenty wide, the rivers of the zone can generally be stepped, or at least jumped, across. They often come perilously close to running dry, especially at the beginning of the planting season before the rains begin, when Yura agriculturalists draw off water for irrigation. Yet these rivers are the lifeblood of the region; without them, human settlement would be very nearly impossible.

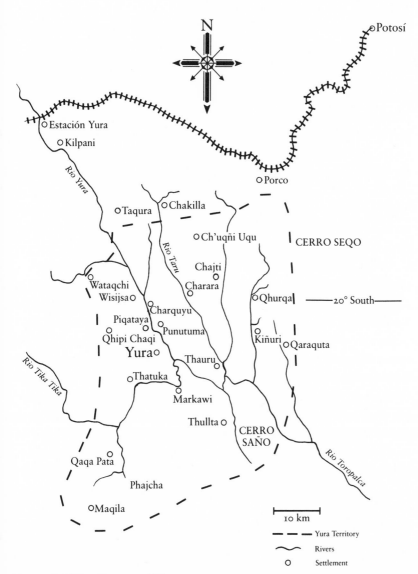

Figure 2.1 The Canton of Yura

As the map shows, the rivers join together as they flow south. The combined watercourses eventually unite with the Pillcomayo outside Yura territory.

In addition to the dryness of the climate—which magnifies the importance of the rivers—the second major factor determining the ecological characteristics of the zone is, of course, the altitude. The lack of very high peaks means that the average range of elevations between mountaintop and the lowest point in the valley floor is only about 800 meters, which is not a great contrast in Andean terms. There are no vast vistas of abrupt altitude changes as seen elsewhere in Bolivia. The rivers of Yura descend only about 700 meters as they flow through the canton, a distance of some 80 kilometers. In the northwest and west, where they enter the area not far from their headwaters, the valleys are situated at about 3,600 meters above sea level. At the southern boundary, when the rivers have all joined together, the valley bottom is still at some 2,900 meters. The bulk of the Yura population lives somewhere in between, from 3,400 meters down to about 3,200.

At 20 degrees south of the equator and 3,400 meters above sea level, annual temperature variation is considerable, although diurnal variations are perhaps more noticeable. From dawn to noon the temperature may rise as much as 20°C, although the season determines the overall range within which this variation occurs. In the rainy season from December to March, which is also the agricultural season, temperatures rarely fall below freezing—if they do, it may portend a catastrophe for farm production that year. By the beginning of May, however, the temperatures dip down to freezing almost every night, and in June and July they may fall by dawn to − 5°C or even lower as a regular occurrence. The high temperature of the day, which can surpass 25°C in the warmer months, may not climb above 12°C in winter. Year-round, the average is in the range from 12°C to 16°C.

Rainfall is seasonal and very low for most months of the year; the best estimates of annual rainfall place it within the range of 125 to 300 millimeters (that is, about five to twelve inches) (Bolivia, MACA 1975:195, 239, 312; Bolivia, Departamento de Meteorología 1974:79). Except for a rare hailstorm or cloudburst there is almost no precipitation in the months from April through October. Occasional rainfall begins in late October and gradually increases in intensity through January and February, when the rains reach their peak. They then decrease again until they diminish almost completely by the end of March.

The Central River Valley

Drought years are not uncommon, and Yura reports several each decade. As long as the rivers keep flowing (which is as dependent on precipitation much farther north as it is on rainfall in the immediate vicinity), a prolonged lack of rainfall does not necessarily lead to the failure of agricultural production for the year. Yet even the rivers eventually run dry, as they did in the planting season of 1983, when agriculture failed almost completely.

The occasional violent hailstorms are also quite serious in the damage they wreak on fields. They can pass through localized sections of the area with frightening intensity. Such a storm may deposit ten centimeters of hail in ten minutes, speedily destroying crops standing in the fields.

As in much of central Bolivia, the area of Yura regularly experiences strong winds in the winter months. These tend to blow in the afternoons and can be predicted by morning cloud formations. Every few years a dust storm lasting several days occurs, when the sand and loose soil from the riverbeds and the bare landscape swirl hundreds of feet into the air and blot out the sun.

The narrow river valleys of the region shelter both the Yura population and their fields. The total width of the valleys, from one extremity of the cultivated fields next to the slopes, across the riverbed and the river itself to the hillside edge of the fields on the opposite bank, may be as little as a hundred meters. The central valley, that of the Yura River, is almost a kilometer wide by this measure. The riverbed often claims a considerable proportion of that distance, however. In many areas of Yura canton the rivers meander across an expanse of sand, stones, and fine gravel which is only filled bank to bank for a few hours during the heaviest rains. This *playa* expands yearly due to erosion; fields tens of meters wide have been lost to the playa within living memory. Yura farmers maintain fields and terraces on the margins of the wide riverbed wherever there is space enough to cultivate. At some points the river rushes against a sheer rock wall, making the construction of fields impossible. At others a wide apron of land next to the playa provides choice farming acreage, and Yura farmers take advantage of the richer alluvial soil for greater production.

Population and Settlement

According to the 1976 census the inhabitants of canton Yura number 6,265 (Bolivia, Instituto Nacional de Estadística 1977:14). Of these, some 1,200 reside in the mining community of Qaraquta on the extreme eastern boundary of Yura territory. Mine officials report that they employ about 270 workers (the bulk of the population is, of course, made up of family dependents), of whom only 50 are originally from Yura.

A second "urban" center is the canton capital, a small village of less than 100 people which also bears the name Yura. About half the residents of the village are indigenous *comunarios* (or, as they also call themselves—and as I shall term them in these pages—"Yuras"), while the other half identify themselves as participants in the urbanized culture of town centers, a social category frequently termed "mestizo" or "criollo." They often refer to themselves as vecinos ("citizens of the town" in its original sense), which is the term I shall use hereafter. I shall return to this important social distinction later in this chapter.

Finally, the settlement of Punutuma, upriver from the village of Yura, currently has some 300 inhabitants. Punutuma was established in the first years of this century to maintain a hydroelectric plant that was constructed on the Yura River to provide electricity to the Huanchaca Company mines at Pulacayo, some ninety kilometers away. The plant is today run by COMIBOL, the nationalized Bolivian Mining Corporation. The recent program to "relocalize" COMIBOL workers has reduced employment from its former 180 people, which included both white- and blue-collar workers, to about two-thirds that figure. Some 80 to 90 percent of the employees are from the area, almost all originally from the comunario social category. Many in fact have kept their houses in surrounding Yura settlements, the reason for the low worker-to-population ratio of the town. Punutuma is in many ways a transitional community, since the industrial work schedule of the plant imposes a time structure on the workers which is alien to those who devote themselves to agriculture. Nevertheless, many employees of Punutuma retain their fields and continue to plant them.

The rest of the canton's inhabitants are the 4,500 comunarios who compose the Yura ethnic group. They live in more than one hundred villages and hamlets (the ranchos mentioned above) dispersed mostly along the river valleys that make up the area. Some of these villages are fairly large: Thatuka, for instance, has seventy-five households and Chikira has over forty. Others consist of only one or two families.

Population has not grown at a high rate in this century. The annual growth from 1950 until the last census in 1976 within the entire province of Quijarro (in which canton Yura is situated) was only .19 percent (Bolivia, INE 1977:18). As for the canton, the 1900 census reported a total population of 3,682 (before the founding of the Qaraquta mine in 1934) (Bolivia 1973:222). In 1950 the canton had 5,990 inhabitants (Bolivia 1955:31). Based on these figures, the Yura have experienced an annual growth rate of only .17 percent since 1950; the annual growth of .7 percent experienced since 1900 is greater due to the influx to Qaraquta.

This slow growth in population is largely explained by the high rate of infant mortality. Our investigation of birth and death records

indicates that probably close to one-half of all children die before the age of five. Added to this is the fact that the Yura have
practically no contact with modern medical treatment. Death is
frequently caused by infections that could be controlled with anti-
biotics, and such endemic diseases as tuberculosis exacerbate this
unhappy situation. Another possible factor for slow growth, permanent out-migration, has played only a small role in population
patterns in Yura; a census we conducted of some ninety-eight households confirms this.

I have said that there are over a hundred ranchos in Yura. It is difficult to give an exact count of such communities because the Yura
view them on different levels. Large ranchos are always subdivided
into smaller, named clusterings of houses. At times the number of
such divisions that one sees empirically differs from the number
conventionally reported to be there, showing that the Yura apply
models of organization to their home settlements which are also
relevant at higher levels. In addition, residence for many families is
not absolutely fixed. Given varied landholdings in several valleys,
some settlements are abandoned except during planting season and
the harvest.

Most ranchos tend to be located in *quebradas,* or dry ravines
(dry, of course, except in heavy rains), along the rivers. In these
ravines rock walls have frequently been constructed to channel
the runoff water and to permit the formation of adjoining fields—
fields that would otherwise be subject to the erosion of water running through the ravine. These small tracts are select garden plots,
covered regularly with loads of manure, sand, and fine gravel. A
smaller proportion of the hamlets are located on outcroppings high
above the river. In areas such as these there is frequently a wider
apron of arable land than is found next to the ravines.

Hamlet houseyards are clustered, and fields are dispersed upriver
and down from the ranchos. Although most Yuras have some of
their lands close to their principal residence, these are normally
intermixed with the plots of their neighbors or those of people from
other valleys.

Agriculture and Economy

In spite of the rigors of the environment and the climate, the Yura have developed a technology of agriculture and herding which permits them to take maximum advantage of the ecological possibilities. The Yura are maize farmers, planting a dozen varieties of corn in their small irrigated plots along the riverbanks. Although they also cultivate broad beans, several varieties of squash, and potatoes, they focus almost all their energies on corn. Corn provides them with the basic elements of their diet such as *mut'i* (loose, cooked, unsalted grains, which the Yura use as a diet staple equivalent to our use of bread), *lawa* (a thick, gravy-like soup made from ground corn flour), and *aqha* (a fermented corn beer).

Due to the aridity of the zone rainfall agriculture is not feasible. The Yura have therefore created an elaborate system of irrigation channels; every valley has several major canals which carry water to all the cultivated fields. While disagreements occasionally occur over distribution, all comunarios have an equal right of access to water and there is no social stratification based on water control. To keep the water flowing when it is needed, the Yura work cooperatively, contributing their labor wherever they have fields. Comunarios are selected to serve as officials to oversee this work. The Yura also employ cooperative forms of labor in many other work tasks.[1]

The resources of individual households are not extensive, and by most accountings the Yura are poor. Land-holdings for crop production fall within a range of one-half hectare to two hectares of intensively farmed fields, with most households possessing about one hectare. The urban-oriented mestizo families in the central village, a total of less than ten households, own about twice that much. A typical Yura family has about fifteen to thirty sheep or goats, five to seven llamas, and perhaps a pig or some chickens. A somewhat better off household may own an ox or even two. A team of oxen, however, represents a considerable investment, and less than half the households have one. In addition, most Yura have rights to several apple trees, and cultivate both poplars and eucalyptus for the wood. They also inherit claims to stands of *churki* (*Prosopis ferox*

[Bolivia, MACA 1975]), a small hardwood mesquite indigenous to the area, which is used for firewood.

With few exceptions Yura have access to land. This is an area of *tierras de origen,* which is to say that the Yura peasant farmers have succeeded in controlling their lands through the centuries, never having had them alienated to haciendas. While the historical records indicate that several small estates existed in the past, and the adjoining herding area of Chakilla was held as an hacienda until the 1950s, the formation of large landed estates has not in general been an important factor in the economic history of the zone. At the other end of the scale of land ownership, informants indicate that formerly there existed a number of landless families. However, the practice of this century, which permits land sales within the ethnic unit, has enabled these to obtain fields of their own.

Most Yura families hold lands in a number of different places in the territory. Although Yura no longer includes as wide a range of altitudes as it once did, there are nevertheless significant variations due to altitude in the ecological potential of agricultural lands in the area. For instance, in the Watajchi Valley on the northwest border of Yura, the 3,600-meter valley floor is just above the upper limits of corn cultivation. The Yura families there plant such Old World crops as barley and wheat, as well as the Andean potato; they secure access to corn from the lower valleys either by controlling fields through marriage or inheritance or by establishing exchange relationships. But even in cases where a family owns several plots in different valleys at approximately the same altitude, the microecology can vary to such a degree that production will differ greatly from one to the next. One area may be more sheltered and therefore warmer (or even colder) than another, or a localized hailstorm might destroy the maturing crops in one valley but not in the next. In narrow valleys the sheerness of the summit walls affects production by reducing the hours of direct sunlight. In addition, the quality of soils and the quantity and mineral content of the water diverge as well. The conditions that the diverse environment creates make dispersed landholdings throughout the zone the best solution both to the insecurities of weather and to the natural contrasts that each area exhibits in terms of its resources.

The Yura take advantage of the altitudinal levels available to them in another economic activity—herding, the second most important element in their subsistence. The apparently barren mountainsides, like the cultivated fields, are all divided among the comunarios; they all have owners. Families have access to these grazing lands either through inheritance or on the basis of kin ties. The boundaries of the lands, which apparently are quite ancient, are known by the owners.[2] The limited use of such lands by neighbors who pass through with their flocks, or by the occasional wandering bull, is not prohibited or closely controlled—a practical impossibility in any case. In Yura eyes, however, the mountain slopes are important resources. Mountain slopes are thus grazed by flocks of sheep, goats, and llamas, as well as oxen and bulls; they also provide other important wild plant products, such as cactus fruit and herbs for cooking.

In a system similar to that still maintained in the northern part of the department of Potosí by the Machas (Platt 1976, 1982) and the Laymis (Harris 1978, 1982a, 1985), the Yura's forebears once had access to lands dispersed over a much wider area than today, in zones both higher and lower than at present. Predecessors of the Yura were to be found in the 1590s both at 3,800 meters above sea level in Chaquí (AGN 13.18.6.4, it. 1:fol. 5v) and at 2,000 meters on the banks of the Pillcomayo River (Mujía 1914:537). The Yura maintained, as the Machas and Laymis still do today, a form of economic organization that John V. Murra has termed a "vertical archipelago," in which the goal is the "vertical control of a maximum of ecological floors" (1975:59–115). Realignments of groupings in late colonial and republican times, and a government policy which consistently refused to recognize such far-flung holdings, have meant that the present-day Yura have lost their rights in these lands.

The present-day economy of the zone could be termed one of regional self-sufficiency; the majority of comunarios provide for their subsistence through corn and broad bean production in their own fields, supplemented by the very occasional slaughter of a sheep or llama. The Yura farmer must manage resources that are spread over several valleys, planting and tending lands inherited from various family lines. Beyond that, the Yura establish a variety of exchange relationships with others of their ethnic group in adjoining valleys, both in labor and in farm products.

In many regions of the Andes the diversity of the ecology makes it possible for peasant farmers who control resources within different microclimates to evade the worst effects of nonproductive periods, such as in winter or in periods of drought. This is done by scheduling work tasks in other ecological zones where productive activities are possible (cf. Golte 1980b). The loss of the more extensive resources within the vertical archipelago that the Yura once controlled suggests that this rationality of Andean organization is less applicable to the Yura than to other cases, in spite of the localized ecological differences. One substitute for the direct control of other levels evident in the historical record is the long-distance trade whereby the Yura of some areas still travel to lower valleys to trade salt and highland herbs for corn.

This disarticulation of the older system may help to explain the rapidity with which certain changes have come to the economy of regional self-sufficiency. In recent decades many Yura have augmented their agricultural and herding activities through a seasonal participation in the national labor market as wage-earning workers in rural areas of the Bolivian lowlands and Argentina. A pattern of temporary migration has evolved through which young men and women leave Yura for several months, or even years, only to return and resume their agricultural activities. Labor migration continues to have important effects on life in Yura.

As for the local market economy, the Yura do not generally sell any of their farm products except dried apples. Their apples are a small, unimproved variety, but they have had steady sales in the city and in the mining centers. The Yura do not supply the urban market with any other agricultural or herding products.

Social Class and Ethnicity in Yura

In the discussion of population above, I referred to the existence of "Yuras" and "vecinos." The population figures have revealed that Yuras, who are the focus of this study, form the overwhelming bulk of the population—close to 95 percent of the inhabitants of the area if we exclude the peripheral enclave of Qaraquta. Yet the intermediate position and the greater economic power of the vecinos make their role more important than their numbers would at first indicate. Furthermore, these kinds of social contrasts are widespread throughout the Andes, to the degree that they have become a major focus of study elsewhere. I therefore conclude this preliminary description of the area with a characterization of these two social classes and with a discussion of their nature for a better understanding of the rural context.

Virtually all inhabitants of Yura are either Yuras or vecinos. Membership in either of the classes brings with it a whole complex of characteristics, both in terms of ideas and values as well as economic position and power, which identify an individual in his relationships with all other social actors and which have far-reaching consequences for every aspect of a person's life.

The two categories can be understood better by juxtaposing the typical actions and orientations of the members of each. I shall portray first the Yura, then the vecinos, in terms of a series of attributes such as economic activities, membership in indigenous groups and the consequent relationship to state-level institutions, dress and body symbolism, and language. Here we only delineate what would be a typical man and woman in each category. We then turn to a consideration of the dimensions of class and ethnicity in Yura and in the Andes more broadly, leaving until later a more complete analysis of the broader sets of meanings which the two groups hold.

The Yura

As we have seen, the Yura are full-time agriculturalists except when they leave the area to seek wage labor. They all control their own lands, which are planted in a kind of communal work festival.[3] The Yura consider it a moral obligation to help their neighbors when asked. Agriculture is more than an occupation for them; rather, it is the activity by which the Yura, both men and women, judge their self-worth and by virtue of which they evaluate others. To be able to plow and to manage a team of oxen is a life goal of all Yura boys; it is hard work, and only robust young men at the peak of their strength can do it well. A man sees as a sign of his own mortality the time, in his late thirties, when he finds plowing too great a burden.

The Yura belong to the traditional groupings called ayllus (vecinos do not) and pay a yearly *tasa,* or land tax, to an indigenous official. Membership in an ayllu implies that one will eventually take on one of the various Yura authority roles described in chapter 4 or one of the kuraqkuna-appointed festival sponsorships. That is, most people assume, either with anticipation or resignation, that they will serve as *alcalde* or *jilaqata* once they have established their households as adults. Ayllu members do not expect to be chosen to take on certain other offices—the nationally oriented local-level political roles of the Bolivian state such as *corregidor* of the canton or mayor of the village of Yura; the selection of these is made largely by vecinos, and it is they who have normally filled the posts.

Ayllu membership has as a corollary a more obligatory participation in festivals than is implied by vecino social identity. Yura couples participate in fiestas either through accepting one of the authority or sponsorship roles or through accompanying someone, a relative or friend, who is filling that role. They see the dancing, drinking, and general rowdiness of the festivals as a kind of sacred duty and look with disdain on the nonparticipating vecinos, who generally stand on the sidelines during the celebrations and whose main interest in the events lies in selling the Yura cane alcohol.

In terms of residence, the great majority of Yuras reside in the dispersed hamlets and villages spread throughout the five valleys, close to their principal fields. While almost all either own or have access to a single-room house in the central village of Yura, these dwellings remain empty most of the year. In spite of the fact that the settlement of Yura is the canton capital, many Yura go there rarely. The comunarios normally travel to Yura only to attend festivals or when they must consult vecino authorities. For most Yuras daily life takes place in the small settlements of the surrounding valleys; the majority are not in continual contact with the vecinos.

Formal education is another index of Yura-vecino status. Most Yuras under the age of thirty have a few years of schooling but their way of life is not conducive to maintaining the skills gained in school. Many Yura parents do wish for a better education for their children, but there is also a sense that the practical experiences of agricultural work and herding are as valuable as the more abstract abilities developed in formal instruction. It is true that the latter is more easily available now to children in the dispersed settlements of Yura than was the case twenty years ago. Yet today only a handful of Yuras have studied at the secondary school level and the pattern remains strong for children to quit school after three to five years of primary studies.

Another important factor in Yura self-identification is language: Yura speak Quechua as their language of choice.[4] It is spoken at home, at festivals, and even at public meetings in the presence of Spanish speakers. Men over forty rarely speak Spanish with any fluency and most women are monolingual in Quechua. The few younger women who have learned some Spanish while working elsewhere or when traveling with their husbands outside the canton are reluctant to speak it in Yura. Some younger men who have worked in Argentina or in other areas of Bolivia speak Spanish with varying degrees of skill; many of their number are fully fluent. But in the case of men, too, Quechua is preferred in daily interactions with fellow Yuras, even by youths who speak Spanish well. Yura Quechua, a dialect which has remarkably few Spanish loanwords, shows every sign of being the mother tongue of the indigenous population for the forseeable future.

Finally, the choice of dress and other body adornments acts as a marker in all societies, providing a means to express one's sense of identity and social affiliation. This is stressed in the Andes, where there is a long tradition emphasizing both the value of cloth (Murra 1962) and the importance of clothing styles and headgear as a marker of ethnic identity in a multiethnic state (Espinoza 1969, I:par. 25; Cieza [1553] 1967:79–80). Most Yura women wear a straight shift of rough manufacture under a wraparound overskirt called an *aqsu*, which they weave themselves. They almost always have with them a carrying cloth, a *llijlla,* which they also weave, and wear a round black velvet hat with a narrow brim that is made locally.

Until some ten years ago Yura men wore a male version of this distinctive costume: the *unku,* a voluminous, woven sleeveless shirt, tied with a woven belt, knee-length homespun pants, and the same hat as the women. As the men traveled to other areas to work, however, they increasingly felt handicapped by the distinctiveness of Yura clothing. In recent years most men have switched to Western-style, store-bought pants and shirts. A visored, brimless riding cap and rubber-tire sandals are now the distinguishing features of male Yura clothing in contrast to the vecinos.

The Vecinos

The vecinos of the central village of Yura, and those who fall in the same category residing in Punutuma, identify themselves not with the large population of rural peasant agriculturalists among whom they live, but rather with the Bolivian urban classes and the national elites. The vecinos see themselves as the bearers of national culture in the face of the backwardness of the rural majority. Nevertheless, social life is always a dialogue, even in cases such as this where the dialogue is fundamentally hierarchical. The vecinos define themselves according to a model drawn from the towns and cities, but this is modified by their intimate interaction on a daily basis with the Yuras.

The vecinos are largely agriculturalists, like the Yura, in that they own fields and have them planted; but they have a more utilitarian approach to agricultural work, and many (though not all) prefer not to spend much time in manual labor. All the vecinos receive the bulk of their income from some additional means at the local level. In the central village of Yura every vecino family has a small general store (a tienda) where they sell the lucrative cane alcohol as well as some canned goods and other household items to the Yuras. The vecinos in Punutuma work in the power plant as employees of COMIBOL and earn salaries. Most also operate tiendas.

The vecinos are not participants in the ayllus, nor do they pay the ayllu land tax, the tasa. Through the years they have converted their landholdings to individual private ownership, and they consequently pay a *catastro* (real estate tax) directly to the departmental treasury in the city of Potosí. Nor do they take on any of the ayllu authority roles: they do not become kuraqkuna. The vecinos do take part in festivals, mostly by assuming certain voluntary festival sponsorship posts that they largely share among themselves. On the other hand, they have until recently held a monopoly on the nationally oriented authority roles of corregidor, civil registrar, and the municipal mayor.

The vecinos as a group tend to have a higher formal educational level than the Yuras. Many have attended high school, and the younger generation frequently attend the university as well. Almost all vecinos are literate, with the exception of a few elderly people.

As we have seen, the residence of the vecinos is largely limited to two places, the village of Yura and the upriver "company town" of Punutuma. Some vecinos have acquired lands in other parts of the region but they do not reside on them. The sons and daughters of vecinos have almost all left Yura to live in Bolivian cities, with no intention of returning.

The vecinos speak Spanish as their language of choice. All know and speak Quechua (except for the youngest generation, many of whom have always lived in the city). With them, however, Quechua carries an aura of ignorance and coarseness. Some vecinos, to dissociate themselves from "Indian" status, affect a lack of facility in Quechua on certain occasions; but their frequent interaction with the Yura obliges them to know the language. Most insist that Quechua is not a language, but only a dialect, and they deny that Quechua can be said to have a grammar. This is a distinction they were apparently taught in school which serves to reduce Quechua to an inferior status in relation to the language of power and culture, Spanish. The vecinos speak Spanish at home and among friends, and most have more facility in it than in Quechua.

In dress, the vecinos wear Western-style clothing; a few older women wear the pollera, which in the cities is thought to be a sign of indigenous identity. However, in the provinces of Potosí it was this form of dress, and not Western clothing, that distinguished

The Town of Yura

mestiza women from Indian women. Both sexes wear shoes rather than sandals, and they either go hatless or wear a fedora of a design common to the entire country.

The two groups of vecinos in canton Yura, those of Punutuma and those of the village of Yura, are quite similar in their relative economic status and their orientation toward the nation. But Punutuma's history as a settlement created to support the hydroelectric plant places it in a special relationship to the rest of the canton. In a sense the very existence of Punutuma has created an increased number of vecino-level slots in local society. It has been possible for some Yura comunarios to go to work in Punutuma and to move themselves and their families gradually into the higher social category without directly competing with the vecinos of the town of Yura (who, as oral history attests, would resist this). Thus the vecino segment of the canton—vecino in terms of the model created above—is today larger than it would have been if Punutuma had not existed.

There are differences between these two vecino groups. The Punutuma employees of COMIBOL are, in relation to the state enterprise that gives them work, a nascent industrial proletariat. The residents see themselves not as the petty bourgeois traders that the Yura vecinos are proud to be, but rather as unionized workers (this in spite of the fact that almost all the wives of the workers also have a small shop or prepare food for sale). The regularized workday schedule (in this case, an eight-to-five shift) has placed—as E. P. Thompson (1967) showed in the context of industrialization in England—different "urban" demands on their time that the vecinos of the village of Yura, with their more flexible daily schedule, do not have to contend with; and this has had an impact on the mutual evaluation of the two groups.

The vecinos of the village of Yura base their claims to high social status either on their supposed descent from Spaniards (many say they are "hijos de cura," offspring of priests) or because their parents were already vecinos of other town centers when they moved to Yura in this century. They are aware of the history of upward mobility of the Punutuma residents and try to assert their social superiority over them in face-to-face interactions. The Punutuma vecinos, on the other hand, are in the contradictory situation of having closer ties to the comunarios than the Yura vecinos (and, again, many Punutuma residents identify themselves as Yura, not as vecinos at all), while maintaining an urbanized orientation that looks to Potosí and La Paz for guides to behavior.

Conceptions of relative status can lead to hairbreadth distinctions; to expand on those here would not be useful to our purposes. The fundamental fact remains that the two vecino groupings, in Punutuma and the village of Yura, while articulated in different ways with the national economy, nevertheless share many common interests which distinguish them from the large comunario population that surrounds them.

Class and Ethnicity Considered

The significant contrasts between vecino and Yura form the context for social interaction between group members, even though most Yuras are not, living as they do in their dispersed hamlets, in daily or even frequent contact with vecinos. For the majority of Yuras it is the internal arrangements of hamlet and ayllu that are more directly relevant to their actions in daily life.

However, most Yuras see relations with vecinos as fraught with tensions. For example, while vecinos do not control major extensions of land, they have been able to acquire choice parcels through purchase or expropriation at the death of comunarios (often justifying the latter by claiming unpaid alcohol debts). They mobilize labor to work their lands through asymmetrical ties of obligation with the comunarios. Such ties are based on common residence, fictive kin ties, and on implied coercion (expressed most often when comunarios come to the central village to carry out official business, such as requesting birth certificates or registering to vote) (Harman 1987).

Vecinos therefore represent, both symbolically and actually, the penetration of the wider society into the countryside, into the heart of the Yura ayllus. Vecinos consider the Yuras uncivilized, ignorant, or, in moments of pique, as *indios brutos* (brutish Indians, a grave insult in Bolivia). The Yura look at the vecinos as rich and powerful, but also as greedy and cruel, with no sense of the proper human values of hospitality, reciprocity, and mutual support. While willing in some contexts to refer to them by the respectful term *wiraqucha,* Yuras also see the vecinos as *q'aras,* people stripped of ethnic identity and of the human qualities Yuras deem essential. These hierarchical and exploitative social relations, although mitigated by certain social conventions such as *compadrazgo* ties, which "personalize" the vertical links, are nevertheless an everyday social reality for most comunarios, a dimension of social life with which they must deal.

Many of the contrasts and conflicts described here between Yura and vecino have also been sketched for other areas of the Andes and, indeed, for Latin America. What seems to be at play is the contrast between American native, European conqueror, and, in the case of the mestizo, their supposed offspring. These social categories thus represent, one would think, the contemporary result of real historical and even biological events.

However, it is important to understand that the two social categories are emphatically not racial categories as North Americans conceive of race. Race in Latin America is, in the first place, a more flexible concept, (see Harris [1964], and Wagley [1965]) than it is in the Anglo-American world. Clearly, as Pitt-Rivers (1971) also has shown, ideas of "race" are frequently used to "mark differences of ethnic identity within the nation," and being an Indian or a mestizo is not a question of biological inheritance, but of social status.

The word mestizo has as one root meaning the genetic sense of "half-breed." Since this biological connotation carries with it a strongly pejorative sense in many areas, I generally avoid the term. But when it is used here (and when it is used by Bolivians) it is not meant as a racial designation. Specifically, some of the vecinos of Yura do approach a European phenotype, but a person who is very clearly of Andean ancestry today finds no barriers to participation in the vecino status if he fits the category in other respects. Likewise, some comunarios appear physically to have a large European genetic endowment, but Yura they remain. Without belaboring the point, the reality of these categories is not a color bar, such as exists in the United States, but a culture and class bar.[5]

Neither is affiliation with either the comunario or vecino group solely determined by one's economic class—one's relation to the means of production. While questions of economic control and power certainly underlie the relationship between the two categories, a strict concept of social class is insufficient for comprehending the relationship between them. There are symbolic elements of social identity, of ethnicity, as well as placement within a social network, that make such simple economic determinism inadequate.

That is, ethnicity, which is a sense of group identity rooted in any number of factors—a common conception of the past, or language, or the symbolism of personhood—is not simply a brute social fact. As Fredrik Barth (1967) and Abner Cohen (1969, 1974, 1976, 1981) have been arguing for years, ethnicity is a strategy adopted when social groups are in interaction. It serves as an informal means of group formation, especially in situations of power relationships where more formal, rationalistic methods of mobilization would be suppressed. Ethnicity marks social boundaries; phenotypical characteristics can be employed as ethnic indicators, but other elements can also be drawn upon to buttress social differences such as economic class.

The latter seems to be the case in the southern Andes where, in a major study of ethnic and class relations in the Cuzco region, Pierre van den Berghe and George Primov have proposed the term "ethno-class" (1977:253)[6] as a conceptual tool for describing intergroup relations. They argue that cultural factors reinforce class inequalities in such a way that the social strata remain rigorously separated, at least as social types. This is clearly the case in Yura; as we have seen, the two categories of vecino and comunario are conceived as opposing categories which conjoin aspects of social class and ethnicity. Paradoxically, as van den Berghe and Primov note, individual social mobility is possible and common between the two statuses, especially through migration on the part of young people (1977:251ff.).

Yet, in seeming contradiction, these authors also emphasize that the various social categories they outline—white, mestizo, cholo,[7] Indian—have no sharp points of demarcation at which it is possible to say that an individual in transition is no longer one and now belongs to another; rather, these social types form a kind of ethnic continuum (1974:204–5). However, van den Berghe and Primov then seem to adopt a reductionist avoidance of the more conceptual complexities of ethnicity by arguing that these complex social identities are correlated with three determining factors: "urbanism, altitude, and distance from the main road" (van den Berghe and Primov 1977:251). That is, these three characteristics, and not the strategies of group interaction, predict social affiliation. They thus abandon a more demanding inquiry which would show the contextual use of class and ethnic identity and return to what we might call a pre-Barthian view of ethnicity as a listing of cultural and social traits.

In Yura, many of van den Berghe and Primov's preliminary conclusions seem valid. Physical features, or phenotype, as they demonstrate for southern Peru (1977:136), are largely peripheral to determining group membership. Likewise, participation in agriculture is a trait shared by both Yuras and vecinos. Moreover, transition and mobility between the categories is possible for some, who gradually adopt the way of life of the desired category. The vecinos, dominant both politically and economically, are anxious to preserve their control and prerogatives and frequently resist any upward moves to their status. Nonetheless, comunarios become vecinos under certain conditions, such as by becoming a school teacher or opening a small store. (The reverse movement, although it is much rarer, also occurs.) Although transitions through two generations are more common, certain highly motivated individuals who were born Yura comunarios have gained, by mid-life, a reasonably secure place in the vecino class. Of course it should not be assumed that all Yura are actively striving to leave their comunario status in order to become vecinos; far from it. The overwhelming majority of the population, as we have seen, are Yura, and they intend to stay that way: this is a basic fact of life which forms the central theme of this study.

A small number of individuals are able to participate in both categories, a situation which seems stable for them. These people tend to be individuals whom one would class on first appraisal as Yura, yet who live in or near the canton capital or who work in Punutuma. These few people are able to maintain comunario ties and yet be accepted as vecinos in certain situations. Such cases are exceptional, but their very existence emphasizes even more the relative fluidity of the boundary between what are conceived to be two very distinct groups.

It is through considering such factors as these that we can argue that van den Berghe and Primov failed to understand ethnic diversity and class relationships in the Andes. They rightly saw that ethnic identifications are both basic to an individual's sense of self and yet mutable. However, their approach was overly "etic" and relied on elements that may be external to the dynamic factors which determine ethnic affiliation. They based their analysis on a rather static conception of ethnicity which failed to take into account both the strategic elements of ethnic identification and the systems of meanings which Yura or vecinos rely upon in order to interpret their experience and the actions of the world around them.

Vecinos in Yura assiduously cultivate their urbanized identity because it helps them to reproduce a structure of hierarchy and domination over the Yura population. The Yuras, on the other hand, retain and modify their own sense of ethnic identity because it roots them in a broad social network which has, overall, given them the group solidarity necessary to retain control of the local means of production, the land. However, in neither case is group identity phrased or conceptualized in such utilitarian and rationalist terms. Rather, the Yura, by participating in the ayllus and in the social and symbolic activities which ayllu membership entails, re-create a sacred vision of the world and their place in it which provides a complex—and presumably satisfying—cluster of referents which they call upon to guide their actions in relation to each other and to the dominant group. The ayllus, then, provide a basis for group identity, and a framework for ritual action.

3

SOCIAL ORGANIZATION
AND THE AYLLU

For centuries the ayllu has been a conundrum for students of Andean society. From the time the Spaniards first arrived in Peru there has been a suspicion that within the range of meanings of this word lies a great deal of the sense of human relationships among the indigenous people of the Andes. Accordingly, many attempts have been made to clarify what is meant by the term.

This is not the place to review exhaustively the history of the word or of its definitions. Nevertheless, a brief sketch of some of the previous dialogue may be helpful as a setting for a discussion of the use of the term in Yura. The early Quechua-Spanish dictionaries from the first decades after the Iberian incursion are a good way to begin.

Fray Domingo de Santo Tomás, a Dominican who became an expert in the Quechua language, defined the term in 1560 as "linaje, generación, o familia" (lineage, generation, or family) ([1560] 1951: fol. 107v). In 1608 Diego Gonçalez Holguín characterized the ayllu as "social segment, genealogy, lineage, or kinship, or caste." In a separate entry he added that "in things, [ayllu means] genus or species" ([1608] 1952:39). The entry in the 1586 "Ricardo" Quechua dictionary reinforces this picture, defining ayllu as "tribe, genealogy, family home" (1951:18). In these we see a general range of meanings that refer to kinship and descent and to social groupings, as well as a more abstract sense of type when it is applied in contexts beyond reference to people.

In this century Bautista Saavedra, a Bolivian scholar who attempted to reconcile his interpretation of the Spanish chroniclers with perceptions current in his day about Aymara rural society, devoted an entire book to the topic of the ayllu. Drawing on the early descriptions of the ayllus and *panaqas* of Cuzco (in which elite interests dictated an explicit descent rule, a tendency that the Spaniards, accustomed to primogeniture, converted in their writings into an inflexible edict), Saavedra concluded that however badly the Aymaras had distorted the ayllu, it was originally and essentially "a tribe, a clan" (1903:107). Saavedra, like the Spaniards, assumed patrilineal descent. Castro Pozo, writing two decades later, simply equated ayllu with community, although he assumed that all indigenous communities are based on consanguinity (1924:7).

Such received wisdom has a way of perpetuating itself. In a recent Aymara dictionary Cotari first defines an ayllu as "a group of families established in one place, linked among themselves by a common trunk of kinship and totemism—tribe, clan." He then goes on to remark that as far as he knows the word has been lost and replaced by the Spanish loanword *estancia* (1978:45).[1]

In spite of this echo of the armchair techniques of the past, in more recent times it has gradually come to be realized that there is no single signification to the term that can be applied to the Andes in general. Recent research has offered us a variety of referents for the term. For example, for Brush and Guillet (1985:21) the ayllu is "the primary kin group." Others have characterized ayllus as groups created on the basis of bilateral kindreds (Isbell 1978:75); larger social groups who hold land together (Platt 1976); units of residential proximity (Palomino 1972); and even nonlocalized groups with no territorial links organized around work tasks (Ossio 1981). Skar found the ayllu in Matapuquio, Apurímac, to be an ego-centered group utilizing diverse modes of mobilization but relying on a conception of opposition, similar to a faction (1981:166–69). Espinoza (1981:101, 116–20) sees the ayllu of the early colonial period as a clan or a consanguineal kin group which functioned as a territorial unit, while Harman (1986) has suggested that in Yura the roots of the ayllu lie in kin relations, but the pressures of colonial rule caused the kinship principle to be lost. In Otavalo, Ecuador, Butler (1985:195) found kinship (with a factor of political control) at the heart of the concept, that is, the ayllu is composed of the bilateral kindred and the close descendants linked consanguineally to a deceased but politically important leader. Urton (1985) offers a more dynamic view of the ayllu in his analysis of animal metaphors among Andean peasants of southern Peru, defining the concept as based on "social relationships and processes of hierarchical group formation merged with the dynamics of the life cycle." Allen stresses the localized use of the term in the Cuzco area when she writes: "An ayllu is created when runa [i.e., Andean comunarios] build a house or houses on a named place. The ayllu does not consist simply of the group of co-resident individuals, nor of the named place by itself: it exists only when these entities—people, houses, the place—are brought into relation with each other" (1986:41). Finally, one of Isbell's Chuschi informants characterized the ayllu as "any group with a head" (1978:105). Indeed, an entire symposium has been published dedicated entirely to defining and delineating the ayllu; and as a result we see a wide variety of different kinds of groupings to which Andean peoples apply this term (Castelli et al. 1981). As Ossio, a participant in the symposium, writes, "It is illusory to try to assign a single meaning to all these [uses of the] term" (1981:198).

In sum, for Andean people the ayllu is a complex concept with a wide range of senses, as inclusive as the English word group. The task before us is therefore not to assume that there is one root or aboriginal meaning for the word, but rather to investigate the specific referents in particular cases.

In Yura, too, the meanings of ayllu are complex and multiple, and yet it is a concept within which one finds the fundamental principles of social relations. In certain contexts, as was the case in Chuschi, ayllu refers to kin or relatives. The use of ayllu that concerns us here, however, refers rather to large groupings to which Yura belong according to the locations of their fields. When contrasted with the kinship senses of the word, these are called *jatun ayllu* (big ayllus).

It is true that people who are kin frequently belong to the same ayllu, since they may have inherited lands from a common forebear. But no Yura asserts—there is no shared cultural conception—that all members of a single ayllu are relatives. Indeed, genealogical reckoning is fairly shallow among the Yura. Most informants find it difficult to trace their kin ties much beyond their grandparents, and they do not normally keep track of links to collateral relatives beyond descendants from common great-grandparents. Nor do they claim ties of kinship among ayllu members without being able to trace them. The ayllus are therefore not lineages, which trace descent matrilineally or patrilineally, or clans, which propose ties from an eponymous ancestor. Nor, as is often claimed for other areas, is there a "totem" of the ayllu in the sense that there is a particular animal, plant, or object associated with each from which members claim mystical descent. In sum, the jatun ayllus of Yura are not kin-based groups as such.

Conventionally said to be four in number, the ayllus form the organizational base incorporating the entire Yura population throughout the two thousand square kilometers of Yura territory. They take the form of named landholding groups whose members join together in rituals and who place themselves under a common set of authorities. Ayllus act as the entities which ensure, through the collection of the tasa (the head tax originating in colonial tribute obligations) and through the highly standardized performance of certain symbolic acts, their members' rights in lands. Given the importance of lands in a zone where agriculture is the fundamental economic activity, and yet at times both extremely difficult and risky, it is easy to understand why working to assure continued dominion over those lands would be a basic preoccupation. The ayllus, then, are the Yuras' response to that felt need. Participation in an ayllu carries with it, however, more than a simple, utilitarian effort to maintain control of lands. It is, as well, a means of categorizing human beings and structuring society.

Each cultivated field in Yura is assigned to an ayllu. The field's owners pay their tasa to that ayllu's officials, and join with the other members of their ayllu in rituals and festivals. Many people, by having landholdings in more than one ayllu, can potentially activate membership in several of them. Nevertheless, Yura tend to limit their principal participation to the ayllu in which they have their largest or most productive clustering of lands; they usually make their main residence close to those fields.

Residence can, of course, change during one's lifetime, especially after marriage. A wife (or, less commonly, husband) may, while still retaining her own lands, reside most of the time with the spouse close to the latter's fields; spouses take part in festivals and daily life with their mate's fellow hamlet and ayllu members. That is, a new residence brings with it new ayllu affiliations. On the other hand, some couples whose ayllus differ retain active participation in the principal ayllu of both spouses.

The organization of these groupings is complicated by the fact that the lands assigned to the ayllus are not necessarily contiguous. For example, in one ayllu, Wisijsa, many miles separate an "island" segment of its lands from the main core of the ayllu's fields. Another ayllu, Qullana, has lands in the southern area of Phajcha and the Thatuka Valley as well as in the Taru Valley to the north (see figure 2.1). The ayllus do tend to cluster, however; and although the large ayllu are not a single unit, they each occupy sizable extensions of the total area.

Ayllu Organization in Yura

If one asks "How many ayllus are there in Yura?" the answer that is invariably given is "four," and most informants follow that with a list: Qullana, Wisijsa, Qhurqa, and Chiquchi. As it happens, however, the system is not that simple, and it turns out that with further questioning one learns that these four groups are in fact intermediate groupings in an ascending hierarchy of four levels. That is to say, these four ayllus are both grouped together into larger entities and subdivided into smaller ones.

At the highest level of generality it is perfectly correct to refer to all of Yura canton as a single jatun ayllu. When comunarios say "Yura kaniy" (I am a Yura), this seems to be what they mean; they are referring to their membership in this maximal ayllu level. This overall unity is bisected into two moieties, the highest manifesta-

Figure 3.1 Ayllu
Organization in Yura

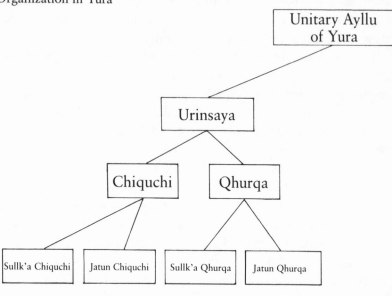

tion of a principle of duality which underlies all Yura concepts of
organization. Qullana and Wisijsa are grouped together to form
the Upper Moiety, formerly (but no longer) called Anansaya, and
Qhurqa and Chiquchi join together as the Lower Moiety, or Urinsaya. Each moiety is next divided in half, into those four ayllus
whose names are customarily given. Finally, these four are divided
once more, Qullana into four smaller ayllus, and Wisijsa, Qhurqa,
and Chiquchi each into two, for a total of ten. The four segments
of Qullana are called Jatun Qullana, Sullk'a Qullana, Qhapaqa,
and Agregado, or Ariaw. Wisijsa is made up of Wisijsa Qullana
and Sawlli. Qhurqa is divided into Jatun and Sullk'a Qhurqa, and
Chiquchi likewise consists of Jatun and Sullk'a sections.

The words jatun and sullk'a can be translated here as "large" and
"younger," respectively. In the three cases of sullk'a ayllus, they are
indeed all composed of fewer members, and in general they seem
to have smaller landholding units than their corresponding jatun

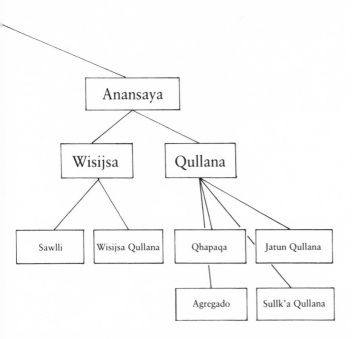

affiliates. The origin of this distinction is not yet clear, although in chapter 6 it will be suggested that this may be related to certain changes of status with respect to the state and within the indigenous population.

For some Yura this system is largely implicit. While everyone knows the four jatun ayllus, some may be able to give the names of the smaller ayllus of the jatun ayllu to which they belong but may hesitate in naming those of the other three. Other informants (here, older people of both sexes) can readily recite a list of the jatun ayllus and their subdivisions. These ayllu groupings provide both a means of self-definition and social categories. The various levels become most evident in the context of certain festivals, as we shall see.

The Yura themselves distinguish the various levels of the ayllus contextually and do not apply special titles to them. But to make our task easier here, I propose to refer to the different levels as

"Yura canton," or the "unitary ayllu"; the two "moieties"; the four "major ayllus"; and the ten "minor ayllus." Figure 3.1, a diagram of the ayllus, is thus an approximation of an overall order that many Yura will describe and have learned, although the form of presentation is not theirs but mine.

To say that individuals belong to the ayllu to which their lands have been allocated is correct as far as it goes. However, the distribution of lands in Yura is not at the level of the four major ayllus, but rather at a step below, at that of the ten minor ayllus. Correspondingly, Yura pay their tasas to an official chosen at the minor ayllu level. Membership in the four ayllus is, in a sense, derivative, since one is first and foremost identified with the minor ayllu to which one's lands have been assigned. This in turn brings with it an affiliation with one of the four major ayllus that results from the groupings of that lower level.

This further complicates the overall distribution of Yura lands into the ayllus. Although the four major ayllus all have core areas where their lands cluster, within these the fields of the minor ayllus tend to be highly intermixed. This means that the fields in a particular zone might all be of the major ayllu Wisijsa, for example, but on closer inspection it turns out that there are plots belonging both to Wisijsa Qullana and to Sawlli.

I mentioned previously that the moiety names—Anansaya for the upper and Urinsaya for the lower—have largely been lost in Yura. Their loss is recent, however, for they appeared in tax documents as recently as a century ago. Some older informants recalled hearing the terms when they were children, and these designations are still used in the neighboring area of Toropalca (which earlier formed a common ethnic group with the Yura). The fading of the terms has not lessened the strength of the groupings, though, for Qullana and Wisijsa still, in the appropriate ritual contexts, act together in opposition to Qhurqa and Chiquchi. As one woman told me, Wisijsa and Qullana are "like brothers," as are Chiquchi and Qhurqa. Even in recent years, Yura of Chiquchi report that at the annual water battle *tinku* (duel, but also joining together of two) between the moieties at San Juan (June 24), when the participants exchange insults as well as water, the Upper Moiety members sometimes shout

"Urinsayas!" at Chiquchi and Qhurqa. The Lower Moiety members do not respond by calling their opponents "Anansayas," of course, since everyone recognizes that the Upper Moiety has higher status. One informant said the Wisijsa and the Qullana are the *umas*, the "heads," of Yura (although, in contrast with the body metaphor that Bastien [1978] found in Charazani, he denied that Chiquchi and Qhurqa are "feet" or any other part of the body!).

The names of the major ayllus do not in themselves have, or at least no longer have any referents for the Yura. When a member of Qhurqa is asked, for instance, what the name of his ayllu means, he will reply, "*Sutilla*" (It's just a name). The name Qullana continues to be widespread as an ayllu title all over the Andes. Zuidema has argued that it carried the sense of "the first, the highest, prominent" and in Aymara thought may be associated with the sun as a representation of divinity (1964:164). Today "Qullana" crosses linguistic boundaries and is found in both Quechua- and Aymara-speaking areas. Furthermore, the link is historical as well; the ancestors of the Yura spoke Aymara in the seventeenth century. A search of Aymara and Quechua dictionaries available to us (Bertonio 1612; Cotari 1978; Ricardo [1586] 1951; Santo Tomás [1560] 1951b; Lira 1944; Lara 1971; Gonçalez Holguín [1608] 1952) suggests no clear derivation for the other three major ayllu names.

To summarize, the Yuras, with varying degrees of explicitness, picture their society as a set of dual divisions arranged in tiers of pairs: the entire Yura ayllu is divided into the two moieties (again, now recognized in ritual action but presently unnamed in speech), each of which is correspondingly segmented into two. Three of these are likewise divided into two groups, while the fourth, Qullana, undergoes a kind of doubling of the dual principle to be divided into four. One way to picture this kind of organization is in the form of a circle, as has been done in figure 3.2. In this manner we see better than in figure 3.1 how one group is embedded within another, such that an individual ayllu member has multiple levels to which he owes allegiance.

Figure 3.2 is a conceptual model of Yura organization rather than a spatial one. There is nevertheless a rough mapping of this elaborate arrangement of groups onto the geography of Yura canton. In

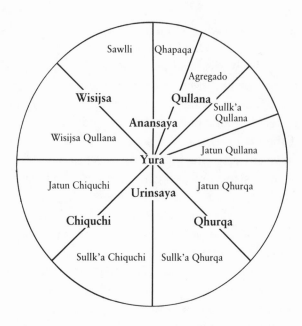

Figure 3.2 An Alternative View of Ayllu Organization

terms of ideas expressed about the ayllus, many Yuras picture them as corresponding in a vague way to the four cardinal directions—or at least as dividing the territory into four slices of a pie. If the ayllu "islands" (those fragments of ayllu set off from the main clusterings) are discounted, then this perception is not without some truth. Starting with Qullana lands and going clockwise, ayllu Qullana occupies most of the land in the southern and southwestern parts of the area. Wisijsa is to be found in the west, northwest, and north, while Chiquchi is centered in the northeast, and Qhurqa controls a broad band in the east and southeast.

This description of Yura ayllus is of course highly reminiscent—although on a much smaller scale—of the organization of Tawantinsuyu, where the huge territory of the Inkas was divided into four sections. Furthermore, just as the four suyus came together at Cuzco in the Inka state, the four major ayllus—indeed, all ten of the minor ayllus—have lands close to the central village and canton capital of Yura. Even within the village itself the houseyards affiliated with the various minor ayllus tend to group themselves by quarter. The renowned *ceque* system (Zuidema 1964, Wachtel 1973) is an analogue (although perhaps a rather distant one) to the actions of the festival of Carnaval, to be described in chapter 10. As we shall see, the ancestors of the Yura *were* incorporated for a time into the Inka Empire, but it was apparently a rather fleeting moment in their history compared to developments before and the Spanish domination afterward. The model of organization may thus have been imported or imposed during that period. However, given the fact that similar arrangements exist in other areas (such places as the Altiplano communities of Huachacalla and Jesús de Machaca [Albó et al. 1972] are instructive in this regard), I believe what we see here are widespread, quite ancient organizational principles which Andean peoples adapted to the constraints resulting from the Spanish policy of centralizing dispersed populations, the *reducción*.

Yet again, when one begins to consider the specifics of the case it turns out that the actual situation is considerably more complex than a simple quadripartite division might indicate. A complete description of the details of minor ayllu distribution in Yura would be too tedious to go into at length, but a few examples will serve to highlight the system.

Among the major ayllus Wisijsa presents an interesting case. This ayllu is conventionally said to be located in the western and northern parts of the canton. That is true—one of the westernmost ranchos in Yura, Qhipi Chaqi, is affiliated with Wisijsa. Another large rancho, called Wisijsa after the name of the ayllu, is located in the north of Yura territory. Yet several populous ranchos to the south which adjoin the canton capital—Churki Pampa, Panawa, and Sitis Mayqa, for instance—have lands belonging to Wisijsa Qullana. Many miles to the southeast, at the end of an arid valley which is Chiquchi along most of its length, is a rancho, Thullta, which also belongs to Wisijsa Qullana; and the minor ayllu Sawlli of Wisijsa has small clusters of lands in the southern herding area of Phajcha and in the Taru River valley (again, consult figure 2.1).

Indeed, Phajcha, near the southern edge of the canton (and in some ways the most isolated part of Yura), has a special place in the organizational scheme. Colder and higher than most Yura river valleys (the tiny fields there are at 3,700 meters, beyond the limits of corn cultivation), it consists of several linked small plains and surrounding hills, with most of its hamlets located at the intersections of the two. Due to the altitude, Phajcha is primarily a herding area. Yet the grazing on these pampas is not especially good because of the aridity. The Phajcha have adapted to this zone by becoming the potters of Yura; by exchanging their cooking, storage, and drinking pots with those of other areas, they are able partially to overcome the limitations imposed by the high altitude of the zone. They usually carry their wares to the lower Yura valleys to exchange for corn.

Most lands in Phajcha belong to the two minor ayllus Qhapaqa and Agregado, both of Qullana. Although these ayllus are found elsewhere, this is said to be their home area. Some Yura speak of a sense of opposition, within Qullana, between the Phajcha pair of Qhapaqa and Agregado and the other two minor ayllus, Jatun/Sullk'a Qullana, which tend to cluster in Thatuka and Taru.

The Obligations of Ayllu Membership

Historically, the most important ayllu duty was to pay the tasa to the ayllu *jilaqata*. Today the tasa has become a minimal expense, but that was not always the case. The ayllus undoubtedly existed in some form long before the Spanish invasion in the sixteenth century; but it was the colonial state structure and its successor, the Bolivian republic, that in a sense froze their form during the four centuries between the first incursion into Inka Qullasuyu by the Pizarro brothers and the present day. This was done in order to ensure the collection of tribute—the tasa—and for other administrative reasons. The ayllus of Yura are today at least partially the result of impositions by the state.

During the colonial and early republican periods the administration of the tasa was highly developed. From 1575 to 1880 teams were regularly commissioned to inspect all the indigenous communities in the provinces. These officials conducted an ayllu-by-ayllu census, a *revisita*, which adopted the existing indigenous social groupings for record keeping. The tasa rates then levied were based on these censuses. We shall examine these revisitas in chapters 5 and 6.

It is clear that the tasa was established as a personal head tax due from all men between the ages of eighteen and fifty, the colonial category of *tributario* (tribute payer). Through time, however, it came to be associated by the comunarios with rights in land. This linkage may of course have been fostered by the agents of the state, something that is hard to determine from the perspective of the local level. But however it came about, we find that by 1830 women's and minor children's names began to appear in the census in place of men who had died. At some point in the past the Yura came to view the tasa as a land tax, not a head tax, one placed on the ayllu and distributed among the households who owned fields within it.[2] By paying the tasa, the Yura ensured their rights in land under the ayllu system.

The tasa was not merely a means to subjugate the populace. It also provided, especially in the early republican period of Bolivia, a major proportion of the state's budget. Recent calculations indicate that for the period from 1831 to 1847 the portion of government income from the "contribución indigenal" averaged 37.5 percent (Sánchez-Albornoz 1978:198). With the development of mining at the end of the last century, the proportion of revenues deriving from the tasa steadily declined. Today the tasa has been abolished in several Bolivian departments, but it continues to furnish Potosí departmental coffers with a share of their receipts.

At the pragmatic level the tasa continues to serve a unifying purpose for the ayllus, although the internal dynamics have changed. The revisitas reveal that, as in the rest of rural Bolivia, three categories of household heads were delineated in Yura: *originarios*, *agregados*, and *forasteros*. Determined by the household's putative local origins (or by its alleged later migration into the community), these categories fixed the tasa rate one paid and, apparently, one's relative social status and security of land tenure. The review of nineteenth-century revisitas of Yura that Inge Harman and I made shows that these categories, thought previously to be inflexible slots which determined a household's social position and rights in land within the community, could, with the passage of time, be manipulated by both individuals and groups.[3] Yet notwithstanding the former importance of these classifications (and their continued existence in many areas of Potosí), these three social categories go unremembered by the Yura today. This fact obscures the analysis of the current tasa system, since the underlying logic of the past tripartite division has been lost.

When republican administrators ceased making revisitas in Yura after 1880, the updating of ayllu changes that had resulted from new revisitas ended along with them. The units that were framed then have continued until today to be the base for the tasa. The three categories have correspondingly lost their relevance as the tasas paid by households have been adjusted by division through inheritance, extinction of family lines, and the buying and selling of lands.

Because of subsequent inheritance and divisions, groups of adult siblings frequently share one unit (or even a half- or quarter-unit); they arrange among themselves how they will pay the tasa they jointly owe. This also accounts for the cases where an individual, through inheritance via different lines, may owe small fractions of tasas to several minor ayllus. There are cases of two families who share a tasa but barely know each other and who are not, as far as they know, related.

The adjustments that have been necessary should not be exaggerated, however, for in many cases lands are still held in the original units, or only one division has been made. Individuals who have inherited lands in the same minor ayllu from two family lines may consolidate these by paying the tasa at a rate appropriate to the larger revisita units. Yura still say that the relative rates they pay were set *visitamantapacha* (right at the time of the revisita) notwithstanding the subsequent divisions and regroupings. By this the Yura recognize that those units served as the starting point for what one finds at present.

Today the tasas are paid at four rates, termed *iskay chunkapi, chunkantin* or *chunkapi, tercio* (in Quechua, *tirsiu*), and *medio tercio*. In 1980 *medio tercio* paid $b5 per year (at the time, only U.S. $.25), *tercio* paid $b10, *chunkantin* $b20, and the very few cases of *iskay chunkapi,* $b40. By 1987 these rates had been adjusted to reflect the rampant inflation of recent years. *Medio tercio,* for example, paid 500,000 Bolivian pesos in 1987; but that was still only US $.25.[4] Again, these are usually paid not individually but by groups of adult siblings. Even before the rapid devaluation of the currency that began in 1983, these sums were practically meaningless in terms of real purchasing power.

Landholders know to which ayllu their tasa is due and how much to pay by inheriting this information from their parents along with the lands themselves. If brothers and sisters decide formally to divide the lands and their tasa (and it is possible to distribute the lands without dividing the tasa), then the tax is adjusted accordingly—and heirs are told by their parents that, for example, the fields are now a *tercio* tasa rather than a *chunkantin.* When the departmental authorities raise the tasa (as has been done numerous ous times in the last twenty-five years), then a simple percentage adjustment is made for the four rates. This is to say that everyone has an understanding of the particulars of the tasa system as it relates to him or to her, but I met no one who could offer, beyond small glimpses, a clear picture of how the overall system evolved to its present state. The description presented here is a distillation of many conflicting views combined with research in the archives.

Beyond paying the tasa, another obligation of ayllu membership is to take on the indigenous authority roles, the topic of the next chapters. Filling these service roles is a major life experience for Yura which requires time, resources, and dedication. Ayllu members who are not in one of these positions during a particular year nevertheless feel obliged to accompany their ayllu's authorities at festival times. Although this norm is most strongly acted upon if one has some other link to the persons serving in the role (through, for example, common hamlet residence or kinship), the inveterate party-goer can always justify his presence in an authority's house-yard by pointing out that they are members of the same ayllu.

Many other potential social obligations are not greatly affected by ayllu membership. For instance, a person is not restricted in the creation of elective social ties, such as ritual kinship or exchange relationships, by the ayllu of the others. Nor is marriage restricted by ayllu membership below the level of the unitary ayllu. Although there is an expressed preference to marry "within your valley," marriages between members of different major and minor ayllus are as common as within any one ayllu. Nor does marriage within one's valley imply that the marriage will be endogamous to a single ayllu. For example, the Taru Valley has lands of Wisijsa Qullana, Sawlli, Jatun Qullana, Qhapaqa, and Jatun and Sullk'a Chiquchi. Marriage between neighbors within the valley would obviously not ensure an intra-ayllu match. However, at the highest-level ayllu, that is to say the ethnic group and canton of Yura, marriage is quite endogamous. If we exclude vecino marriages and those where both spouses came from outside the canton (as is the case at some small mines), the endogamy rate is very high indeed. There are occasional marriages with "outsiders," but they are rare. Yet membership in an ayllu is, as we shall see, still a major factor in defining one's public identity and, along with that, a whole range of social characteristics.

We shall return throughout these pages to the question of ayllu organization and obligations and their importance in Yura social life and in the system of authorities. This introduction, however, should serve as a general orientation to the nature of ayllus in Yura as we turn to a discussion of the ways that such groups find their expression in social action and ritual.

4

THE KURAQKUNA OF
YURA TODAY

Characteristics of the Kuraqkuna

The organizational sketch of the ayllus of Yura presented in the previous chapter also gives us a model of the *kuraqkuna*, the indigenous authorities, for they correspond to the levels of the major and minor ayllus. In fact, it is through this correspondence that most people conceptualize the ayllu order. As the sets of roles exist today, there are ten *jilaqatas*, five *alcaldes*, and four *kurakas*. There are also two *jatun alfereces*, who are special festival sponsors, and, until 1975, there were eight *postillones*.

Jilaqatas serve the minor ayllus, one couple from each of the ten. The postillones were also chosen at the minor ayllu level. The alcaldes are selected at the level of the four major ayllus, with a fifth coming from the "auxiliary" Qullana region of Phajcha. The jatun alfereces are also selected at the level of the four major ayllus. The four persons who take on the posts of kuraka, the supreme ayllu authorities, also serve at the level of the major ayllu.

Although the authority roles differ in the specifics of their activities, they share many characteristics. Before turning to a consideration of each post separately, I shall sketch some of these more general attributes. For the purposes of ethnographic completeness the postillón role as it functioned up until 1975 will also be described. For many men who are adults today, the expectation of serving as postillón had always been a very real prospect in their lives, and its recent demise has left a strong imprint in their memory.

Among the kuraqkuna, the highest authority is the kuraka. He and his wife, who serves jointly with him, are chosen by their fellow ayllu members in a public meeting to which everyone in the ayllu has been invited. The kurakas are in turn responsible for assuring that all the other ayllu positions listed above are filled. All the roles are taken on a rotational basis, although the term of office and the dates for the renewal of the posts vary, as we shall see. Every Yura expects to take on at least one of the roles during his lifetime.

In general the three kuraka-appointed service roles can be taken on voluntarily at any point in adult life after marriage. Although the particular work task (*kamachi*) associated with the role (such as the service that the alcalde provides the vecino corregidor) will be carried out by the husband, Yura are unanimous in their opinion that all the kuraqkuna posts are assumed by the couple, and not just by the man. In decades past both husband and wife worked, even in the two posts that required direct labor service to vecino officials (the postillón and the alcalde). Today, although the wife of the alcalde no longer has to work in the corregidor's household, preparations for fulfilling the festival obligations of all the roles fall more on the women than on the men.

This sharing of responsibility is also suggested in the titles granted to the participants. Just as men receive the title "Tata Alcalde" and "Tata Jilaqata" (tata meaning father), their wives are addressed as "Mama Alcalde" and "Mama Jilaqata." As one informant said, "Qhariwarmipuni pasanku, khushka jina machakuspa, khushka jina ch'allakuspa; machasqalla sapa dia pasakuna a." (It's always the husband and wife who serve in the post together, drinking together, pouring libations together—just drunk every day we celebrate.)

It follows that an explicit norm exists that kuraqkuna should be married, and the overwhelming majority are. Nevertheless it is possible for a single person, including unmarried women, to fill any of the three service roles. In these cases someone stands in for the nonexistent spouse at the festivals—a sibling, a cousin, or a parent.

One young unmarried woman who became alcalde at age twenty asked her father to take on one of the month-long periods of service for the vecino corregidor, while she did another one herself. If, as happens regularly, a spouse dies during the period of service, the survivor asks a relative—perhaps even a son or daughter who is still a child—to substitute at the festivals.

If no one volunteers for a particular post, the kuraka has the right to impose these roles on individuals who have been reluctant to take them in the past. His decision is influenced by many factors, such as the positions in which a couple has already served, how much land they own and their relative wealth, and their familial and hamlet situation (that is, whether there are others available from whom they can expect help). Normally, if one person from among a set of adult siblings takes on one of the roles, other ayllu members (and the kuraka) will consider that sufficient contribution from the sibling group as a whole; no other brother or sister will be obliged to take on the same role. They might, however, be asked to take on one of the other posts, depending largely on the quantity of lands the sibling group controls.

It is therefore the case that these posts do not have to be filled in any strict order. The kuraqkuna of Yura do not constitute a civil-religious hierarchy as is found in Mesoamerica, where each person must fill one role before moving on to the next (e.g., Carrasco 1961; Cancian 1965; Smith 1977; Mathews 1985). It is not necessary to have been a postillón or jilaqata, for instance, to be alcalde. Furthermore, some couples serve as jilaqatas twice (though never in the same minor ayllu). They either take on the posts in the principal ayllu of both husband and wife, or in two ayllus where one of the spouses happens to have lands. In such a case as this, the couple would have amply fulfilled their communal obligations and, if they choose not to, might never take on any other roles beyond those. Other couples who have been married for some years and are well endowed with lands may be asked to serve as alcalde without ever having been either postillón or jilaqata.

Although a person or couple may volunteer for any of the positions chosen by the kuraka, and can do so without following a prescribed order or passing through them in a stair-step way, there is an agreed-upon hierarchy of relative prestige in the roles which does influence the age at which one takes them on. The postillón, now abolished, tended to be filled by young men, primarily because of the immense physical requirements of the post. In addition, the term of office was shorter, such that the outlay of resources needed was less for them than for those who would accompany their fellow kuraqkuna through a whole annual cycle of festivals. This, too, was attractive to young households of limited resources. Those who owned little land might go no further in the series than this position.

Jilaqata is next in the progression of roles, both in terms of the age of the incumbents and in the relative wealth to be expended, since the jilaqata is the primary host at only one large fiesta. Alcalde comes above that. Until 1979 the alcalde had to host two major fiestas and part of a third.[1] The alcalde has the added prestige of his work for the corregidor. Notwithstanding the example of the twenty-year-old female alcalde, most people who take on service roles or the sponsorship of festivals are usually older than that. The average age of the jilaqata falls somewhere in the late twenties to early thirties, while the alcaldes—who may or may not have served in some other post before—are often in their late thirties. Most adult couples who have been married for at least five years have taken on one service or sponsorship role. By age forty, many have filled two.

The kuraka also appoints two jatun alfereces (or major hosts), one couple for the festival of Encarnación and another for Corpus Christi. At the former festival a number of other alfereces, all of whom have volunteered as a personal act of devotion, also celebrate without the kuraka's intervention. At Corpus there are no other alfereces beyond the appointed one, but the jatun alférez shares sponsorship duties with the jilaqatas. These jatun alférez positions, which rotate among the four major ayllus, are not prerequisites for any of the three service roles, or vice versa. Chances are that if a couple had already served as postillón or jilaqata the kuraka would not choose them as jatun alférez unless they volunteered.

There would always be others who had done less. Some people have expressed the opinion that the jatun alférez post should be taken on before becoming alcalde or kuraka, but this was not a generally accepted rule. I met several people who had become alcalde without having served as jatun alférez.

This contrast between the Yura system of passing through the authority roles and the more rigid civil-religious hierarchy of Meso-america (where participants must pass through each of a sequential set of positions) may have to do with the fairly small number of offices in Yura to be shared among a large potential population. Another factor accounting for this contrast with the Mesoameri-can practice is the sense of the unity of the adult sibling group, which considers participation of brothers as counting for each other. Taking on the role is never automatic. A final distinction is the fact that these roles, except for the jatun alférez, are civil rather than religious—or, to avoid that confusing terminology, all have a civil component in addition to festival sponsorship. Many couples who are chosen as kurakas of their major ayllus have not served as jatun alférez, and have correspondingly filled only "civil" roles.

Both age and the completion of at least two service positions (or, in other cases, one and a jatun alférezship) make a couple eligible to take on the responsible post of kuraka. However, reputation is another important factor in choosing the kuraka (and here the husband's qualities are usually emphasized). Such a reputation is, of course, only established through time. Most couples serving as kurakas are in their forties or fifties.

I have mentioned the need on the part of those who assume the service roles to amass considerable resources in order to sponsor the festivals. The quantities needed are large: five hundred pounds of corn for beer, firewood for heating hundreds of gallons of water for days for beermaking, and assistance in serving guests for a week. But this is not done alone; rather, the work is accomplished through reciprocal exchange of labor and goods, established with neighbors and kin. The nature of this sharing of labor and the mutual obliga-tions created by it have been described and analyzed in some detail by Inge Harman (1987).

Description of the Kuraqkuna Roles

We now turn to a description of the particulars of each of the kuraqkuna posts. Although they share many characteristics, each also has its own distinct set of obligations and activities.

The Postillón

The duties of the postillón perhaps do not qualify it to be called an "authority" role at all, since the primary task of the post, until it was abolished, was to carry the mail. This mail varied from simple letters to payrolls and even large packages. The origins of the institution may well be found in the Inka *ch'aski* system (as described, for example, by Cieza [1553] 1967, chap. 21:70–72; and by Polo [1561] 1940:140). The form of postillonaje found in Yura, however, was almost certainly established early in the colonial period and then modified as different population centers in the region grew or declined in size. It was a state imposition, used primarily by literate, urban-oriented Bolivians and supervised, at least in this century, by a vecino official at the local level.

In Yura, this vecino position was called the *postero* or the *correista*. The person who was appointed always held the job for several years. Although the post involved only the collecting and sorting of correspondence and packages, it gave the correista temporary control over the labor of those Yuras serving as postillones in what was frequently an exploitative and abusive relationship. Until the early decades of this century both the postillón and his wife were required to live in Yura during their periods of service.

Each postillón served a term of six months, and four people took on the post for every six-month period. The kuraka chose postillones from all ten of the minor ayllus. The four postillones from the Upper Moiety began their term of service at Christmas and served until San Juan (June 24), while the four from the Lower Moiety worked from San Juan until Christmas. This meant that in the three major ayllus composed of only two minor ayllus, both of the latter provided a candidate for postillón every year. In practice, this meant that in the Lower Moiety's semester postillones were recruited from Jatun Qhurqa, Sullk'a Qhurqa, Jatun Chiquchi, and Sullk'a Chiquchi. In the Upper Moiety's half-year, Wisijsa Qullana and Sawlli each provided a postillón each year, but in the case of Qullana, which is composed of four minor ayllus, Jatun Qullana provided a postillón yearly while Qhapaqa, Sullk'a Qullana, and Agregados took turns filling the second slot.

The postillones worked in monthly cycles; that is, the wife acted as servant to the postero for two weeks at a time, and the husband served the vecino postero for one week and carried the mail for another week; then for two weeks they were free to return home to their own work. They also planted and tended the fields of the vecino postal official. Due to the half-year schedule of the moieties, it was always those from Chiquchi and Qhurqa who planted the postero's fields in October. The postillones from Qullana and Wisijsa were responsible for the work of irrigation and harvest.

In the week of labor service that each postillón performed for the correista prior to carrying the mail, no separation was made by the vecino postman between tasks related strictly to the mails and personal tasks of his household. For instance, the correista required the postillón to carry several loads of water—each load being two sixteen-liter cans—from the river to his house before setting off on his long, difficult trip to Potosí. One Yura, who regarded water consumption for anything besides making corn beer as extravagant, remarked ironically that "the correista must really have stunk" to need so much. During these weeks the postillón was treated as a personal servant, like the hacienda *pongos* who served the landowners, and was even loaned to other vecinos to work for them.

The journey carrying the mail was made on foot. The postillón hurried along the mountain paths and roads, usually traveling alone through the night. He was accompanied only by his *pululu*,[2] a bugle made from a bull's horn, which he sounded in villages and hamlets. Until some twenty years ago the trip was especially arduous: during the course of some five days, he was required to run round trip between Yura and Potosí (a total of some 220 kilometers), then continue directly on to Tomave, located another 60 kilometers to the west. If an exhausted postillón felt it was impossible to complete the trip, he might ask a relative or friend to stand in for him as his replacement, his *mink'a,* for one of the legs of the journey. In the last years before the post was abolished, the trip was shortened by half and the runners could leave the mail at Porco, midway on the trip to Potosí.

The journeys made by the postillón were considered to be—and were—a great sacrifice of effort and time. But the postillón felt protected by his pululu, which he saw as a companion and as a guardian against dangers from men and spirits. Informants referred to the pululu as the "mamita," the same term that is applied both to Earth Mother (see chapter 10) and to the patron saint of the territory. Yet when the post was abolished, no one lamented its passing. Many, however, were sorry to lose the festivals associated with the change of runners at Christmas and San Juan. The Yura are unanimous in agreeing that the work involved in the role was a terrible, painful task, and they were glad to be rid of it.

The Jilaqata

The jilaqatas are the kuraqkuna most oriented to festival activities; and they play a major role in the fiestas of Corpus Christi, Encarnación, and, formerly, Navidad. There is, however, an important civil aspect to this post. The jilaqatas are responsible for collecting the tasa, the indigenous land tax described in chapter 3 which the Yura believe ensures their access to lands.[3] They take the tax from the members of their minor ayllus and then turn it over to their ayllu's kuraka. The way in which the jilaqatas go about the collection of the tasa reveals in some ways how the Yura comprehend the relationship between the community at large and those serving as kuraqkuna.

The ten jilaqata couples (chosen, like the postillones, by their kurakas) serve for one year. Their terms of office begin and end according to the moiety affiliation of their minor ayllus. The six jilaqatas of the Upper Moiety ayllus of Qullana and Wisijsa turn over their posts to their successors on the Saturday after Corpus Christi (Corpus is, of course, always on a Thursday), while the four jilaqatas from Chiquchi and Qhurqa of the Lower Moiety are installed the month before at the "big festival" of Nuestra Señora

A Jilaqata Couple with
Pululu and Staff of
Authority

de la Encarnación, the patron saint of Yura. At present they serve almost overlapping terms. A few Yuras related a tradition that long ago the Lower Moiety jilaqatas entered their posts at Christmas. If that is true the changes would have occurred by moiety almost on a semestral cycle, similar to the postillones. However, I have not been able to confirm this.

In their role as ayllu tax collectors, the jilaqatas must observe one unfailing rule: they must never ask anyone directly to pay what they owe. The tasa must be offered voluntarily by all, without any requests or reproaches from the jilaqata. One older man in ayllu Chiquchi put it in forceful terms when he said: "Manaña, manaña, ima p'inqaywaq mañasun? Jina lastipullanchis, chinkachipullanchis sina, mañasun. Ima nispa mañamuwaq? Niña mañanakuq kanchu kasun." (No way, no way. With what shame [how shameful it would be] will we ask for it? That's how we damage things, that's how, it seems to me, we end up just losing things [our traditions]. What would you say when you went to ask? There's just no way we can ask each other [for the tasa].)

Although the paying of the tasa is considered a serious duty, and Yuras sense strong pressures to fulfill the obligation, naturally there are always some who are unable or unwilling to pay their part. When that happens the jilaqata must make up the lack from his own pocket, *wulsanmanta*. By acting as a liberal and generous host at festivals, he hopes to encourage his fellow ayllu members to remember their tasa obligations. But it is the responsibility of the role to assure that the minor ayllu tasa is covered, no matter how. The sum today is relatively small: for example, the jatun and sullk'a segments that make up ayllu Chiquchi paid only $b1,385 in 1978 (at exchange rates in effect then, that represents about U.S. $70, though that tells us little about local purchasing power). In the past the amount, in real terms, was considerably greater. If the jilaqata's obligation to complete the total payment was the rule then, it would have represented a great economic burden even if only a few households were unable to pay.

By accepting to pay for all who cannot, the jilaqata, whose social existence is required through impositions of an "alien" state, acts to foster and protect ayllu unity and integrity against such impositions. Someone who identified with the state could create divisiveness if he, for instance, reported to Potosí treasury officials that "our tasa is incomplete because the following people failed to pay their share . . ."

There is one exception to the prohibition on requests for payments. Most minor ayllus are highly dispersed over the territory of Yura, and sometimes isolated segments become less diligent in making the tasa payment. In such cases a jilaqata may ask his kuraka to establish a commission to go to each delinquent household and remind them that they are behind in their tasa and should pay either then or at the next festival. The landholders normally agree to do so, unable to deny the kuraka's request. The jilaqata does not join this delegation and is accordingly spared the embarrassment of requesting the payment himself.

One aspect of the role of jilaqata is, naturally, to keep track of the tasa payments as they are made to him. Before the fruits of literacy were extended to the Yura some forty years ago, all accounting was kept in the head. Older people who have seen the feats of memory of their parents and grandparents that were required by the ayllu record keeping recall with wonder such lost abilities. These earlier jilaqatas were aided in their task by a mnemonic system in which tasa households were recorded through the use of maize. Each tasa unit was alloted two corn grains; the pairing was probably due to the fact that the tasa was paid in two installments at six-month intervals. The number of corn grains was carefully monitored and controlled in order to be consistent with ayllu membership, and they and memory together served to keep track of the entire ayllu's tasa payments. Today the corn grain system has been retained, but names and amounts are also noted in writing. The corn grains, while still symbolizing the unity of the ayllu and the tasa units, no longer demonstrate the mathematical exactitude of before. The jilaqata couple, or more precisely the *contador* (accountant) appointed to keep the records for them while they celebrate, now simply writes down the payment in a school notebook.

The lands owned by vecinos, and a small portion of those of the comunarios, have been taken out of the ayllu tasa system (in which an ayllu's lands are treated by the state as a single unit) and converted to an individually titled status. In these cases the owners pay a *catastro*, or private land tax.[4] At a public meeting in January 1979 the corregidor read a statement from the Military Geographic Institute in La Paz that ordered every peasant landowner to report to Potosí to have all lands converted to individual catastro.[5] To those familiar with rural Bolivia this is a ludicrous prospect. To do the job in a minimally legal way, hundreds of thousands of small farm plots would have to be surveyed around the country. Even in periods of political stability the resources needed for such a task ensure that it will not be done in this century. Furthermore, the comunarios themselves would resist a shift to catastro taxation, since the individualized direct taxes are much higher than the tasa.

In June 1984, five years after the order, no one had moved to follow the institute's edict. A number of the Yura agreed, however, that if the tasa were to disappear, then the primary function of the jilaqata would be lost and the post would be abolished. No one could really foresee such an occurrence; everyone who expressed an opinion said they would be reluctant to lose the fiestas that the jilaqatas host. But the abolition of the jilaqatas, just as the postillón had been abolished before, was nevertheless felt to lie within the range of real possibilities.[6]

The Alcalde

The alcalde (the Quechua form is *alkanti*) is the post among the kuraqkuna that we could best characterize today as having power, in the sense of the capacity to affect the conduct of others and to require obedience from them. The alcalde's primary civil task is to serve the corregidor, the local-level vecino post whose incumbent is the chief administrative and judicial figure in the canton recognized by the Bolivian state. During his kamachi, or term of service, the alcalde acts as the corregidor's constable and messenger, and places himself at the disposal of the vecino official for any purpose that may arise. The alcalde becomes in many circumstances the basic link between the police power of the state and the comunarios. Yet the alcalde, too, has a significant role to play in the festive life of Yura ayllus, and his exercise of power as the corregidor's agent is circumscribed and reinforced by ritual commitments.

The indigenous alcalde is the structural descendant of an office that was established early in the colonial period. In 1575 Francisco Toledo issued regulations for Charcas (what is today central Bolivia), relating to the election of an indigenous official bearing the same title. This post was empowered to hear certain civil and criminal disputes among those indigenous folk who were not of the local hereditary elite (Toledo [1575] 1925:304ff.). The role of the alcalde is listed in the revisitas of Yura as early as 1602 (AGN 13.18.6.4, it. 3:fol. Br) and alcaldes reappear in the documents throughout the centuries. Today the alcaldes of Yura continue to be authorities involved in the settlement of disputes, now, however, under the supervision of a vecino corregidor.

Each of the five couples who serve as alcaldes fills the post for one year, entering and leaving office on January 7 at the festival of Reyes (Epiphany). The ayllu kurakas are responsible for choosing those who take the office. The Qullana kuraka selects two alcalde couples, one from the jatun/sullk'a pair of minor ayllus, and a second from the isolated southern region of Phajcha, from the minor ayllus of Qhapaqa and Ariaw. The other three kurakas choose one couple each as alcaldes for their major ayllus.

The husband of each alcalde couple serves at the corregimiento (the vecino corregidor's office) for a total of two months and fifteen days, except for the Phajcha alcalde, who serves for only two months. The labor service, or kamachi, is performed on an elaborate rotational calendar. The kamachi year actually begins on December 1, over a month before the formal installation of the new alcalde. The alcalde who works that first month is called the *originario*, and is now appointed from among the major ayllus according to a simple four-year cycle in the order of Qullana–Qhurqa–Wisijsa–Chiquchi.[7] Regardless of who the originario is, the Phajcha alcalde always works fifth, last in the kamachi round; he cannot be originario.

An example will clarify how this works. In 1986 the Qullana alcalde was originario, and he carried out his first month's kamachi in December 1985. In January the Qhurqa alcalde served, in February the Wisijsa, and in April the Phajcha. Then the cycle repeats, with the Phajcha alcalde serving his second month in September. Two months remain until December 1, when the new originario will take over, and these are divided up into half-month *yapas* (added amounts) by the alcaldes of the four major ayllus.

Labor requirements in the present system are considerably reduced from the past. As late as the 1930s, all five alcalde couples, both husband and wife, had to spend the entire year in Yura at the disposition of the household of the vecino corregidor. The wives were expected to assist the corregidor's wife in the preparations necessary to feed all these people. The alcalde couples would return home during the year only to oversee planting and to carry out the minimum chores needed to keep their crop production going. This represented a real control of surplus labor for the corregidor which, in this agrarian economy, would have significantly improved his position in the urban markets and as a local nexus of redistribution. This large labor burden was gradually reduced, apparently after the 1952 MNR Revolution, to the current system of turns.

The alcalde serving his kamachi undertakes a range of activities. On one hand, he acts as a policeman. If, for instance, there has been a fight in a distant rancho between husband and wife or between neighbors, one of the people involved might go to the corregidor to lodge a formal complaint. Depending on the seriousness of the case, the corregidor may decide that he must see the defendant in order to hear the opposing view or to levy a fine. In such a case it is the alcalde who brings that person to the canton capital. The alcalde carries with him his *kinsa rey,* the wooden staff of office that will take on increasing importance in our discussion. Due to the respect that Yuras express toward the alcalde, and especially toward the staff, people very rarely, if ever, go against the alcalde's wishes.

The alcalde also serves as a general courier throughout the canton in order to relay to the ranchos the news of upcoming meetings in Yura. He usually delivers the message, often in written form, to the comisionado in the larger ranchos.[8] The alcalde may be sent to any part of the Yura territory where he is needed, not just to the lands of his own ayllu. He is not, however, asked to go outside canton Yura, for example, to make trips to the cities.

At public meetings during festivals in Yura (the normal time for them to be held), the alcalde travels from houseyard to houseyard in the central village to ask people to attend. He also serves as doorkeeper and sergeant at arms at the meeting, ready to fetch people or carry messages if it becomes necessary. On the other hand, a great part of the alcalde's efforts are dedicated to the personal service of the corregidor. Like the postillón, he also carries water for the vecino's household. He cleans and sweeps the corregidor's office. He also attends to the corregidor's fields by irrigating them, weeding, contributing his labor toward keeping the irrigation canals open, and harvesting the crops.

I have mentioned that the Yura plant their fields in a kind of cooperative work festival, the *mink'a*.[9] A special form of this, called a *yanasi mink'a*, is organized for all the kuraqkuna, as well as for the alfereces of certain festivals, by their fellow rancho members. While the regular mink'a is highly egalitarian in form, the yanasi —along with a few other specialized mink'as—introduces a note of hierarchy between those who offer it and those who enjoy its benefits. In the case of the members of a hamlet who fête one of their number who has become jilaqata or alcalde, this stratification aspect is not highly accentuated; to the degree that it is, it serves to express the community's gratitude and respect toward those who have agreed to take on the post.

The alcaldes, however, are also expected to offer the corregidor a yanasi mink'a. In the past, when all five alcalde couples lived in Yura, this was an elaborate, costly, and exploitative institution. The alcaldes provided everything—the human labor to carry out the work, the animals for plowing, and all the other elements for the highly ritualized undertaking. In more recent years the alcaldes have been able to lessen this burden through a kind of passive resistance, and today only the alcalde carrying out his kamachi is expected to help out in the planting of the corregidor's fields.

Yet in other respects the corregidores continue to exploit the alcaldes' labor. Alcaldes may be sent on missions that have nothing to do with the official aspects of the post, but rather with the private affairs of the corregidor or his family. For example, the mother of one corregidor manages a store in the central village of Yura, where she sells considerable quantities of alcohol. A comunario in a settlement some thirty kilometers to the south of the village was late in making payment on the credit account he kept with her. The storekeeper had her son order the alcalde to walk to the man's hamlet to collect the debt he owed.

The corregidor, like the postman, formerly felt he had the power to loan alcaldes to other vecinos when they had some special work task. The alcaldes, who have generally been willing to carry the burden of serving the corregidor, always resented being required to work at the personal tasks of other vecinos. This practice has largely ended, except for special community visits by government notables.

This description has emphasized the service, almost servile, relationship between the alcaldes and the vecino corregidor. Such an emphasis results from discussing only the kamachi of the alcalde and is, as we shall see, something of a distortion. In the description of the festival of Reyes to come in chapter 8, it is clear that the kamachi is only one element of the post. Yura generally picture the labor service as almost a necessary evil which is accepted with equanimity in order to carry on with the more important and fulfilling aspect of the role, that of festival sponsorship.

If indeed the alcaldes once had greater independent powers to adjudicate disputes on their own, they have lost them. Yet it may well be that, in spite of Toledo's edicts, the alcalde was never able to exercise such prerogatives. It seems evident that Toledo intended to create the alcalde in the sixteenth century as a counterweight to the hereditary kurakas; but if that was the case, in Yura, at least, his hope remained unfulfilled. Early on the incumbents, if they were commoners, found themselves under the influence of those very leaders; and in some cases the post was filled by members of the hereditary elite itself. Two centuries later, when this superior stratum was finally destroyed, the alcaldes seem to have transferred their loyalty to the new vecino authorities. But that is a story that will be developed in its proper place.

The Kuraka

In many ways the post of kuraka is the most intriguing of all the kuraqkuna. As opposed to all the other kuraqkuna, the four kurakas are elected and ratified by their major ayllus in a general meeting. Neither do they serve a fixed term of office. Three to five years is the normal period of time in the post, but kurakas have served from as little as one year to as many as ten. With no set date for entering the post, no festival is specifically theirs. On the other hand, they attend all the festivals sponsored by other kuraqkuna and by the jatun alfereces; in fact, they are obliged to accompany the others in all their ritual activities.

The kurakas also serve as a couple, and husband and wife hold the post jointly. Yet, when candidates are discussed for the post, it is my impression that the husband's personality and qualities are of principal consideration. This is not to deny what is a strong current of approximate equality between the sexes in Yura social life, but rather represents the widespread tendency of human societies in which males predominate in the public sphere. In this post, where one sees more discretionary possibilities for expressing public leadership, this tendency, largely submerged in other realms, seems to come more into the open. On the other hand, the kuraka's stated judgments and actions often result from joint deliberation between husband and wife. The wife's role in those ritual activities involving the kurakas is crucial.

The kuraka couple is in many respects the moral leader of the ayllu. The husband must be seen as a *k'acha runa,* a man of admirable character. In this he differs from the other kuraqkuna, who are chosen not because of their leadership abilities or intelligence, but rather because they have lands in the ayllu and it is their turn. In contrast with the kuraka, anybody can be jilaqata or alcalde. The kuraka, however, should ideally be a person who is not argumentative or prone to violence, who is honest, who can speak well and command respect. A sense of personal dignity is also important, but not in the sense of pomposity—the kuraka should be *ancha humilde,* a *runa cabal,* a man circumspect, not overbearing, in his dealings with others. Other informants added that the kuraka should have a superior memory and be acquainted with more members of the ayllu than is true of most men.

These kinds of characteristics as sources of leadership ability and individual prestige may be widespread in the southern Andes. Webster (1974) has analyzed the factors that determine relative status in the community he calls Cheqeq in the department of Cuzco, where he found that, in spite of an ideology of egalitarianism, a certain degree of internal differentiation existed. Relative wealth was one determinant of status; but more important were the kinds of personality traits—being well-spoken, mature, tranquil, yet one who "gets things done"—which Yura suggest are necessary for the kuraka. In Cheqeq, as in Yura, participating in the indigenous authority system was a principal means by which couples gained prestige and raised their status.

The kuraka is theoretically confirmed by the subprefect of Quijarro province in Uyuni and sworn in by the canton corregidor in Yura. Although the legal status of indigenous authorities such as these is ambiguous in Bolivia, in the department of Potosí, at least, they receive some recognition of their service in a simple typed memorandum that appoints them to their post. When the ayllu meets to select a new kuraka, the incumbent turns over a list of three nominees to the corregidor. But the primary candidate is always clearly designated and invariably appointed. Any politicking and muted competition for the position occurs before and during the ayllu meeting. The candidate named there is selected by consensus, and any further jockeying ends. Of course the final confirmation by the subprefect in Uyuni could provide the vecinos a chance to block the appointment of someone whom they did not wish to see in the post, but I know of no case within recent memory where this has occurred.

At times a man who is chosen by his ayllu is unwilling to serve. The position requires a steady and constant expenditure of time and resources, and many feel the rewards—which consist largely in the satisfaction of being in a position of respect and responsibility —are not equal to the sacrifices. In rare cases the husband of the couple named just disappears. He may, for instance, go off to the cities or to some agricultural area to work in wage labor. This happened in 1978, when the person selected to be kuraka of Wisijsa promptly left for Santa Cruz to work in the sugar cane harvest. But in the great majority of cases the couple, after some initial reluctance, accepts. Most are convinced, according to informants, by the fact that the ayllu at large chooses them. Although they may argue that their resources are inadequate, the outgoing kuraka and the corregidor remind them of the support the ayllu has shown them, and they put up no further objections.[10] At other times several men are anxious to be kuraka, and some will go to the person in office and propose to take over the post from him. Yet the community must agree, and if ayllu members hold strong reservations about a man's character, he will never be selected no matter how much he wants the job.

The kuraka owes no kamachi, or labor service, to vecino officials as do the alcaldes and the postillones. The relationship between the corregidor and the kuraka is not always free from questions as to which is the higher authority. Observation of events indicates that in fact the corregidor has more power than the kuraka: the vecinos, by their ability to manipulate the urban levers of departmental government, through their predominant position in the money economy, and because of their ethnic identification with the urban classes, are able to use the office of the corregidor to influence events in their favor at every opportunity. But as an ideological statement of how the relationship should work, one former activist kuraka, speaking in a mixture of Quechua and Spanish, put it this way: "Corregidorqa ni ima ruwayta atinchu, porque kurakaq nisqampi corregidor kanan tian. Kuraka es más autoridad que todo el campesinado, autoridad. Kurakaq nisqampi corregidor kanan tian ari." (The corregidor can't do anything [as far as obliging the kuraka to work for him] because the corregidor must be under the mandate of the kuraka. The kuraka is the primary authority of all the peasantry. The corregidor has to be under the authority of the kuraka.)

The kuraka, free from any direct obligation to the local vecino elite, attends to a wide range of activities. First, as we have seen, it is the kuraka who selects all the other kuraqkuna. This is to say that it is in fact the kurakas who maintain the entire kuraqkuna system; without their administrative efforts the other posts would not be filled. To choose fellow ayllu members for these roles the kurakas must keep track of who has served and who has not undertaken their obligations to the ayllu. They must evaluate the relative wealth of different families and have some idea of the amount of land they own overall. They must also be willing to apply moral pressure to individuals who resist when they are selected.

In the past such pressure was not necessary. Many informants recounted how the kurakas were frequently besieged with requests from couples who wanted to serve in a post. The kuraka memorized long lists of candidates and was forced to mediate fights between people who were eager for their turn to come. Sometimes posts were assigned years in advance. This is no longer the case, although people do continue to ask to fill a role for the following year. In general, however, the new opportunities in wage labor elsewhere in the country, which take both men and women away from their homes for months at a time, have made many couples less willing to take on the commitment of a kuraqkuna role.

The kuraka now frequently has to obligate some ayllu members to accept one of the positions. There are several steps a kuraka can take to convince a recalcitrant ayllu member to accept the post. He first points out to the person resisting the appointment that he is obliged to fill the position because of his use of lands assigned to the ayllu. One kuraka described this in terms of an imaginary dialogue:

"Jilaqata kanayki tian. Qan kay terrenuta tarpunki."
"Tasata yupashani."
"Tasata yupay; piru chay jilaqatata tantanayki tian. Chaytaq, jilaqata, pitaq?"
"Tarpullasaq; ñuqataq tasata yupashani."

("You have to serve as jilaqata. You are, after all, planting this field."
"I'm paying the tasa."
"You may well pay your tasa; but you have to take on the post of jilaqata. If not, just who will be it?"
"I'm just going to plant; I'm paying the tasa.")

The kuraka concluded, "Obliganan tian runasta. Kantumanta ruwananku tian." (He has to oblige people. Everybody has to do it.)

When such arguments fail, the kuraka may take the reluctant candidate to the corregidor to enlist his aid. The vecino official also tries to convince the person, or he may even order him to accept. Apparently many people give in before going to the corregimiento, while others refuse until confronted by the vecino official.

Other kurakas, rather than involving the corregidor, threaten to take away the lands of the couple who refuse to serve. The kuraka tells them not to plant that year; those fields will be given to whomever takes the post that the candidates are evading. One former kuraka said that if a neighbor of the couple wanted to take on the post, then he would simply annex an adjoining field of those refusing the kuraka's appointment to the lands of the person who said he would accept. Everyone agreed, however, that this is a final threat, and no lands have ever actually been taken away, at least in the last fifty years (which is as far back as the memories of the older informants reached). As one person said when I asked when a kuraka had last transferred land in this way, "*Manaraqpuni, nisqalla*" (Up to now, never; it's just said [that he will]). The person who had declined to accept the post invariably takes it when the kuraka threatens to assign his fields to someone else. This presents us with a tantalizing possibility in which the kuraka, acting for the community, claims prior land rights of the ayllu over the family which actually controls them.[11] Yet it remains a claim which has never been (or is no longer) effectuated. The threats are, nevertheless, still made.

In the end most people do not resist to the point where such threats are necessary, since taking on one of the roles, in spite of the costs involved, has its rewards. Furthermore, the request of a kuraka carries weight in itself and, Yura agree, is not usually made lightly. As one man put it, "Jinapi pasaykuyku; kurakas churapuwayku, yastá, imanaykumantaq. Imanasuntaq, churawaqtinchis kurakaqa. Mana kurakata atipay atiykuchu. Chay comunarios kayku, a la fuerza chayman pasanayku tian." (So in that way we just enter in to serve. The kurakas suddenly choose us, well there you are, what option would we have? So what can you do if the kuraka selects you? We can't beat out the kuraka. Those of us who are comunarios, we have no choice, we just have to take them [the kuraqkuna posts] on.)

The kuraka's importance in maintaining the system is seen most clearly in his role in the inauguration festivals of the different posts. In each case the kuraka couple is obliged to "lead" (*pusay*) those that are about to enter the posts and to "accompany" (the Spanish verb is Quechuized to *akumpañay*) those who are filling or about to leave them. The result of this is that the kurakas must attend the whole range of festivals and provide at least some food and drink at all of them. Although there is no single fiesta at which the kuraka has to provide the quantities of corn beer and alcohol that, for instance, the jilaqatas have ready at Corpus, they must make at least one *wanta* (batch, using about fifty pounds of corn) of corn beer for, as a minimum, six different occasions; and several other events have recently been abolished. They do this in order to be able to adequately accompany the other kuraqkuna and alfereces they appointed.

In special cases the kurakas are responsible for mobilizing their ayllus for public works projects in the central village of Yura. For example, in the construction of the canton central school some years back, it was decided that all Yura households would contribute a day's labor. The kurakas were those charged with organizing their fellow ayllu members to carry out the work. A similar arrangement was used for the construction of a paramedic clinic, an office for the corregimiento, a building for the municipal government, a two-room hotel, and a later addition to the central school.

Similarly, the kuraka may mobilize labor to clean the rough dirt roads of the canton. The rural indigenous population is yearly re-quired to offer their *prestación vial* labor service (while urban Bolivians free themselves of the obligation by paying a small sum). Most Yura take part in the three days of labor with pick and shovel in order to obtain the receipt issued at the end which confirms their participation. This document can be demanded by any uniformed official when Yuras travel outside the canton—a form of harassment that all country folk learn to endure.

As a "moral voice" to the ayllus, the kuraka is sometimes called on to settle disputes among individuals. The kuraka does not pun-ish, nor can he impose fines. He rather admonishes others to do better. The word universally used here is *k'amiy,* which carries the sense of "scold" or "reprimand." A former kuraka said that he might say to two men who are fighting: "Wawasniyuqña kan-kichis, ededña kankichis, cargu pasaqña kankichis. Mana allinta portakunkichischu, portakunaykichis allinta a." (You already have children, you are adults now; you've served in cargos. You've be-haved badly, and you really ought to act right.)

The kuraka tries to "make people understand," to mediate arguments and settle differences by compromise. Yet if the conflict is serious, such as one in which an injury has resulted, or if the two disputants are from two different ayllus such that the kuraka has less moral authority over one of them, then the individuals involved, or the kuraka himself, will go to the vecino corregidor. The corregidor has the power to make judgments in disputes and can levy fines or impose punishment, usually in the form of work such as cleaning the public areas of the central village. He can also put offenders in jail for a few days and, in very serious cases, deliver them to authorities in Potosí. If the kuraka feels that the disputants are not going to listen to him, he can insist that they go with him to the corregimiento or have the alcalde order them to Yura.

It may be that the kuraka's authority is less in this regard than it was in the past. Most people with complaints against others will go directly to the corregidor and ask the kuraka to mediate only in exceptional cases today. However, one man described a trip with his brother, who was Qullana kuraka at the time, to the Phajcha area. Phajcha is more isolated and, some say, more traditional than the central valleys. In Phajcha the Qullana kuraka was called upon to settle a whole series of disputes. The father of an adolescent son, for instance, would tell the kuraka: "Jinataq, mana kasuwanchu kay waway; k'amirparipuway." (And so my son here doesn't listen to me; please straighten him out for me.) The kuraka might then take the boy aside and tell him to behave in terms such as these: "Imarayku machu-machu chay jina kanki? Imaraykutaq qan jinata portakunki? Jovenraq kanki. Ajina purinayki. . . . Kasunayki tian tataykita." (Why are you so vehement that way? Why are you behaving like that? You're still just a youngster. This is the way you should conduct yourself. . . . You have to obey your father.) It is clear, then, that for the Phajchas the kuraka was a figure who could be called upon to improve relations even among family members. Yet if this aspect of his job has been diminished somewhat as more and more people turn to the corregidor to resolve disputes, the kuraka is still called upon to reprimand those who fight in his presence. The person of the kuraka is always to be respected.

The kuraka acts as a direct link between his ayllu and the outside, both in relations with the urban governmental sphere and with neighboring ethnic groups. Once the jilaqatas turn over the tasa they have collected to him, the kuraka is responsible for carrying the sum to the departmental treasury in Potosí. Activist kurakas have also confronted government officials over problems that affect their communities. I was told that one Chiquchi kuraka, for instance, traveled to La Paz some years back to speak to officials in the Agricultural Ministry and the Mining Ministry about the medium-sized antimony mine of Putuma, located along the southern Taru River. The mine had been dumping its wastes into the watercourse, damaging agricultural production downstream. Since urban government officials tend to treat country folk either with undisguised contempt or as curious trained bears, the kuraka's efforts unfortunately had little practical effect: the mine continues to dump its tailings into the stream. Nevertheless, the fact that he had made the trip was universally known, and his attempt was cited as exemplary action by a kuraka. Other kurakas have also traveled to La Paz; a former Qullana kuraka is frequently mentioned in this regard.

The kuraka must represent his ayllu in boundary disputes with neighboring groups. The *mojones,* or boundary markers, of Yura are well established, and the Yura possess documents handed down through the generations which verify their locations. Nevertheless, other groups sometimes try to "advance" onto Yura territory. In recent years, one former kuraka told me, there have been disputes with the Chakillas (an ex-hacienda) and the Phurqus (Porcos) on the northeast, the Charcas, or Toropalqueños, on the southeast, the Tolapampas on the southwest, and the Tomaves on the west. Whenever such boundary conflicts arise, the kurakas of the ayllus involved (both from Yura and from the neighboring group) go "in commission" with their land titles, usually with their alcaldes. One former kuraka mentioned that it was also necessary to have an *allin liyiq* along, someone who can read well. The two groups of officials then walk off the boundaries according to the records and reestablish the boundary markers.[12]

Of course such land disputes are not always resolved so peacefully. In one dispute with Tolapampa the Yuras fought to reset the old boundary and pushed their opponents back with force. The most famous local example of a land battle was with Chakilla in the late sixties. Chakilla is a high, lush plain that supports thousands of grazing animals. A stream crosses the pampa, passing through a *bofedal* (an area covered by a thick carpet of mosses and humid grasses)[13] situated on a southern finger of the plain. The stream then flows off the tableland and into the Yura valleys, becoming the Taru River. This bofedal, called the Churu, by all accounts belonged to Yura as the upper extension of the Taru. A list of boundary markers dating from the 1590s (found in the Corincho document discussed in chapter 5) quite definitely places the Churu within Yura territory. However, the area was at some point alienated by the Chakilla hacienda. When the hacienda was turned over in the 1950s to the families living on it, they decided to hold on to the Churu. The Yura kurakas finally gave up on regaining possession of the area peacefully, and, with the support of the corregidor, assembled a small army to take it. When the Chakillas saw the arrival of the massed Yura, they responded in force. A rock battle broke out which ended when a Chakilla exploded a stick of dynamite among the Yura. Suffering several injuries, the Yura called a retreat. The police, then the army, were called in to restore peace. In spite of the early documents the Churu remains a part of Chakilla to this day.

The position of kuraka is full of fascinating contradictions. It is the most exalted of the roles, yet those who fill it are expected to act the most humble. The kuraka's moral authority, and the respect due him, is higher than for any other of the kuraqkuna, yet his ability to impose actual sanctions is very circumscribed. In a society where frequent festivals are an essential part of sociality and serve as a marker of the assumption of special communal statuses, the kurakas, alone among the kuraqkuna, have no fiesta of their own. We shall return to these points in the course of the coming pages as we examine the role of kuraka both in its historic as well as its symbolic contexts.

Vecino Authorities

Some posts held by vecinos have been mentioned in passing in the preceding discussion. Let me describe very briefly the three posts that vecinos fill at the local level in canton Yura: the civil registrar, the corregidor, and the municipal mayor.

The civil registrar is in charge of keeping demographic records in the canton, and in this capacity he also performs civil marriage ceremonies. Although this position carries with it no powers of punishment or legal adjudication, the vecino status of the office-holder permits him to wield considerable influence over the lives of those comunarios who find it necessary to turn to him in such cases as the legitimacy of children, inheritance, and the need for official documents. The registrar was also responsible for the inscription of comunario voters in Bolivia's recent elections, three between 1978 and 1980, and again in 1985. In the earlier cases this enhanced the power of the vecino incumbent to exact personal services from ayllu members. The civil registrar, appointed in Potosí, has no fixed term of office. The predecessor of the present official held the post for more than a decade before his death. Since 1984 a young and capable Yura has taken on the post, although his tenure is now challenged by a vecino contender.

The municipal mayor (usually termed the *intendente*) focuses on activities in the central village where the vecinos reside. In recent years the mayor has been responsible for the construction of a number of public buildings. Theoretically, his (or, as has often been the case, her) responsibility extends to rulings on disputes involving damages by farm animals throughout the canton. The vecino mayor acts at times as a voice of the vecinos in general before the Prefecture in Potosí.

The most important vecino authority is the corregidor. In almost all cases of civil or criminal disputes or offenses it is the corregidor who decides the issues and renders an opinion. The corregidor has the power to impose fines, to punish through labor service, and to imprison. He is also responsible for organizing public meetings, delegating labor for certain public works, and acting as a representative of the community before higher authorities in the provincial and departmental capitals. The holder of this post is very much an intermediary figure, for although he is elected from the vecino group, he is then appointed by the central government. Many of his tasks of office relate to the Yura, primarily due to the fact that the comunarios form the great majority of the total population. As I described above, he relies on an indigenous staff of five alcaldes for a great deal of the actual labor of the posts. The corregidor is, however, in the position of making and putting into practice basic decisions which affect the comunario group.

This concludes the discussion of the civil aspects of the kuraqkuna and a survey of other authority roles at the local level. What has been described is a view of the elders as they exist today, largely divorced from time and with only a few hints at the complex of meanings that surrounds them. I stated earlier that I consider discussion of both civil and symbolic aspects to be essential for an adequate understanding of the institution of the kuraqkuna. We will now look at the past of the kuraqkuna, where we shall see how the Yura, through time, have governed themselves and have dealt with the impositions of the state. Historical research reveals the dynamic nature of authority among the Yura, and suggests why the present constellation of features evolved. Later, we will return to the present with an investigation of the systems of meaning that the Yura associate with their authorities (and which are based largely in the kuraqkuna's participation in ritual), in which a substantial part of the explanation for the continuing relevance of the roles is grounded.

PART 2

INDIGENOUS AUTHORITIES
OF THE PAST

Five centuries of change in the Yura system of native authorities are explored in the two chapters that make up this section of the book. Archival research, reported upon in chapter 5, permits us to reconstruct aspects of the preconquest social organization of the Yuras' ancestors, known as the Wisijsas, and examine as well their responses to the Spanish invasion. A wider view of the Andean ethnic groups of the region during the early years of Spanish colonial society provides the basis for extending Yura history even further into the past, back to early state formations—the Aymara polities that coalesced in the southern Andes in previous centuries and which were later incorporated into the Inka Empire.

In spite of the Spanish incursion into the southern Andes, the Wisijsas were at first able to retain their native identity; however, the internal organization of their ayllus was soon modified by the pressures of Spanish attempts to resettle and concentrate the dispersed Andean populations. Little by little the more extensive political structures that had existed before the arrival of the Spaniards were fragmented. The idea of being a Yura, and the restructuring of the ayllus around the colonial settlement bearing that name, finally replaced the earlier and more inclusive social order of the Wisijsas.

Throughout most of the colonial period the Wisijsas and their successors, the Yuras, were governed directly by their own hereditary kurakas. These native leaders formed an elite stratum both economically and politically; they were the primary mediators between the comunarios they ruled and the Spanish administrators who controlled them. These patterns, formulated early in the colonial period, remained in place through the end of the eighteenth century.

In chapter 6 we examine the extraordinary events surrounding the insurrection of 1781: the assassination of the Yura hereditary lord, the resulting reorganization of the ayllus, and the abolition of the hereditary principle of succession in favor of a fully rotational, egalitarian set of indigenous authorities, the direct precursors of today's kuraqkuna. In this analysis we uncover the continuities between past and present-day structures, while at the same time revealing the fundamental transformation that has taken place in the nature of indigenous authority.

This section concludes with a brief consideration of the events of the nineteenth and early twentieth centuries. From this time, in spite of repeated attempts by republican governments to alienate indigenous lands throughout Bolivia, the Yuras, both in their ayllu structure and in their political organization, emerged largely unscathed.

5

INVASION AND ADAPTATION TO THE COLONIAL SYSTEM

In this chapter we examine the past of the authority roles of Yura during some three centuries, from the little that we know of the pre-Inka polities before the Spanish invasion through the early eighteenth century. We shall also describe the mechanisms imposed on the native populations by the Spanish conquerors to control them and extract resources from them. This will be nothing more than a brief sketch, for records, sparse as they are, nevertheless reach back over four centuries to the first decades of European domination and even beyond. To discuss in depth all the sources available would be a task beyond the scope of the present study. In spite of the incompleteness of the historical record, we are able to draw some conclusions about the changing relationship between the ancestors of the Yura and the colonial state.

The discussion begins with a consideration of the larger clustering of ethnic groups of which the Yura once formed a part, and the participation of that grouping in an even more encompassing pre-Inka polity. The Spanish invasion and the subsequent creation of colonial institutions of labor extraction—the forced labor of *mita*, the concentration of populations into the *reducción*—are treated next. The colonial regime that was established by 1600 retained many of its characteristics for the next two centuries. These institutions formed the backdrop to the struggles fought and the accommodations made between the indigenous authorities and their

European rulers. The mode of presentation followed will be to select several "moments" in time, almost in the form of snapshots,
by drawing on information from censuses (revisitas) and litigation
records. We end this chapter with a look at Yura in 1726.

As we shall see, the institution of the indigenous authorities has
endured for centuries even while the roles and status of the kuraqkuna have changed through time. This evolution came about
both in reaction to impositions from the state and as a result of
the Yuras' perception of new, or newly intolerable, conditions. By
examining the past we can see the contradictions inherent in the
authority roles. Briefly put, the kuraqkuna are today demonstrably
the bearers of a profoundly indigenous organizational tradition and
are a symbol of ethnic resistance to assimilation. Yet the historical
record reveals that in the past they were effective agents for state
mechanisms of extraction while, at the same time, they adapted
to the dominant elite's demands and attempted to influence their
actions.

A major result of this research has been to demonstrate that
in early colonial times the authorities were the most hispanicized
group in Yura society. Yet those roles have became the primary
means chosen by the Yura to stress their Andean identity in the
face of the national society and in their struggle to retain a certain
degree of autonomy, even of self-determination, in an oppressive
colonial system. This was a strategy they continued to follow after
independence from Spain. During those centuries, when elements of
the authority roles became repressive or no longer seemed relevant
to their social reality, the Yura have acted (sometimes with violence)
to change them. But to begin at the beginning, let us turn briefly to
the indigenous polity that the Spaniards encountered when they first
entered what is today central Bolivia.

The Confederation of the Charcas

The ancestors of the Yura, along with several other dispersed populations in the area around the Spanish mines at Potosí, were once
members of an ethnic group known as the Wisijsas.[1] The Wisijsas
were only one of a number of ethnic groupings which, before the

Spanish invasion, made up a large polity that comprehended much of the territory of what is today central Bolivia, including most of the departments of Potosí and Chuquisaca, and parts of Tarija. Following the lead of the early Spaniards and indications of the ruling kurakas of the day, Platt (1978:3) has termed this polity the "Confederation of the Charcas."

Recent research on the Charcas Confederation will be available in a volume published in Bolivia, so a detailed explanation of Charcas organization is not required here.[2] The Charcas followed the widespread Andean pattern of dual division, or organization into moieties, with the Upper Moiety, or Anansaya, also bearing the name Charcas, while the Lower Moiety, Urinsaya, was collectively called the Cara Caras (Espinoza 1969, I:par. 50). The Cara Caras were apparently composed of seven, or perhaps eight, component groups of diverse populations and territories: Macha; Vissisa and Caiza (that is, the Wisijsa); Chaqui; Muru Muru; Colo and Caquina; Picachuri; a group of "lesser" Cara Caras; and Tacobamba (Capoche [1585] 1959:137). How these groups were arranged within the overall Cara Cara moiety is not clear, although it seems likely that dual division was once again apparent, with Macha the principal unit in Anansaya and the Wisijsas dominating the Cara Cara Urinsaya.

Any reconstruction of the original territories of the various ethnic groups relies on the later arrangement of the reducciones established by the Spaniards. The weight of evidence however, supports the conclusion that European administrators used the organization extant for their own bureaucratic purposes. It is apparent that, although each group had an identifiable core area where its villages and fields were clustered, it also operated an elaborate "archipelago" economy of the kind that Murra (1975:59–115) described for peoples further north. The component groups were thoroughly intermixed among themselves, as well as living among (and sharing strategic resources with) groups from outside the confederation. This was especially true in the case of maize production, here as elsewhere a prestige food product (Murra 1960).

The chiefs of the larger ethnic groups of Charcas were apparently powerful leaders long before they led their groups to become part of Tawantinsuyu (an event that preceded the Spanish invasion by perhaps only fifty years). Although we have as yet no detailed information on Wisijsa leaders before the arrival of the Europeans, genealogies of Macha and Charcas lords indicate the existence of a distinct, self-conscious elite who were recruited to membership through hereditary succession. The Charcas lord Ayaviri, ruling in Sacaca in 1582, claimed that "for more than two hundred years up to now my ancestors and predecessors were lords, before the Inkas and after them" (Espinoza 1969, II:par. 2). Later, the Cara Cara lord Ayra de Ariutu detailed his descent through five generations on both his father's and mother's sides, reaching well before the time of the Inkas (AGI Charcas 56:fol. 3r).

When incorporation into Tawantinsuyu finally occurred, it may have been a voluntary move on the part of the ethnic lords. Ayra de Ariutu reported the tradition that one ancestor of his had traveled to Cusco as an emissary from the Cara Cara king. Later, the king's son had himself visited the Inkas and was awarded the hand of one of Wayna Qhapaq's daughters. It was this son who ruled the Cara Caras in the time of the Inka Waskar, when the Spaniards invaded (AGI Charcas 56).

In spite of the special role that the Charcas and Cara Cara groups seemed to have played in the Inkan armies as renowned and feared warriors (Espinoza 1969, I:par. 45; AGI Charcas 56:fol. 9r), their inclusion in the Inka Empire did not seem to change in fundamental ways their forms, organization, or economy. The clear outline of the Charcas polity was still very apparent when Tawantinsuyu succumbed to the army of Pizarro.

The Spanish Invasion and the Establishment of the Colonial System

In 1538 the Charcas and Cara Caras found themselves confronted with the overwhelming military force led by the two brothers of Francisco Pizarro, Hernando and Gonzalo; they were quickly defeated (Hemming 1970:245–47; Espinoza 1969, I:par. 48), leading to the establishment of European domination in Charcas. Two years later the confederation was given in encomienda to the Pizarro brothers. Most of the Cara Cara moiety was apparently assigned to Gonzalo (AGI Charcas 56:fol. 41). However, his political ambitions and his eventual rebellion against the Crown led in 1548 to his defeat and execution at the hands of Royalist forces. That portion of his encomienda which included all of the Cara Cara (except for one ethnic group, the Muru Muru) was then granted to Pedro Hinojosa, one of the commanders of the viceregal troops who had captured the rebel Gonzalo at the Inka fortress of Sacsahuaman (AHP Cajas Reales 18:fol. 216r; Garcilaso de la Vega [1609] 1960, book 5, chap. 34:382).

In the two years before a new tribute list was set in 1550, Hinojosa managed to extract vast amounts of wealth from the indigenous groups under his "care" (Barnadas 1973:325). Even after the tribute owed him was reduced in 1552 he still managed to claim a major segment of the total agricultural production and large sums of cash (Platt 1978:34). In 1553, however, Hinojosa was, in his turn, killed after reneging on his promised participation in another plot against the Crown (Zimmerman 1938:34). Rather than being assigned to another Spanish warrior, the Cara Caras (with the Wisijsa among them) were then incorporated into the domain of the Spanish Crown. Their tribute would go directly into Spanish coffers, at first to support the colonial militia, then later into the general revenues (AHP Cajas Reales 18:fol. 216r; Cajas Reales 328:fol. 118r). Even after a new, lower tasa was established for them in 1553, the groups of the Cara Caras together were still required to pay 14,650 pesos each year. As was true in other Andean areas (Assadourian 1983; Stern 1982), most of the burden of mobilizing these resources fell on the backs of the native lords, and required ingenuity and adaptability in the new context of the incipient colonial society. Such a sum as the Wisijsa had to pay indicates that they, and especially their kurakas, were deeply involved in the nascent money economy only fifteen years after their defeat by the Spaniards (Platt 1978:38).

From the earliest years of Spanish domination, the Crown and its representatives attempted to concentrate indigenous populations and to institute programs of conscripted labor for the mines. Indeed, members of Andean communities were being sent to Potosí on a regular basis by their Spanish encomenderos before 1550 (the mines at Potosí had only begun to be exploited in 1545) (Zavala 1978:9, 13, 15, 30, 45, 243). By the arrival of Viceroy Francisco Toledo in Potosí in late 1572, the mechanisms for forced indigenous labor in the mines were, for all practical purposes, already in place (Bakewell 1984:39–46, 56–59). However, Toledo, who was viceroy of Peru from 1568 to 1581, was a consummate administrator, and it was he who succeeded in putting into effect on a massive scale such projects as the concentration of native peoples into new towns and the regularized provision of laborers for mining (Levillier 1935; Zimmerman 1938; Cole 1985). Toledo succeeded in institutionalizing in the Viceroyalty of Peru the framework of extraction that was employed (at least rhetorically and as a norm) throughout the rest of the colonial period.

The Reducciones and the Wisijsa

In order to see the impact on the Wisijsa of the evolving colonial system, we must examine several of the policies which the Spanish viceroy Toledo imposed on the Andean peoples, and the impact it had on different groups.

Toledo's Policy of Reducción

One of Toledo's primary objectives was to bring hamlet-dwelling Andean people into new towns in order to control native populations more easily for tribute and labor mobilization (Málaga 1974; Zavala 1978:68ff.). This policy of reducción, which regularly ignored ethnic realities in its efforts to reach bureaucratic goals, also brought with it the suppression of many traditional authorities and the creation of new indigenous officials in Charcas. These were to be centered in the reducción itself, based on a model derived from the Spanish *cabildo* (town government). The creation of new posts like alcaldes did not imply, however, the abolition of the hereditary leaders, even if the tone of Toledo's ordinances does suggest that the kurakas and the new cabildo authorities were expected to be in conflict. The reducción alcaldes were to be the creatures of the new

Spanish regime, conceived as an adjunct and a counterweight to the hereditary leaders (Toledo [1575] 1925:304–82). The kurakas were warily tolerated; especially in the early years, the control (or at least direction) of the means of production remained largely in their hands, and without their cooperation the Spaniards would not have been able to gain the tribute. Indeed, Stern speaks not of servile relations between hereditary kurakas and the new Spanish overlords, but of alliances (Stern 1982:27–50).

Later documents suggest that the newly created officials of the reducciones eventually found themselves under the sway of the traditional hereditary authorities (as we shall see below in the case of the Wisijsa),[3] and in this Toledo's plans were unrealized. The larger goal of circumscribing the kurakas' range of power succeeded, however, both geographically and socially. Even if the Spaniards left the indigenous elite largely in place, Toledo's furtherance of the process of "destructuration" (Wachtel 1977:chap. 3)—of fragmenting ethnic groups and curbing the scope of authority of hereditary leaders—gradually took its toll on native society.

The same can be said for the reducción itself. Although large numbers of people apparently did move temporarily from their hamlets to the new Spanish towns, they did not remain there long. Yet when Andean peasants returned to their former hamlets the reducciones did not disappear, but rather took on the role that many still have today as festival centers and seats of local government, the place of linkage to the state and the residence of the maximal authorities (Gade and Escobar 1982). Their impact on indigenous populations perhaps became even more important with the passage of time, since they provided a new focus for creating a sense of ethnic identity and brought about alterations in the internal organization of the ayllus, as the Wisijsa case reveals.

The Wisijsa "Reduced"

Along with other groups inhabiting what is today central Bolivia, the ancestors of the Yuras—the Wisijsas—were also concentrated after 1575 into new towns. The core territory of the Wisijsa ethnic group was a region of high, arid valleys encompassing some 6,750

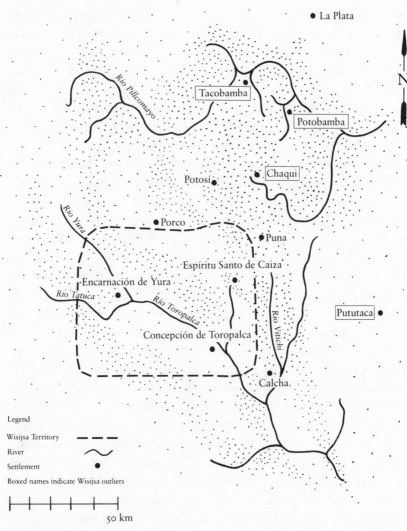

Figure 5.1 Wisijsa Territory in 1590

square kilometers, an area larger than the state of Delaware. The Wisijsa, like other Cara Cara groups, managed a vertical economy, and their outlier settlements were far from the core area. For example, a contingent of Wisijsas resided in 1592 in what was the core of the neighboring Chaquis to the east; they presumably had been there for some time (AGN 13.18.6.4, it. 1:fol. 72r).[4] Other Wisijsas resided in the lower valleys of the Pillcomayo River in the administrative division set up at Tacobamba, close to the reducción of Potobamba (AGN 13.18.6.4, it. 4:fol. 5v) and in Pututaca, in today's Nor Cinti (Mujía 1914:537). Figure 5.1 is a tentative map of Wisijsa territory.

Some time before 1575 the Wisijsas were "reduced" to two towns, "Nuestra Señora de la Concepción . . . and another town called Nuestra Señora de la Encarnación" (AHP Cajas Reales 18:fol. 217v).[5] Encarnación was and is Yura, and in this reducción all the Wisijsa of the western half of the core area were expected to build their houses. It would be in this town, later referred to as "the capital of the *repartimiento*[6] of the Wisijsa" (AGN 13.18.6.4, it. 4:fol. 5v), that the subject population would have to offer labor service in the mines, pay their tribute, and attend to their religious education. The second reducción, Concepción, later Santo Matías, was established at Toropalca, seventy kilometers downriver from Yura; it was intended for the eastern half of the central area. A population of 402 tributarios (that is, able-bodied men between the ages of eighteen and fifty) was reported for Yura in 1575, while 620 tributarios were "reduced" at Toropalca. The total population for the Wisijsa repartimiento, including all categories of persons, was reported to be 4,000 (AHP Cajas Reales 18:fol. 217r).

Part of the Wisijsa group assigned to Toropalca gained permission soon afterward to found another reducción, Espíritu Santo, thirty-five kilometers further north at Caiza. Caiza was high, cold, and arid; but it was closer to the important valley fields in the east and only "seven leagues from the Villa Imperial of Potosí on the royal road to the province of Tucumán" (AGN 13.18.6.4, it. 4:fol. 2v). The valley lands were soon alienated by Spaniards, however, and by 1610 Caiza was said to be "deserted and depopulated" (AGN 13.18.6.4, it. 4:fol. 3r). It exists today as a small provincial settlement.

The repartimiento (administrative division) of the Wisijsa, itself defined as a geographic or territorial unit enclosing the core area, was divided into three ecclesiastical *doctrinas*, each based in one of the three reducciones and presided over by two, then three, Mercedarian friars (AGN 13.18.6.4, it. 4:fol. 4r; AHP Cajas Reales 18:fol.

219v). A list from the 1590s of peaks given as the landmarks, or mojones, enclosing the doctrina of Yura is identical to the boundary markers delimiting the canton of Yura today (Corincho 1905:fols. 30r–v).

The Wisijsas, themselves a subdivision of the Cara Caras, were, like the contemporary Yura, divided into a number of component ayllus. As in contemporary Yura, the ayllus were not territorially cohesive units; rather, the same Wisijsa ayllu appeared in Toropalca as in Caiza and Yura. Census records show that the most inclusive level of ethnic organization was that of the entire repartimiento, which was subdivided into the moieties of Anansaya and Urinsaya (although these latter may have gone by the equivalent Aymara names, since the Wisijsa apparently spoke that language for many decades after the arrival of the Spaniards). In 1592 the Upper Moiety of Anansaya was made up of the ayllus Collana, Saulli Soroma, and Capacanaca Tiquiscaya; while the Lower Moiety comprised ayllus Araya and Manaya Chacti, Araya and Manaya Corca, and Checochi (AGN 13.18.4.1:fol. 10r). The principle of dual division, found both at the level of the entire confederation and repeated in the Wisijsa ethnic group, was extended into the lower-level ayllus as well. For example, in 1592 the ayllu Saulli Soroma had two headmen in one of the reducciones: one for Saulli and another for Soroma; and its members were listed separately. The dual pattern was repeated in ayllus Corca, Chacti, and Capacanaca Tiquiscaya; however, these ayllus were treated as single units in the document and no distinctions were made in its members (AGN 13.18.6.4, it. 1:fol. 38r). Thus the distinction between major and minor ayllus described for the Yura of today in chapter 3 was not clearly drawn in the 1590s, although a parallel may exist in this division into moieties apparent in four of the six major ayllus. Figure 5.2 provides a diagram of Wisijsa organization at this time; a mere glance at these names points to organizational continuities within the Yura group today.

The earliest records presently available show that the organization of leadership among the Wisijsas was quite complex. Two chief kurakas ruled each moiety; the one ruling over Anansaya was also classified as the principal kuraka of the entire group. There were

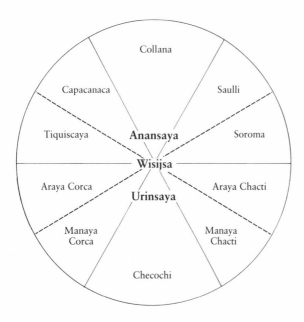

Figure 5.2 The Ayllus of the Wisijsa in the Sixteenth Century

also moiety leaders for the various Anansaya and Urinsaya ayllus clustered at each of the three reducciones. In addition, each ayllu segment, centered on a reducción, had a designated principal (AGN 13.18.6.4, it. 1; AGN 13.18.6.4, it. 2; AHP Cajas Reales 18:fol. 222r).

State Exactions and the Wisijsa:
Tasa and Mita

As we have seen, all the ethnic groups of the Cara Cara moiety were already paying a heavy burden of tribute before 1550, when they were assigned in encomienda to Pedro Hinojosa. Nevertheless, Málaga argues that no one was successful in implanting a truly functional tribute system until the viceroy, Toledo, created the reducciones after 1572 (1972:603–9). Tribute, which in this part of the southern Andes had to be paid in cash at seven pesos of assayed silver per male tribute payer, required an ever greater involvement in the market economy (Wachtel 1977:118; AHP Cajas

Reales 18:fol. 218v). In the rural repartimientos it was treated as an obligation of the ayllu, not of individuals: the amount an ayllu owed remained fixed from one census to another, regardless of any decrease in the actual tributario population in the interim (Málaga 1972:611).

Likewise, Toledo was regularizing the mobilization of labor for the mines at Potosí and Porco at a time when production was once again soaring due to the introduction of an amalgamation process using mercury (Lohmann Villena 1949:55; Bakewell 1984:18–30). The viceroy established the mita (from the Quechua word *mit'a,* used by the kurakas when they spoke of their men coming to take their turn at mining), a labor draft which, in its 1578 version, required a total of 14,296 men to go to Potosí each year (Cole 1985:17). A thousand more served in Porco. The *mitayoc* (mita workers) were drawn not only from all the indigenous repartimientos in the area of the mines, but also from native groups as far away as Cusco and Arequipa (Capoche [1585] 1959:135, 143; Cole 1985:9; Saignes 1985b).[7]

In the early years the indigenous people seemingly did not object to the work in the Potosí mines. As the richest veins were exhausted and as new techniques were introduced, however, the labor became harder, more dangerous, and less rewarding (Bakewell 1984:33–60). Many people in areas subject to the mita fled their homes and families rather than work in the mines. They went to other communities where they would not appear on the tax and mita rolls, or to zones beyond those subject to the mita (Kubler 1946:337–39; Evans 1986; Saignes 1983). After 1575 the fiscal category of *forasteros* (strangers)—people who had moved away from their natal homes—formed an increasing percentage of the total population (Sánchez-Albornoz 1978:32).[8] Paradoxically, some went to Potosí itself, where they became assimilated into the urban economy as "free" daily wage workers. These *mingas* (stand-ins) earned more and could avoid the most dangerous jobs, and they apparently broke the ties to their group of ethnic origin (Bakewell 1984:81–136). They are said to have numbered some 40,000 by 1600 (Fernández de Santillán [1601] 1868:453) in a total population of over 120,000 (Hanke 1959:9).

These population shifts took place, however, in an overall context of population decline in the Andes, from the catastrophic losses of population in the coastal areas to lesser, but still considerable, losses in the southern Andes. A chief factor was the introduction of European diseases; epidemic after epidemic swept through the Andes in the colonial period, even preceding the physical arrival of the Spaniards (Dobyns 1963). Whatever the population of the Andes may have been before the Spanish invasion (and estimates run from 37 million [Dobyns 1966] to 6 million [Rowe 1946]), it had fallen to about 1 million by 1570, and perhaps to only a little more than half that by 1620 (Cook 1981:253).

The Native Lords and State Exactions

For those who remained in their home ayllus the role of the kurakas took on primary importance, for the burden of tasa collection and the mobilization of corvée labor for the state fell squarely on the backs of the native leaders. How they worked to accomplish those ends has become the center of some debate, however. Verlinden, for example, has argued that the kurakas were simple puppets of the state who abused power and served as nothing more than tax gatherers (1960:133). Wachtel has argued that the ideology of reciprocity and redistribution employed by the Inkas was "perverted" by the kurakas under the Spaniards into a unidirectional extraction of wealth (1977:129–31). In her earlier writing Spalding stressed the ability of the kurakas to take advantage of their traditional position in the community to accumulate wealth and power in the new economic order (1974:80–82, 172–76) and has documented how the higher-level kurakas of a zone outside the area subject to the Potosí mita were, as a class, "gradually incorporated into the group of provincial merchants, administrators, and landowners" (1973:596).

Others provide similar interpretations. Stern, writing about the kurakas of Huamanga in the early years after the Spanish invasion, argued that they "were the best equipped to take advantage of new opportunities"; he has shown that the kurakas were able, in their alliances with Europeans, to "'privatize' their traditional land use rights" (Stern 1982:38, 134). Larson (1979) has stressed the role of the "collaborating caciques" who worked to accumulate commercial capital for their own personal wealth and who passed on tribute debts to other members of their communities. And Choque Canqui (1978:28–32) has described how Pedro Chipana, a cacique in the late seventeenth century in the Altiplano of La Paz, so severely harried his people in search of tribute funds that many fled the community.

Certainly such cases as these confirm that many kurakas were violent, overbearing, and exploitative leaders who constantly worked to extract as much wealth as possible. Yet there is also evidence for another perspective on the kurakas, one that pictures them as more generous and protective. Both Stern and Spalding, for example, temper their depictions with more benevolent cases. Stern found certain kurakas of Huamanga acting as "guardians and representatives of the community" (1982:44). Spalding, in her recent detailed study of Huarochirí, has described the long and ambivalent relationships between the Andean elites and the ruling Spaniards as something more complex than a simple case of collaboration and cooptation. She points to instances where "kurakas also used their personal estates to buffer their communities from the excesses of the system" (Spalding 1984:228).

Other studies draw similar conclusions. Rivera (1978), in her examination of a wealthy kuraka of Jesús de Machaca, found that through his large-scale (and very successful) commercial activities he was not only able to "capitalize" other Andean leaders in their efforts to meet state exactions, but he was also able to slow the general process of communal disintegration apparent in his own group after the first century of colonial rule. Murra's study (1978) of the commercial operations in Potosí of a powerful Lupaqa lord from the Chucuito district of Lake Titicaca reinforces this view.

Phrasing the contrast as we have, between "good kurakas" and "bad kurakas," reveals the conceptual weakness of such a dualism. We can expect to find evidence to support both sides of the debate. A more useful approach would be to recognize the dynamic factors which constrained the activities of kurakas at different times, attempting to take into account the particular economic and ethnic factors, as well as changes in the global situation, facing various regional ethnic leaders through time. More research will have to be done in order for us to conclude which of these tendencies—those of exploiting the community or those of protecting it—prevailed generally, or were more prevalent at certain periods than at others. In their efforts to mobilize resources to comply with the requirements of the state, some kurakas no doubt did abuse their position; but theirs was a balancing act between powerful conflicting demands. If they were agents of the state, it is clear that they were also more than that.

The Wisijsa and the State

Because of their proximity to the mines, the Wisijsa were especially subject to the strict labor requirements of the mita. They were obliged to maintain in Potosí one-sixth of their total tributario population of 922, or 154 each year. At any one time, and for a week at a stretch, one-third worked in the ordinary mita (Capoche [1585] 1959:137).

Consistent with demographic losses elsewhere, census information from 1575, 1592, and 1610 reveals that the Wisijsa suffered a drastic population decline in those years[9]; by the later date only 522 tributarios were to be found in the three main reducciones. In Yura alone the tribute-paying population declined by almost 60 percent, from 402 to 174, although the census records indicate that much of that decline must have taken place before 1592, since the figures between that date and 1610 changed very little. (See table 5.1 for figures from Yura.) Yet the mita obligation was actually increased in 1592, to 165 per year (AGN 13.18.6.4, it. 4:fol. 8r). Given the 1610 population figures, this meant that the Wisijsas were required to provide 30 percent—almost one in three—of their active male population to Potosí alone. Nor did their labor obligations end there. In all, the Wisijsas were expected to provide 98 men for the ordinary mita (AGN 13.18.6.4, it. 4:8r–v). According to the policy by which the mita workers served only one week of every

Table 5.1 The Doctrina of Yura: Originario Population, 1592 and 1610

| | Tributarios | | Total population | |
Ayllu	1592	1610	1592	1610
Anansaya				
Collana	52	54	208	259
Saulli Soroma	25	21	115	107
Capacanaca/				
Tiquiscaya	20	19	104	79
Urinsaya				
Corca	15	20[a]	98	112
Araya Chacti/				
Manaya Chacti	62	55	290	248
Checochi	10	5	32	37
Total	184	174	847	842

a. Includes five "absent" tributarios, who may be drawn from the entire lower moiety.
Sources: AGN 13.18.6.4, it. 1; AGN 13.18.4.1.:fols. 99ff.

three, 294 men would have to be ready to serve each year. Simple arithmetic shows that to fill such a labor requirement every Wisijsa tributario would have to work in mita labor every other year.[10]

In addition to the mita labor service, the Wisijsas were required to pay a large sum annually in tribute. In 1575 this was set at 6,422 pesos (AHP Cajas Reales 18:fol. 218v). Although this sum was altered as population losses became apparent in the revisitas of 1592 and 1610 (others followed at irregular intervals throughout the colonial period), the economic burden that this represented was proportionately even greater, given the mita requirement. How did the Wisijsa face such an overwhelming demand on their human resources?

Part of the story can be told by examining the actions—or what little we know of the actions—of Alonso (later Juan Baptista)[11] Choquevilca, the principal kuraka of the Wisijsa, confirmed in office by Toledo and the bearer of a name which was to have historic consequences for Yura. In 1583 he was said to be "more than seventy years old" (Mujía 1914:537); thus we can assume that he was born in the second decade of the sixteenth century, before the Spanish invasion. If the date is at all accurate, he would have been an adult by the time the Spaniards first arrived in Charcas.

When he succeeded to his role as head of the Wisijsa is not recorded in the sources available. In 1564 Choquevilca and one Francisco Xarajuri are identified as "kurakas of Chaqui and Macha," Spanish shorthand for the Cara Cara moiety; but this is, of course, almost twenty-five years after the encomienda made to Gonzalo Pizarro. In 1575 Toledo took note of Choquevilca's status by confirming him in his role as the principal kuraka of the Wisijsa "whom the Indians of the repartimiento of Chaqui and its annexes also obey." In addition, the viceroy granted him the highest salary of any of the kurakas of the Cara Caras, even higher than the supposed maximal leaders of the grouping, the rulers of Macha (AHP Cajas Reales 18:fol. 222r). Choquevilca was clearly the head of the entire Wisijsa repartimiento, but he was also "the kuraka whom the Indians of the parcialidad of the Anansayas of all this province relating to the Charcas respected" (AGN 13.18.6.4, it. 4:fol. 6v). What this special relationship to the Anansayas means for our understanding of Charcas organization is still to be determined.

In addition to the salary, Choquevilca was, along with the other kurakas of the Cara Caras, granted rights to the labor of members of the ayllus. His actual access to human resources is unknown, but the compilers of the tasas in 1575 permitted him to call upon the community in order to plant "two anegas of maize and eight of potatos" (AHP Cajas Reales 18:fol. 226v). Choquevilca was required to provide the seed and to offer food and drink during the planting "as is customary." He was also authorized the services of three different categories of community members for his household: eight *reservados* (those men over fifty who were not required to pay the tasa) for his house and animals; six women "above suspicion" to assist his wife; and two boys under sixteen. Other community resources were probably also at the Wisijsa lord's disposal.

By 1592, when Choquevilca was an old man indeed (the census suggests he is 110!), his household was by far the wealthiest of all the Wisijsas. When most peasant families claimed to sow "two measures [*almudes*] of maize," he planted perhaps a hundred times as much, twenty-five sacks of seed. His potato production was perhaps twenty times that of the average household, and he claimed to own four hundred sheep, fifty mares, and thirty-one head of cattle, among other livestock (AGN 13.18.6.4, it. 1:fol. 8v). This wealth in agriculture and animals surely represents a larger input of resources and labor than that granted him by Toledo, even given the community work days, and is some indication of the internal stratification that existed.

Choquevilca, like other principal kurakas, was the primary agent responsible for assuring community compliance with the demands of the colonial state. While the data are incomplete, it is possible to draw some inferences about the strategies that this kuraka followed to confront state exactions, from the use of the Spanish legal system to commercial and entrepreneurial activities.

In the first case, several sources indicate that Choquevilca joined with the leaders of other ethnic groups to protest excesses of the tasa and mita. He is the third signer of a lengthy petition from Charcas leaders drawn up in 1582; his name appears after the head of the Charcas moiety of the old confederation and one of the principal kurakas at Macha (Espinoza 1969, I:par. 53; AHP Cajas Reales 18:fol. 222r). The Memorial is a litany of complaints against the arrangements for labor and monetary taxation, and places the blame for the flight of native populations on the Spaniards.

Choquevilca and his fellow Wisijsa kurakas alone were responsible for another petition the following year. They reminded the Crown that "our ancestors" controlled the rich and productive mine at Porco before the Spaniards arrived; further, they pointed out that "recently the mine of this Villa [Potosí] was discovered in our lands and next to our fields" (Barnadas 1973:591).

This direct appeal to colonial authorities and even to the Crown was a common enough tactic on the part of Andean kurakas. Many others resorted to the court system (although we have not yet found evidence of Alonso Choquevilca instigating formal legal suits). Stern, for instance, has described how the Andean lords in the Huamanga region around Ayacucho used the colonial judicial system (1982:114–37): the native leaders discovered that they could stymie some state demands by entangling them in endless litigation. Further research will no doubt reveal similar attempts by kurakas such as Choquevilca in the Potosí area to employ the same tactics.

Although they learned to use the Spaniards' own legalism against them, most kurakas, Choquevilca among them, tried for the most part to comply with the requirements imposed on them by the European authorities. He displayed his interest in preserving his own prerogatives when he joined other native leaders in 1582 in decrying the state's threats to remove them from office or send them into exile if they failed to deliver the tasa on time (Espinoza 1969, I:pars. 7 and 8). In their intermediary role between ethnic group and colonial state, the kurakas saw that the new administrative apparatus could be a powerful force supporting their own superior status.

The commercial activities that Choquevilca engaged in to help finance the payment of the tasa can only be hypothesized until we have more data.[12] What seems clear is that soon after the mita was established—perhaps not while Choquevilca was still alive, but soon afterward—the money earned went not only to pay the tasa, but also to contract the services of mingas in Potosí to stand in for ayllu members in the mita. Even before 1620 up to half the effective mita in Potosí was delivered in silver, not in workers (Cole 1985:37–42; Zavala 1979:68–69). The degree to which different ethnic groups chose either to send silver in order to hire mingas or actually to send their own people varied. By 1617, according to Saignes's data, most of the Cara Cara groups chose the former course. The entire mita (153 men) that the Wisijsa were obliged to provide that year was paid in money (1985b:70–71, 74). This option increased the need for ways to raise cash through participation in the money economy.

Corn from the Wisijsa valleys was one item which would have entered into the commerce with Potosí from the beginning. No doubt some portion of it was consumed as cooked corn grains (*mut'i*) or in other ways as everyday food, but a great percentage of it was destined to become *aqha*, corn beer. Capoche, writing in Potosí in 1585, complained of the "perpetual drinking sprees" of the Andean population in the city ([1585] 1959:141). The writer of an anonymous "Descripción" of Potosí in 1603 also reported that "each year such an infinity of chicha is made in this town . . . that it seems impossible to imagine; how much more so to calculate the quantity that is made." He went on to report that 50,000 fanegas of corn were used in the city for the sole purpose of making corn beer (Anonymous [1603] 1965:380). Since Potosí is located at 4,200 meters above sea level, where no corn grows, such heavy beer consumption would have required a vast supply imported, as Capoche put it, "from the valleys" ([1585] 1959:141).

Another source of cash income came from charcoal production and firewood, taken from the hardwood mesquite trees, the *churkis*, of the Wisijsa area. A 1610 document describing the ways the different Andean groups met their mita obligation stated that the Cara Caras dealt in "firewood, charcoal, and *ichu*," or bunchgrasses used in thatching (Saignes 1985b:66). That same year the Wisijsas complained that Spaniards from Porco and Potosí were coming to their valleys to exploit the hardwood without the kurakas' permission, thus reducing their sales (AGN 13.18.6.4, it. 4:fol. 9v). Nevertheless, charcoal remained an important commodity for commercialization in Choquevilca's time, and continued to be so for long afterward; an observer at the end of the eighteenth century still lists the former Wisijsa area as a major center for charcoal production (Cañete [1797] 1952:367).

Yet another source of income for the Wisijsa is recorded in 1583, when Choquevilca was called upon, along with other indigenous leaders, to testify in the colonial capital of La Plata. It seems that the Chiriguanos—Guaraní-speaking peoples of the eastern lowlands—had been attacking the herding settlement of Pututaca. This estancia was located far to the east of the core area of the Wisijsas; but they retained an interest in it (Mujía 1914:533–37; see figure 5.1). Later, in 1610, the Wisijsas' one-third share in Pututaca was rented to a Spaniard, and the income was applied to their head-tax payments (AGN 13.18.6.4, it. 4:fol. 9r).

Yet another means to meet the demands may have been through deception. This is of course much harder to document. But one familiar with the brokenness of the terrain and the difficulties of travel even today can only wonder at the effort it must have taken to carry out the successive censuses in the sixteenth and seventeenth centuries on which were based the taxes owed the state (at least as far as the head tax was concerned). Many of the censuses, in spite of the appearance of a household-by-household inscription, must have relied on the various levels of leaders as informants. Even in the event of an actual visit, it would have been all too easy to hide family members, especially adolescent boys who would have been inscribed as future tributarios. There are constant complaints, questions, and suspicions on the part of Spanish authorities concerning the accuracy of the censuses (cf. Cole 1985:107–10 for a later period).

These different strategies—the protest of abuses, attempts to strengthen their own positions through petitions and claims, compliance through commercialization and pressure on the community, and the potential use of deception—form the core of the Andean kurakas' options under the new regime. Alonso Choquevilca and the other kurakas of Wisijsa, under even greater domination due to their closer location to Potosí, were no exception to this.

The Evolution of Leadership

We have examined the situation of the Wisijsas and their kurakas at the inception of the colonial system, especially in reference to the state-imposed extractive mechanisms. The remainder of this chapter and the next take a more "processual" view by considering the evolution of the ethnic group and the kuraqkuna through time. The story begins with a sketch of Yura in the full flower of the colonial regime.

The Kurakas in the First Decade of the Seventeenth Century

By 1610 the organization of authority among the Wisijsa had been thoroughly reoriented around the three reducciones of Yura, Cayza, and Toropalca. Two principal kurakas presided over the entire repartimiento as a unit: one over ayllus of the Upper Moiety, or Anansaya, and the other over Urinsaya, the Lower Moiety. There also appear to have been two moiety leaders in each of the three reducciones governing the ayllu members of their moieties who were "reduced," or concentrated, there. Another kuraka ruled over those Wisijsas outside the core area who were settled in the town of Chaqui and in the fields of Potobamba (AGN 13.18.6.4. it. 2:fol. 5v; AGN 13.18.4.1:fol. 160r; ANB ALP Minas, t. 125, no. 1118:fol. 8v). We see, then, a potential of nine high-level kuraka posts in the whole repartimiento: two repartimiento moiety leaders, six reducción moiety leaders (that is, the heads of Urinsaya and Anansaya in each of the three reducciones), and the Anansaya leader over the Wisijsas inhabiting the agricultural "islands" in Chaqui and Potobamba. However, a review of censuses from the period reveals that in 1610 there were only seven, not the potential nine, kurakas. One sees in this what seems to be an extension of a Charcas organizational principle whereby individual authorities, due to the dual model, could occupy positions simultaneously at different points in the hierarchical arrangement of posts.

The relationship described to exist among some of the leaders confirms the importance of the rule of hereditary succession. The Spaniards rigidified this Andean principle, however, in their demand for primogeniture in the inheritance of offices and in the strict limitation on the number of kurakas who could be exempt from tribute. The principal kuraka of the Wisijsa in 1610 was Juan Seco, who also served as chief of the Urinsaya ayllus. Seco, according to the record, had succeeded his brother, Carlos Seco. Yet although he served as leader of the Wisijsa for many years, his tenure was always considered temporary, as one "who holds and exercises [the post] because of the death of don Carlos Seco, his brother, until don Gabriel Hurtado de Mendoza, legitimate son of the said don Carlos, is of age" (AGN 13.18.6.4, it. 3:fol. 24r). While Juan Seco may have been illegitimate in Spanish eyes, the obstacle to recognizing his permanence seemed to lie in the rule of succession which passes the post to the eldest son rather than to a brother.

The Anansaya chief of the repartimiento, Diego Hamamani, is identified as a grandson of the same Alonso Choquevilca we have just discussed. Hamamani is said to be an *indio ladino,* a hispanicized native; in 1610, because of his youth and inexperience, he was judged to be incompetent to rule by the Spanish inspector Balderrama (AGN 13.18.6.4, it. 4:fol. 6r).

Below this level of the repartimiento elite came the *principales*, the leaders of the reducción ayllu segments. In 1600 in Yura, for example, ayllu Collana was ruled by a single principal, as were Saulli Soroma and Capacanaca Tiquiscaya (see figure 5.2). Governing kuraka Juan Seco was the foremost leader of ayllu Araya Chacti–Manaya Chacti for all the Wisijsas, and another man from the same ayllu served as Urinsaya leader of the Wisijsa ayllus clustered there; but the two halves (the araya segment and the manaya segment) of this Lower Moiety ayllu also each had their own principal, or leader. Ayllus Checochi and Corca also each had a principal centered in Yura (AGN 13.18.6.4, it. 1:fol. 64v; it. 2:fols. 3r–4v; it. 3:fols. 4r, 24v; AGN 13.18.4.1:fol. 101r). Toropalca and Cayza had the same organization of ayllus and principales in 1610 as Yura, except for the addition of ayllu Mitma in Cayza (AGN 13.18.4.1:fol. 10r; 13.18.6.4, it. 2:fols. 3r–4v). Further research will be necessary to determine whether or not these lesser authorities—the ones ruling the smaller ayllu units—formed part of the hereditary class, or whether these roles were already rotational, as they were later. Figure 5.3 draws on the census records to provide in visual form a view of the structure of formal authority roles among the Wisijsa in 1610.

One aspect of Andean leadership patterns that does not appear in the records available to us for the Wisijsas is the role, or even the existence, of women kurakas. Given the significance of women and the married couple for the Yuras' conceptualization of the kuraqkuna today, as well as the importance of women in authority roles in the past (see especially Silverblatt 1987), we can only conclude that the absence of any mention of women here is an artifact of the records. Spanish colonial authorities would have been particularly insensitive to the role of Andean women in the public sphere; their male bias and their low estimation of Andean peoples in general would have constructed a double barrier to the recognition of women in positions of power, especially if there was a man avail-

Figure 5.3 The Authorities
of Wisijsa in 1610

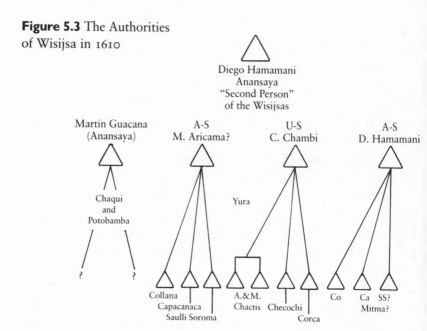

able to be assigned to the post. Clearly, for the Wisijsa case, further research is required on this point.

An examination of the census material suggests that the high-level kurakas, if not the principles, were very careful to delineate their chiefly status from the *indios particulares* (commoner Indians), their subjects. This is most apparent at the level of the repartimiento, where several leaders bolstered their claims to legitimate succession by reference to fledgling genealogies beginning with Alonso Choquevilca and the "original" Carlos Seco. There is some evidence that even at the level of ayllu segment principal, hereditary factors came into play. For example, the principal of ayllu Capacanaca Tiquiscaya in Yura in 1592 was followed in the post by his son ten years later (AGN 13.18.6.4, it. 1:fol. 162v; it. 2:fol. 1v; it. 3:fol. 23v). Later these posts were apparently appoitive (Larson 1979:223); whether they were at this early date or not is unclear.

One conclusion that has to be drawn from the sources is that the form of the system of kuraka posts is very much a colonial product, resulting from the requirement to mold the internal orga-

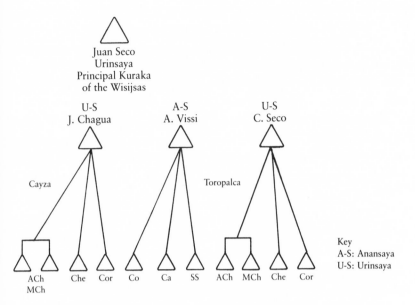

nization of the Wisijsa ethnic group to the fiscal demands and categories of the Spanish regime. This is clearest in the restructuring of the ayllus around the reducciones. Indeed, the fact that such detailed census records exist for the early seventeenth century from which we can extract a model of indigenous leadership confirms the overwhelming interest of the colonial regime in such issues for the Andean population. Although localized ayllu segments probably had leaders before the Spaniards, it is obvious that the specifics of the 1610 arrangement reflected the state's policy of using the reducción as the point of entry into the indigenous labor force and into their larder. The Wisijsa responded to the extractive demands by employing their own organizational principles, the ayllus, but subdividing them according to their proximity to the reducciones. They retained the basic Andean premise of dual organization, using it both at the level of the repartimiento and at that of the reducción.

The state's manipulation of the indigenous authorities is also seen in the curious situation in which a Urinsaya lord, and not one of Anansaya, in 1610 held the position of principal kuraka. Given the ceremonial preeminence of the Upper Moiety, the post should have gone, in strictly Andean terms, to Choquevilca's successor. One can only imagine that administrative considerations were at work as the Spanish rulers confirmed Urinsaya leaders Carlos Seco and then Juan Seco as governors, even if this were considered an interim move.

The kurakas, especially those at the higher levels, were a focus of wealth and of social relations that set them apart from the rest of the peasant households. A good example of this is the case of Juan Seco himself, the principal kuraka of the repartimiento. Like Alonso Choquevilca before him, Juan Seco had access to community labor and to lands which permitted him to plant enough maize to yield one hundred cargas. He also harvested one hundred cargas of potatoes and owned fifty llamas, fifty goats, ten milk cows, and other livestock. By way of comparison, two nonkuraka households which follow in the record reported harvests of only seven and nine cargas of corn, ten each of potatoes, and only a few animals (AGN 13.18.4.1:fols. 100v–101v). In this light Seco's hundred cargas of corn represent considerable wealth. This extensive grain production also points to an active participation in large festivals when it would have been converted to corn beer for the community, and, as we have seen, to a likely role in commerce in which part of the corn would have been sold in Potosí.

In sum, we see evidence in the early seventeenth century for the continuation among the Wisijsa of a definable and self-conscious status group that was confirmed in its roles by the Spanish authorities; wealth and hereditary succession support the first part of that conclusion, while the second seems demonstrated in the unusual situation in which the culturally less prestigious Urinsaya leader was serving as principal kuraka. The particular form and number of the kurakas in 1610 was, again, closely related to the exactions of the Spanish regime and to the existence of the reducciones. What had evolved was a kind of hybrid—ayllus based on dual organization confronting a policy of forced resettlement. The kurakas paid special attention to recruitment to their elite group, in which elevation to office was based on an ever stricter rule of primogeniture. This group still had access to greater resources (both physical and human) and possessed more wealth than the commoner Wisijsa household.

The Growth of Indian Hispanism

Another element that should be considered as we examine the leaders of the Wisijsa after the Spanish invasion and as the colonial system became institutionalized is the development of what Stern (1982) has called "Indian Hispanism," in which the Andean hereditary lords had begun to straddle the cultural gap between the Spanish rulers and their own constituents. This had begun quite early: in the northern Andes, for example, the chief of the Cayambis, close to Quito, was born the year before Pizarro landed at Tumbez; yet he was taken as a small child into the Franciscan monastery and received a European education before returning to rule over his people (Espinoza 1980:90–91). In the south the first bishop of Charcas wrote as early as 1552 of his hope to create a school for the sons of kurakas who would be trained to become preachers and clerics (Barnadas 1973:277). Such schools did not open, however, until after 1618, first in Lima, then in Cuzco and Chuquisaca (Duviols 1972:263–69).

Perhaps most interesting in this regard was not just the opportunity for formal schooling for young members of the kuraka class, but the attempts made by several Andean intellectuals to forge a real intellectual synthesis of the Andean worldview with that of the European. Few examples remain today of this more formal symbolic and literary undertaking; but the result, according to Salomon (1982), was the creation of a "literature of the impossible," in which the "cultural doubleness" of the Andean and European worlds confronted each other but which were ultimately irresolvable as long as both modes of discourse retained their essential integrity. The most renowned example of this kind of work was the thousand-page letter to the king written by Felipe Guaman Poma de Ayala ([1613?] 1980), which Adorno (1986) shows was deeply grounded in the classical and ecclesiastical thinking of Europe but, at the same time, provides invaluable insight into an Andean conceptual world.[13]

This kind of activity was essential for those Andean peoples who felt the need to clarify the relationship between the two cultural frameworks by means of intellectual production. But the same attempts at clarification, as well as struggles to synthesize conflicting values and to work toward a cultural hegemony, must have gone on all the time in terms of a symbolic dialogue of self-identification. For the pressure for assimilation was, of course, felt not only in the attempt to introduce the children of kurakas to Spanish culture or in the efforts of Andean intellectuals to articulate their understanding of the events of conquest and colonialism. The new cultural models were all around the kurakas as they interacted with the Spanish overlords; having been so recently defeated by the force of Spanish arms, they saw the culture of their conquerors as an attraction (Stern 1982:165–73).[14]

The adoption by the kurakas of Spanish models of dress, ornamentation, etiquette, and lifestyle represents this ambivalence toward Spanish culture. Guaman Poma bluntly denounced those assimilationist kurakas who were not "true lords, nor did they do good works" (quoted in Spalding 1984:223), and emphasizes in his drawings the degree to which many of the more powerful kurakas had adopted Spanish dress styles and European vices (Guaman Poma de Ayala [1613?] 1980:776, 786). Capoche, thirty years earlier, spoke of the kuraka who was serving the Potosí mita as a *capitán enterador,* a native administrator in charge of mobilizing and directing indigenous laborers in the city, as one who had "studied in the school of the Jesuits and goes around dressed in our style, with lots of silk." He adds that this leader did not get along well with his charges and his evident hispanophilism won him no friends even among the Spaniards ([1585] 1959:137).

On the other hand, others seem to have adopted Spanish cultural forms while still maintaining good relations with their communities. In the late seventeenth century Pedro Fernández Guarache, and later his son, Joseph Fernández Guarache, both served as kurakas of the Altiplano district of Pacajes. Each had attended school; the son was a great supporter of the church, and in 1720 colonial authorities awarded him the title of "Magistrate of the Four Quarters" (Alcalde de los Cuatro Suyus), an honor harkening back to the

Inka Empire. Father and son were apparently highly respected both by their ayllu subjects and by Spanish officials (Urioste de Aguirre 1978:36). Finally, Stern recounts the story of a hispanicized indigenous lord in Ayacucho who made it his special duty to protect commoner Indians and complain about abuses committed against them. In spite of his adoption of Spanish symbols of identity, he was such a thorn in the side of the provincial upper classes that he was finally murdered by the corregidor and the priest (Stern 1982:182).

Cultural assimilation and Indian hispanism among the Wisijsas in the early seventeenth century cannot be explored in any depth due to a lack of good sources. As we have seen, the Spanish *visitador* Balderrama was rather contemptuous of one of Alonso Choquevilca's grandsons, the *indio ladino*. To what degree the adoption of hispanic cultural forms was generally true is difficult to say. In 1602 six kurakas of the seven in attendance at the verification of census figures could sign their names (some, admittedly, more confidently than others). Only Juan Seco, the principal kuraka, did not know how (AGN 13.18.6.4, it. 3:fol. 33v).

The Decade 1675–1686

The contraction in population that the Wisijsa had suffered from the time of the Spanish invasion continued throughout the seventeenth century. Recalling that the number of tribute payers in the doctrina of Yura had declined from 402 to 174 between 1575 and 1610, it is perhaps not surprising that the Mercedarian priest resident in Yura in 1645 recorded only 139 tributarios, of whom fully 52 were listed as "absent" (AGN 9.17.4.1).

This generalized drop in population led to a drastic decrease in the number of mita workers being sent to Potosí. The mine owners, ostensibly worried about the reduced number of workers, complained loudly to colonial authorities. Of course they were no doubt more concerned about the loss of money they derived from the mita as the population base shrank, for, as we saw, a significant portion of the mita obligation was paid early on in silver, not work.

When the duque de la Palata was designated viceroy in 1680, he saw the reorganization of the mita as the primary task before him.

Table 5.2 The Doctrina of Yura: Originario Population by Ayllu in 1688

	Tributarios	Total population
Ayllu		
Anansaya		
Collana	74[a]	350
Saulli Soroma	25	125
Capacanaca	7	45
Urinsaya		
Araya Chacti	12	77
Checochi	4	27
Manaya Chacti	9	65
Corca	3	16
Subtotals	135	705
Forasteros	28	84
Absent	1	
Total	164	789

a. Plus the kuraka and a *preceptor,* or teacher.
Sources: AGN 13.18.7.3:fols.214v–234r; AHP CGI 95.

This required a new visita in order to determine the subject population. This time all forasteros, those "stranger" commoners whose numbers had swelled in some areas as people fled their home communities to avoid mita service, were to be systematically included (Vargas Ugarte 1966:361–63; Cole 1985:105–22).

The figures of the census subsequently carried out on Palata's orders show, for the Wisijsas, a continued, though now less dramatic, decline in population. In 1686 only 130 tributarios originarios (native tribute payers) were counted in Yura, some of whom (although a much smaller percentage than in 1645) were absent or in Potosí. As table 5.2 shows, Ayllu Collana of Anansaya had some 55 percent of the total tribute payers. Urinsaya consisted of only 28 tributarios and 185 people, divided as before into Araya Chacti, Checochi, Manaya Chacti, and Corca. The total number in the originario category was 705 people (AGN 13.18.7.3).[15]

But for the first time among the Wisijsa we also have (as Palata had ordered) an accounting of the forasteros, who had not appeared previously in regular censuses. Many of these outsiders had indeed left their natal homes to avoid the mita; and they had not been required, in most places, to pay the full tasa. It is likely that many kurakas had already insisted that forasteros resident in their communities contribute resources for the rental of laborers in Potosí (Cole 1985:40). If this was the case, they may have resented the viceroy's efforts to regularize the census counts as much as the forasteros did. Nevertheless, it was the duque de la Palata's goal to change that in order to draw on the labor of these less-taxed groups (Sánchez-Albornoz 1978:69–78). A summary enumeration of forasteros in Yura revealed 28 tributarios and an overall population of 84.[16] The total of the two groups, 789 for the doctrina (or 770 by the CGI figure), still shows a decline from the 842 originarios present in Yura in 1610.

In terms of ayllu organization, the Wisijsas were largely unchanged from the model described for a century earlier, except perhaps that the ayllus seem more clearly centered on the three primary reducciones. The arrangement of kurakas also changed little. Over the doctrina (and possibly over the entire Wisijsa repartimiento) was the head of ayllu Collana and kuraka principal don Juan Baptista Choquevilca; listed with him is a *segunda persona*. Ayllu Collana also had a principal, whom I take to be the *cobrador de tasas,* or tax collector, much like today's jilaqata. Saulli Soroma lists a principal while Capacanaca Tiquiscaya, with its skimpy six tribute payers, does not. In Urinsaya, Araya Chacti, Checochi, and Manaya Chacti also list principales, while tiny Corca goes without one (AGN 13.18.7.3:fol. 233r). Yet in spite of the increasing fragmentation due to the reducciones, the leaders of the repartimiento were still a self-conscious group linking the different component Wisijsa groupings. For example, one source, dated after 1665, refers to the Toropalca kuraka Bartolomé Gonzales as the "principal kuraka of the Indians of Toropalca, Cayza, Yura and the Wisijsas of Chaqui" (ANB ALP Minas, t. 125, no. 1118:fol. 53r).

This same document also describes the hereditary succession of Wisijsa kurakas following the death of Yura's Juan Seco, the Urinsaya chief who, it will be recalled, ruled the repartimiento in 1610. His brother's son, Gabriel Hurtado de Mendoza, had taken the post and governed until the early 1640s. Mendoza's residence was in Toropalca, however, and not in Yura. When Mendoza died without an heir, the old men of Toropalca and Yura met and selected Simón Aricoma, the "great grandson of don Juan [i.e., Alonso] Chuquivilca, governor . . . named by the viceroy don Francisco de Toledo" (ANB ALP Minas, t. 125, no. 1118:fol. 10r), to succeed him. Aricoma, who died in 1658, was followed in the post by his brother, Gerónimo Porotaca. Porotaca died in 1664 and was replaced by his son, Bartolomé Gonzales. With Aricoma's accession, Anansaya was, in Toropalca at least, once again in the primary ruling position (anb, alp Minas, t. 125, no. 1118:fols. 8v–10v). By means of this document, then, we know that throughout the seventeenth century the Wisijsa continued to pass on the leadership posts by means of hereditary succession, both from father to son and between brothers.

The nature of the relationship between Gonzales, the Toropalca head who claimed the status of leader of all the Wisijsa, and the ruler and Anansaya chief living in Yura, Juan Baptista (or Juan "Roque") Choquevilca, who held the post at the same time in the 1660s, is not clear. A man named Pablo Choquevilca of ayllu Collana was ruling Yura two decades before that (Corincho 1905:fols. 39r–40r). Pablo was apparently the father of one Juan Baptista Choquevilca, who in turn was the father of the man of the same name ruling in the 1670s and 1680s (AGN 13.18.7.3:fol. 214v).

The ins and outs of these matters are obscured by the fact that personal names were fluid at this time and surnames were often not passed on. It seems probable, however, that given the mobility between the reducciones, this line of Yura Choquevilcas was descended from Caiza's Diego Hamamani, Anansaya chief of the repartimiento in 1610 and grandson of Alonso Choquevilca. The emphasis on both the principle of hereditary succession to high office and on growing class stratification is therefore notable.

Real insight into patterns of power and social hierarchy existing between the kurakas of Yura and their subjects is available in the form of a litigation record compiled a few years before the 1686 census ordered by the duque de la Palata. This suit (ANB EC 1679, no. 22) details the charges of abuses committed by the kurakas against ayllu members as well as the kurakas' justifications for their actions.

The court record begins with a formulation of charges against three kurakas, one of whom was the Anansaya leader Juan Roque Choquevilca mentioned above. The accusations themselves are grouped into three categories: charges of physical abuse that the kurakas committed against a number of ayllu members; misuse by the kurakas of the labor of the comunarios, both in concert with Spaniards and for their own benefit; and misuse of community lands and of income derived from them.

Testimony by commoner Yuras makes it overwhelmingly clear that principal kuraka Choquevilca and his alcalde mayor Diego Hamamani did not hesitate, in the 1670s, to use physical violence to impose their will on ayllu members in order to force them to mobilize resources needed to fulfill outside exactions. In the main case under investigation, though, the story that can be pieced together suggests that the situation was more complex than simple ill will, and that the issue revolved around the forastero-originario contrast. Two brothers, Pedro Paca and Joseph Ramón, would not accede to the demands of the kurakas for payments toward mita and tasa in a sufficient amount to satisfy their leaders. The kurakas retaliated by putting increasing pressure on the two, up to imprisonment and, according to the witnesses, beatings of them and their wives and family. Both the kurakas and the brothers told Spanish authorities that they felt justified in their actions.

Although the mother of brothers Paca and Ramón was from Yura, the father, according to one witness, came from outside the region, from Tinquipaya. Yet the same witness affirmed that one of the sons had been born in Yura, and that both were present some fifteen years before when an earlier revisita was carried out (fol. 50r). Their status was ambiguous enough, then, for the brothers to argue that their father's affiliation and forastero identity relieved them of full taxation as Yuras. But the kurakas, for their part, rejected the claim to exemption and prodded them to pay. They based *their* demand on place of birth and the brothers' long residence in Yura.

From the point of view of the kurakas, the whole continuity of the system relied on the people's compliance with the extreme tax burden. Any attempts to subvert it had to be met with strong sanctions. Furthermore, Choquevilca felt pressure from above as well. In a complaint against one of the brothers, whom he claimed had physically attacked him, he argued that their efforts to convince others not to pay their mita and tasa obligations had led to significant shortages in both forms of revenue, "and they [officials in Potosí] have sent out judges for the mita on me, causing me expenses" (fol. 20r).

In spite of all the beatings and disputes, the issue was finally resolved around access to community resources. In the end the courts forgave the kurakas much; but the one thing that was imposed on them was the requirement that they assign Paca and Ramón both fields and scrub forest lands for charcoal production "within three days" (fol. 99v).

In the course of the suit between the leaders and the brothers other aspects of the kurakas' activities also came to light. One such dispute arose around the rental of lands to Spaniards. A witness charged that Choquevilca had just begun to rent the lands of Paccha (today's Phajcha) to one Francisco de Bega (fols. 15v, 16v)—very likely of the same Bega family that controlled a hacienda called Yauricoya.[17] Although the witness implied that Choquevilca was using the money for his own ends, Choquevilca responded by pointing out that Paccha and other lands had been the object of a suit between a Yura and Bega. The tactic of charging Bega rent was, from his point of view, a suitable compromise in order to retain control of the lands and to avoid further disputes (fols. 66r, 67v, 69v).

Choquevilca's solomonic leadership may have been less disinterested than he made it seem, however, for other charges lodged against him made it clear that the kurakas often put the interests of Spaniards very high. They apparently also tried to associate themselves as closely as possible with their European rulers. Space does not permit a detailed examination of this theme; however, one witness argued that Choquevilca had ignored previous court orders in favor of his subjects precisely "because he has the corregidor and the Spaniards on his side—he pays [us] no heed and does not concern himself at all" (fol. 4v). Another testified that "the said kurakas take advantage of the money and work of the Indians and the community as well as being powerful and well-established with the corregidor and the Spaniards, with whom they have tight relations" (fol. 6r). How far the effort to curry favor went is difficult to determine; but one person charged that Choquevilca had gone to the extreme of giving two girls to Spaniards (fol. 47r).

These references to Spaniards remind us of the previous discussion above of Indian hispanism and the question of to what degree the kurakas saw their own interests, after nearly 150 years of Spanish rule, as reflecting the goals of the colonial state. Further, claiming community resources as either private property or as subject to alienation to Spaniards for the rental moneys gained (here, renting the Paccha grazing lands) was a widespread practice during this period (Larson 1979).

One set of alleged abuses, however, was not related to outside impositions and contacts. Rather, the authorities were accused of using the labor of indigenous folk for their own benefit. The kurakas had a very particular way of obliging people to work for them. As people left mass on Sunday, the leaders ("and especially don Juan Roque Choquevilca") would stand by the church door and grab the carrying cloths and cloaks of the men and women who passed through. To reclaim their belongings, the people "requested" to work in this manner had to labor for the kurakas the following day, receiving no pay for their toil (fols. 4r, 5v, 7v). One kuraka responded in his defense that in fact this was the case, "that he has made them work in a mink'a, giving them food and drink, and it has been only a few times" (fol. 68r). Another said it was the custom to take the cloaks when the irrigation canals needed cleaning in order to make everyone work "for the common good of the community" (fol. 69r). Several others agreed with him. One said that "for many years it has been the custom" to provide the authorities with labor at planting and at harvest, as well as to oblige people to maintain the irrigation ditches by using this method (fol. 60r). Given what we know about Andean concepts of reciprocity within the community, it seems clear that such community labor prestations to local authorities were indeed traditional.[18] It does explain, however, the references to punishment meted out to those who did not want to go to mass (fols. 14r, 15r). One suspects that the problem here had as much to do with labor conscription as with religion.

The Kurakas and Their Subjects: Consent and Conflict

The suit against the kurakas of Yura in 1679 provides many more details of these Andean leaders' actions than can be discussed in the space we have here. The record allows us to conclude, however, that they were powerful, autocratic rulers, free to impose punishment with impunity and according to their whims. The evidence suggests that their overwhelming and ever-present concern was the mobilization of resources to fulfill the voracious demands of the colonial apparatus. They were also entrepreneurs of a sort, having developed a variety of strategies for raising the monies required of them. Finally, by their efforts to mold themselves to the ruling Spaniards, the kurakas placed themselves in a culturally (as well as structurally) intermediate position between the Andean peasants over whom they ruled and the European elite to whom they were subservient.

For the most part the Yura peasants seemed to acquiesce in the demands made on them. Sometimes, however, the usual support of the people for their kurakas broke down and the kurakas' authority was directly challenged. Such was the case with the Wisijsa lord from Toropalca mentioned previously, Bartolomé Gonzales. In 1667 he was in charge of the mita for the entire repartimiento of the Wisijsa, including those residing in Chaqui and Potobamba as well as those in the core areas of Yura, Cayza, and Toropalca. In his attempt to mobilize the laborers necessary for the mita, he went to the valley of Orca (today's Horcas?) where two Wisijsas resided on the land of a Spaniard. Although they had been born there, they were registered among the Wisijsas of Chaqui. When Gonzales attempted to force them to return to their home district by holding their sister hostage, they attacked him and his party and drove them away in a hail of rocks (ANB ALP Minas, t. 125, no. 1118, fols. 7r–8v).

Similarly, the 1679 court case in Yura recounts that Juan Roque Choquevilca was attacked by two men in the rancho of Tatuca. Here the act of violence was not between an unknown kuraka and people alienated from their home community; rather, it was between intimates, a lifelong kuraka and members of his ayllu. Choquevilca had ordered one of the men to undertake a long journey to the Lipes on the Altiplano to the west. The details of the confrontation are not recounted, but the man obviously considered the demand to be unreasonable, for he grabbed the kuraka and beat him, and his companion joined the fray. If the Andean ideal of at least an appearance of reciprocity between ruler and ruled still held (and there is no reason to assume that it did not), then when that ideal was too grievously wounded by what were perceived as oppressive actions, the reaction was to deny the kuraka basic respect toward his person. In this case the response was violence (ANB EC 1679, no. 22: fols. 20r–24v).

Why the Wisijsas and their descendants, the Yuras, were willing to submit, for the most part, to their kurakas still requires further research. But there is an aspect of social life which goes almost unmentioned in the kinds of documents we have at our disposal from the colonial period, and that is the role of the kurakas in rituals, festivals, and other kinds of cultural performances. Today, three hundred years later, Yura ritual life is rich and diverse; a major aspect of the present-day kuraqkuna's duties is that of symbolic action in the fiestas they sponsor. Unfortunately, the document from 1679 reveals nothing of festival life in Yura, festivals in which the elite must have played an essential role. Yet other evidence suggests that communal celebrations were an important part of the kurakas' duties. Such ritual action would have given the kurakas a certain legitimacy in spite of their abuses.

This is not to say that the ayllu members accepted continual oppression because the kurakas provided them with corn beer from time to time. Rather, I am arguing that the knowledge "built into" the ritual action of the kurakas was, and is, a fundamental underpinning of the Wisijsas', and the Yuras', understanding of the world (both physical and social) and their place in it. The world construction of this Andean group must have largely resided, then as now, in the institution of the authorities. If the hereditary elite was not a priesthood (as was true to some degree of the Inkas), it is nevertheless plausible to suggest that a central role in ritual would have served their interests, just as the attempt to fulfill the extractive demands of the Spanish regime did.

If this is true, however, then the "notorious bind" (Larson 1979: 214) within which the hereditary elite lived becomes even more contradictory. If present-day patterns serve as a guide, the kurakas exemplified the group's unity and integrity in the face of a hostile world. On the other hand, the continual demands from the kurakas, their abuses, and their evident contentment with European contacts conflicted with that integrative role. There was, in the seventeenth century, no simple resolution of that contradiction.

Yura in 1724–1730

For the first decades of the eighteenth century we have at present considerably less information than for the preceding periods. What does seem true is that the general lines of internal organization and the links to the state seem little changed. The revisitas do suggest that in the decade after 1700 the population began to expand for the first time since the invasion, only to be pushed back to its 1686 level by a serious epidemic that occurred between 1718 and 1722 (probably the Andean pandemic described by Dobyns [1963:511–14]).

After the loss of one-fifth of the male tributario population, the structure and relative size of the ayllus in 1724 is very similar to the situation thirty-eight years earlier. Table 5.3 summarizes the ayllu population figures and the set of authority roles. The "repartimiento of Yura," as it was known by then, continued to be faced with mita and tasa demands. Based on a prorated figure, the tasa owed yearly was 1,604 pesos; and there were continual disputes about its payment.[19] In 1701 the kurakas of Chaqui complained to the courts about what seemed to them arbitrary increases in the tasas after the census of the duque de la Palata (ANB EC 1701, no. 3). The epidemics made tax collection even more difficult, so that in 1724 a Spaniard, Captain Francisco Gómez de Cabrera, requested that the

Table 5.3 Yura Population by Ayllu in 1724

Ayllu	Tributarios	Total population
Anansaya		
Collana	79	368
(absentees)[a]	(18)	(26)
Saulli Soroma	11	92
(absentees)	(13)	(17)
Agregados to		
Saulli Soroma	26	67
Capacanaca	13	80
Urinsaya		
Araya Chacti	10	61
(absentees)	(18?)	(24)
Checochi	6	54
(absentees)	(1)	(1)
Manaya Chacti	10	62
(absentees)	(4)	(5)
Corca	7	26
(absentees)	(2)	(8)
Total	162 (218)	810 (891)

a. Figures in parentheses represent persons who were not present at the time of the census and yet were still considered part of the ayllu. In the totals, the number in parenthesis is the sum of those present and those absent.
Source: AGN 13.18.8.3.

special commission of lieutenant governor be granted him in order to take control of the collection of the mita and tasa in Yura and Porco, both plagued by *quiebras* (shortfalls) (ANB ALP Minas, t. 46, no. 264).

Yet even after a reduction of the tasa in 1731, one Yura kuraka complained that the many errors, duplications, and mistaken identities "that this accounting puts on me makes the total burden grow excessively, so that it is impossible to deliver it all, exposing me to total ruination" (ANB EC 1731, no. 4).

Another Yura kuraka named Choquevilca took part in a suit against abuses in the administration of the mita in 1727. Juan Baptista Choquevilca, governor of the town of Yura, joined with kurakas from Tomave and Puna to argue that certain improvements in pay and working conditions promised in a 1697 reform of the mita had never been implemented; Choquevilca offered his copy of the 1697 laws as evidence (ANB ALP Minas, t. 126, no. 12:fol. 28v). When the courts sided with the kurakas, the mine owners and mill operators threatened to close down their enterprises if the provisions favorable to the Yura and other Andean groups were enforced. Once again powerful mining interests defeated the indigenous opposition, and the new regulations were abolished (ANB, Mano de Obra catalog, SG 1339).

An innovation in extracting "surplus" from the indigenous communities had also been developed by this time. This is usually termed the *reparto de efectos* or the *repartimiento de mercancías,* which can be roughly translated as "the (forced) distribution of consumer articles." In this practice the Spanish provincial corregidores —who after 1678 paid high prices for their posts in Spain and even then had only a five-year term of office to make their fortunes in the New World—required indigenous household heads to buy certain items whether they wanted them or not (Larson 1979; Larson and Wasserstrom 1983; Moreno Cebrián 1977). As early as 1701 the Chaqui kurakas were denouncing the actions of the corregidor of Porco for the forced sale of mules, wine, iron blades, and cloth, all at what were perceived to be exorbitant prices (ANB EC 1701, no. 3:fol. 3v). The Yura, living in the same province (and with some of their Wisijsa fellows even residing in Chaqui) were also subject to these forced sales.

Among the Yura kurakas, it seems that by the seventeenth century a pattern had developed in which members of the hereditary elite of kurakas did not necessarily take on the paramount position of *cacique principal* for life. By 1685 the Juan Baptista Choquevilca of that day had held, then relinquished, then held again, the chief position of the Yura (ANB EC 1679, no. 22:fol. 63r; AGN 13.18.7.3:fol. 214v). Prefatory material to the census carried out in 1724 reported that the man who had been filling the office of *gobernador,* one Lucas Copacaba, no longer wished to do so "due to finding himself very far behind in the tasa and mita payments." He asked to be relieved of the post. The "people" were asked who should replace him, and those present, as well as Lucas Copacaba, suggested Juan Baptista Choquevilca "since he is a descendent of the legitimate kurakas of this town" (AGN 13.18.8.3, it. 2:fols. 1r–v). Choquevilca accepted the post. In 1731, however, Lucas Copacaba claimed once again to be principal kuraka, also asserting his own descent from the hereditary leaders (ANB EC 1731, no. 4). Juan Baptista Choquevilca lived on, however, and apparently regained the chief position (ANB EC 1797, no. 14:fols. 9v, 11v). He is listed in the 1764 census as a man of seventy years, still married to the same woman as in 1724; he is the only one in the "reserved" category (that is, those men relieved of mita and tasa duties due to their hereditary kuraka status) who is referred to as "don" (AGN 13.18.9.5:fol. 11v).

The scope of powers of the kurakas had been reduced by this time in terms of the territory under their jurisdiction and in their untrammeled right to act as intermediaries in the mobilization of resources for the state, but the kurakas still worked to maintain the principle of limiting access to the positions via hereditary succession. Even if the position might not have been for life in this period, it still revolved within, and was shared among, a very small group. Perhaps the person who was ultimately responsible for turning in the tasa and mita to the Spaniards rotated while yet remaining within the elite; but from an internal point of view it might have been quite clear to all who the "real" principal kuraka actually was. Nevertheless, as the gap between extractive demands and resources grew too large—especially with the additional burden of the reparto de efectos—it would have been impractical to have one person responsible for attempting to fill it year after year. It therefore appears that this liability was shared. Certainly the very large number of men listed as "absent" in 1724 must indicate a reaction to continued high taxation. The kurakas continued in the 1720s to be the main group attempting to secure compliance with the two main exactions of the state, the mita and the tasa. Although they did object to the size of the impositions, a fundamental challenge to the system was not yet to come from them.

In this review of the history of the Yuras' ancestors through the early eighteenth century, we have described a process of fragmentation whereby larger ethnic identities—and their organizational concomitants—have gradually been broken up into smaller ones. At some point there are no longer references to the Wisijsas as a group. When did that loss of identity occur?

Documentary references to Bartolomé Gonzales and his predecessors as "kuraka principal" of all the Wisijsas in 1670 suggest that the links among the reducciones and with their ecological outliers continued to be relevant at that time. The reality of the present day tells us, however, that at some point such a consciousness of wider ethnic identity was lost; new loyalties based on the reducciones evolved, demonstrating a more localized sense of ethnicity.

When it was that Wisijsa "became" Yura or Cayza is not clear from our sources. My present conclusion is that the Wisijsa identity survived the seventeenth century. However, censuses and taxation records (such as the notations in the Cajas Reales of Potosí)[20] suggest that by the 1750s the wider sense of loyalty had disappeared. *Why* this reduction in the scale of group identity occurred is as difficult a question to answer as when, and we can be no more certain of our response. Several factors were probably at work. The growing importance of the reducciones meant that both tasa and mita collection were centered there. Those kurakas who were moiety leaders in these towns probably saw no advantage in continuing to defer to two of their number as chief Wisijsa lords. If the reducción moiety leaders had difficulty mobilizing sufficient resources to avoid the dreaded quiebras, then the repartimiento leadership posts, with more encompassing responsibilities, would not be offices that many would seek. Although the range of authority of the kurakas was reduced, so would have been their vulnerability to charges of failing to meet state demands.

As for the nonkuraka ayllu members, the kinds of events that brought people together, such as fiestas, now took place in the reducciones and were linked to the church and the religious calendar. The opportunities for ritually renewing group identity as a Wisijsa must have gradually decreased. Wisijsa identity, however it may have first coalesced, was a vehicle appropriate for group interaction in the context of competition and self-determination that existed in the Charcas Confederation. It was not particularly suited to the colonial situation, where outside control was the order of the day.

It was in this way that Toledo's reducción policy was a success, and not in its original intent to permanently relocate indigenous populations. One consistent Spanish policy through the centuries was that of turning Inkas and Wisijsas into "Indians"—the goal of conquest through homogenization and destructuration. However, while the European rulers did manage to expunge ethnic identities in many other areas, here their success was only partial. For while the Wisijsa identity was gradually eroded away, the Wisijsa began to identify themselves as Yura, Cayza, or Toropalca. To be sure, a more delimited ethnic sense was adopted, but it was one which did not strip them of their past affiliations and modes of organization.

Yet the pressures of the colonial system weighed heavily, and by the late eighteenth century there were growing pressures for change. Let us turn now to the events of the 1780s and the modifications that took place in the system of authority in Yura.

6

TRANSFORMATION OF THE KURAKASHIP
From Kurakas
To Kuraqkuna

Beginning in 1779, the southern Andes were engulfed in a series of indigenous insurrections, which at their height in early 1781 included the entire zone between Cuzco and Potosí. While these were not the first rebellions by native Andean peoples (Kubler 1946:385; Spalding 1984:270–93; Varese 1967), none became as generally widespread as those of 1781, in which one estimate suggests that as many as 100,000 people died in a total population of only 2 million (Cornblit 1976:131). While other sources doubt the death toll was as high as that, it is nevertheless clear that many thousands perished.

Indigenous resistance to colonial institutions developed in three major regional foci, even though other areas (such as Oruro, Cochabamba, and Atacama) also experienced revolts (see, for example, Cajías 1983; Hidalgo 1982). The rebellion most widely remembered today was that of the charismatic José Gabriel Túpac Amaru, which began in the reducción town of Tinta in southern Peru and spread to take in a major portion of the diocese of Cusco (Campbell 1976, 1979; Flores Galindo 1976; Lewin 1973; O'Phelan Godoy 1979; Valcárcel 1970). A second major uprising occurred in Upper Peru (modern Bolivia) soon after Túpac Amaru's death. An Aymara speaker from Ayo Ayo named Julián Apasa (but who adopted the nom de guerre Túpac Catari) mobilized an army which laid siege to the city of La Paz from March to June of 1781 (Valcárcel 1970: 282–83; Grondín 1975).

For our purposes, however, the rebellion centered in Chayanta holds the most interest. It was in fact chronologically the first, having begun in 1779. Tomás Catari, a kuraka of Anansaya and a member of ayllu Collana of the Macha ethnic group, had already struggled for years for some solution to the many abuses committed by the Spanish corregidores in the capital of the repartimiento, also called Macha.[1] In 1778 he and a companion had even walked to Buenos Aires to take their case directly to the Spanish viceroy. In spite of the sympathetic hearing Catari received in that distant city, on his return he suffered continual harassment and imprisonment. Finally, the struggle crystallized in a violent confrontation in late 1780, at the northern Potosí town of Pocoata, between Spanish authorities and Catari's indigenous supporters; three hundred peasants and thirty Spaniards died.

This event served as a general call to arms. Soon Spanish towns throughout northern Potosí, as well as those in surrounding provinces, came under attack by the Andean populations around them. The kuraka Tomás Catari was killed in early 1781, but his two surviving brothers, Damaso and Nicolás, kept the resistance alive. They too, however, soon met their end; in April the people of Pocoata, perhaps tired of the conflict, turned the two over to Spanish authorities. They were tried and executed in the Audiencia capital of La Plata.

The peasant movements of the 1780s shook the foundations of Spanish colonial society. Some writers saw the rebellions as examples of the irrational or vengeful actions of an Andean peasantry which had never been incorporated into Spanish culture and thus were still uncivilized (e.g., Konetzke 1965, quoted in Golte 1980a:10–11). A more traditional interpretation of their import has been to see them as forerunners to the later wars of independence resulting from colonial oppression (Lewin 1973; Fisher 1976). O'Phelan Godoy (1976) points to the disruptions caused by the expulsion of the Jesuits and the Bourbon policy of extending tribute to new categories of taxpayers. Szeminski (1984) has chosen to emphasize the cultural continuities from pre-European times, arguing that the sentiments that provided the motivation to rebel were grounded in Andean, even Incaic, concepts of time and space that rejected the imposed worldview of the Europeans. Each of these (except the first), while incomplete in itself, adds to our understanding of the complex causes which led to revolt.

Still, one factor which participants mentioned repeatedly (and one that has recently been the subject of a major study of the period [Golte 1980a]) was the growing weight of the reparto de efectos (the forced purchase of designated consumer goods). The reparto, illegal until 1756, had grown to monumental proportions in spite of the Crown's attempt to control it (Fisher 1976:115; Golte 1980a; Larson 1984:139–64; Valcárcel 1971:246). The practice of selling the post of corregidor in Spain had continued. Those provinces with the highest indigenous populations had the highest fees, and those who secured them redoubled their efforts to make as much during their stay in office as they could. The corregidores received the most benefit, but close behind them were the commercial elite of Lima, who oversaw much of the trade through their ties to transport and finance and who may have provided part of the credit that made the purchase of the corregidorship possible in the first place (Larson 1979:217–18).

It was not only the native population that found itself confronting the reparto. Petty merchants could not compete with the large-scale commerce organized by the corregidores, and other social groups, such as mestizos and criollos (those of Spanish descent born in Peru), found themselves forced at times to accept, or were threatened with the prospect of accepting, the goods as well. At the same time many kurakas, in spite of their frequent cultural assimilation to Spanish society, were themselves under great pressure from the corregidores as they struggled to distribute goods and collect money from their own people on the corregidores' behalf (Golte 1980a:153–56, 180–91). Furthermore, native communities were still subject to the ongoing exactions of mita and tasa.

Indeed, one of the more intriguing issues concerning the rebellions of 1780 is the role of the kurakas. Both Tomás Catari and Túpac Amaru were hereditary kurakas and yet were the main instigators of the rebellions. Many other kurakas joined them in the revolts; in fact, Rowe has argued that the nationalist ideology that sustained the movement was a special preserve of the kurakas, possible only due to their education and literacy in the traditions of Garcilaso de la Vega and other literary sources (Rowe [1954] 1976). On the other hand, many kurakas remained loyal to the Crown and to the colonial order and rejected participation in the rebellion (cf. Larson 1984:157–61).

In Yura, too, we find a struggle with the exploitative reparto de efectos. The complaints had become so generalized in the province of Porco that in 1771 the Royal Audiencia required the corregidor to make a detailed accounting of his distribution of goods that year. Colonial officials in La Plata, aware of the potential for open rebellion, finally began to consider ways to correct the abuses of the system and hoped, through the accounting, to avoid "the frequent and continuous petitions that the Indians of the major part of the provinces of this district make to this Royal Audiencia" (ANC EC 1772, no. 105:fol. 2v). For Yura, 115 adults (including both women and older men in the reserved category) were listed as having received mules or other items in the reparto that year (ANC EC 1772, no. 105:fols. 33r–34r). Of course, they were also still obligated to pay the tasa as well.

In Yura we find a kuraka who remained loyal to the Crown. The group had been ruled for several decades by yet another Choquevilca, this one named Pablo. The Pablo Choquevilca of 1780 was the son of the long-lived Juan Baptista who was ruling in 1724 (ANB EC 1797, no. 41: fols. 9v, 11v). In 1764, when Pablo was already forty-three years old, he was identified in the census of that year as Yura's "governing kuraka and recognized proprietor by the Royal Audiencia of La Plata" (AGN 13.18.9.5: fol. 6r). As was the case in 1724, Choquevilca shared authority with a single kuraka, Luis Argote, who ruled over all the Urinsaya. Argote was said to be the "second person and governor of this moiety, from ayllu Corca" (AGN 13.18.9.5:fol. 18r).

Yura in the Time of the Rebellions: Organization and Demography

The 1764 census offers a view into the changing Yura social order. In the Upper Moiety the three major originario ayllus—Collana,

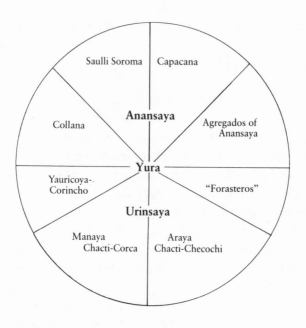

Figure 6.1 Ayllus of Yura in 1764

Capacana, and Saulli Soroma—continued as before. Urinsaya, however, had been reorganized: by 1764 the four (now quite small) ayllus of the Lower Moiety had been reduced and combined into two. The continued decline in population had made necessary the reduction of the complexity of the system. It is nevertheless interesting to note that the paired ayllus that were collapsed, Araya Chacti and Mana Chacti, were not simply lumped with one of the other two. Rather, their internal dual division came into play and they were separated and grouped with the two survivors. The record thus lists "Ayllu Manachacti and Corca" and "Ayllu Araya Chacti and Checochi" (AGN 13.18.9.5:fols. 18r, 20v). We still have no clear evidence for the hierarchy of groupings, the distinction between major and minor ayllus that is the case in Yura today. (See figure 6.1 for a visual representation of this.)

Another interesting shift in the census record is the increasing detail on the non-originario population. Although the people aggregated to Saulli Soroma in 1724 go without mention in the 1764

Table 6.1 Yura Population in 1764 and 1792, by Ayllu

Ayllu	Tributario		Total population	
	1764	1792	1764	1792
Anansaya				
Collana*	85	107	467	455
(absentees)	(2)			
Saulli Soroma	36	38	166	133
(absentees)	(3)			
Capacana	9	16	61	53
(absentees)	(1)			
Anansaya forasteros	?	29	?	102
Urinsaya				
Manachacti-Corca**	25	40	141	201
(absentees)	(5)			
Arayachacti-Checochi**	26	45	113	181
(absentees)	(2)			
Corincho	19	17	81	79
Agregados	4		13	
Yauricoya	13	22	81	104
Urinsaya forasteros	?	12	?	34
Total	230	326	1,123	1,342

*Originarios paid a head tax of ten pesos per year. Those listed as agregados and forasteros paid seven pesos; while the yanaconas of Yauricoya and Corincho paid 3 pesos, 1 real.
**The component names of these two ayllus were reversed in the 1792 census to read "Corca Manaya Chacti" and "Checoche Araya Chacti."
Sources: AGN 13.18.9.5; AGN 13.19.1.2.

revisita, they reappear in later documents. On the other hand, there are now seven tribute-paying households identified as forasteros agregados who are appended to the record after Urinsaya. In addition, for the first time the two groups of *yanaconas* at Yauricoya and Corincho appear together with the originarios. This category paid the least amount of tribute due to their more dependent status on a Spaniard or an estate.

Two sets of population figures are available for the period around the key events of 1781: from 1764 and from 1792. Table 6.1 summarizes the population figures from those two censuses. The non-originario population in 1764 is difficult to estimate accurately; but the seven agregados mentioned, plus the thirty-two yanaconas in the haciendas of Corincho and Yauricoya, indicate that the total population may have been about two hundred people more than the figure given. The more complete figures from 1792, the last colonial census, would confirm this. The 1792 figures show that in spite of the years of war—and contrary to suggestions of considerable population losses elsewhere—the population continued on an upswing. The figures also reveal that by this time almost one quarter of the households of Yura were classified as either forasteros or yanaconas. With these demographic and organizational issues as a background, let us turn to the critical events of 1781.

The Uprising of 1781 in Yura

In early 1781 the Catari rebellion was at its height. Although Tomás Catari had been killed in January, the leadership of his brother Damaso, as well as the news arriving across the Altiplano of the continuing successes of Túpac Amaru, kept this long-withheld reaction to the abuses of the colonial system alive and growing.

For many Yura their principal kuraka, Pablo Choquevilca, had come to represent that system. His wealth, his efforts to assist in the exactions of the state and of the corregidor, his abuses of the Yura to secure those taxes—all these contributed to the resentments that many held against him (ANB EC 1781, no. 61:fol. 23r).[2] Early that year, at some point when people were gathered together (perhaps at the festival of Carnaval), some decided to take action. As Pablo Choquevilca, mounted on his mule, passed by a group from the northern area of Yura, Ventura Pinto (a member of the Anansaya ayllu of Saulli) stepped out of the crowd with his sling at the ready and sent a rock flying at the kuraka. The rock struck him in the head. With another blow to the back Choquevilca was thrown from the mule, and the crowd surged around him, finishing the job by stoning him to death. Hours later his son Asencio was also killed by stoning; his two remaining sons, Lucas and Sebastián, were hanged (fols. 2r, 6v, 26v, 27r). Choquevilca's head was cut off and carried by Ramón Paca, the local leader of the revolt, to Macha, which had remained the center of the Potosí rebellion even after Tomás Catari's death. Paca and Ventura Pinto, who accompanied him, found themselves unwelcome in Macha. The alcalde there wanted to charge them to bury Choquevilca's head rather than, as they had expected, receiving them as heroes (fol. 5r). They hurried back, dumping the head on the way home.

Other guerrilla actions followed. Paca and several supporters attacked a mule train carrying mercury for Potosí and threw the mule driver in jail (fols. 2r, 2v). They forced the widow of Choquevilca to return that year's tasa by handing over all his llamas and mules to those in Anansaya who had paid their tribute (fols. 3r, 7r, 7v, 20r–22v). The priest was attacked at mass and forced to read an "edict from Catari" (fols. 2r, 3r, 3v, 7v).

A confrontation with the colonial authorities was inevitable. In late April Spanish troops moved on the town and quickly overwhelmed a canyon ambush, killing many Yura in the process (fols. 4v, 5r, 6v, 7r, 7v, 8r). By the next day the town and the province were in the control of Spanish forces. The subsequent inquest revealed that the Yura leaders had not acted alone but had indeed been in close contact with the Catari movement. It turned out that Ramón Paca had been to Macha not once, but three times (fol. 5v). Several people testified that Paca had been ordered by Damaso Catari to kill Choquevilca; certainly this is what Ventura Pinto, who struck the first blow on Paca's command, believed (fols. 27r, also 2v, 6r). When Paca and Pinto were in Macha with Choquevilca's head, Pinto later testified, Damaso Catari himself ordered him to assist Paca in the uprising (fol. 27r).

These allegations were greatly reinforced by a series of letters sewn into the litigation record which demonstrated some of these contacts. One, dated March 5 in Macha, is from the "governor and principal kuraka Damacio Catari" who warns "all the community to be ready with their provisions to go to battle when I inform you to" (fol. 10r). Other letters implicated the Yura leaders more deeply. There were also references to the feared Túpac Amaru of Peru. One witness testified that Paca brought a message from Macha which he claimed was directly from "Tupamaro." In the letter Túpac Amaru supposedly warned the people of Yura that if they did not join the uprising he would annihilate them (fol. 7r). Another letter, asking for assistance to fight the growing Spanish army at Esmoraca, requested the "well-armed soldiers" that had been ordered by "our Inka King don Joseph Graviel Tupamaro, Trunk and Strong Yoke" (fol. 16r). In a letter to Paca in opposition to the rebellion, one writer referred to "Túpac Amaru, your viceroy in revolt" (fol. 18r). Ventura Pinto later confessed that Ramón Paca had told him his king was Túpac Amaru. He said that he had heard that Carlos III of Spain had died, and added rather lamely that he understood Túpac Amaru to be king through succession (fol. 27r).

On one hand, the events in Yura were the manifestation of a widespread process in the southern Andes. However, an examination of the court record reveals that the particular course of events in Yura responded as much to internal divisions and loyalties as to outside pressures. For example, questions of ayllu organization underlay many of the points of conflict. In the first place, it is clear from the investigation that Urinsaya—the ayllus of Manaya Chacti–Corca and Araya Chacti–Checochi—did not take part in the rebellion against Pablo Choquevilca. The resistance came directly from members of his own Anansaya.

The internal organization of Collana also comes to the fore. Before 1781 census records do not indicate any internal subdivisions within the highly dispersed, large ayllu of Collana (that is, today's Qullana). Geographically, one large cluster of Collana households was located in the Thatuka River valley; this is where Choquevilca made his home (AGN 13.18.9.5:fol. 6r). Another cluster was in the northern area which bears the old ethnic name, around the hamlet of Wisijsa. The 1764 census gives a consecutive listing of Collana hamlets and villages throughout the entire territory that shows no particular order; in terms of Yura geography it seems quite random (AGN 13.18.8.5:fols. 7v–8r).

Ayllu "Saulli" (the Saulli Soroma of the past) is more localized than Collana and is found in the north and northwest reaches of Yura territory, interspersed with the Collana households there. The third Anansaya ayllu, Capacanaca, is centered in the 1764 census (as it is today) in the area of Phajcha far to the south and in Taru;

a few households are also situated south of the hamlet clustering of Wisijsa (AGN 13.18.9.5:fols. 16v–17v). (See figure 2.1 for a map of Yura territory.)

All those involved in the murder of Pablo Choquevilca were, as far as it is possible to determine, from Saulli, Capacanaca, and the northern "Wisijsa" clustering of Collana. Of the twelve persons in the court record who were said to be actors in the rebellion listed in the earlier 1764 visita, eight were registered in ayllu Saulli, one was from Capacanaca, and three were listed as members of Collana. Two of the latter three were from the hamlet of Wisijsa and one—Ramón Paca, the ringleader—came from the Huatacchi (or Watajchi) River region (AGN 13.18.9.5:fols. 7r, 10r, 12r, 13v, 14r–17r). Huatacchi is a narrow, high valley on the northwestern border of Yura territory in which the settlements on the south bank belong to Yura, while those on the north form part of Aymara-speaking Tomave (again, a look at the map of present-day Yura, figure 2.1, will be helpful here). The action against the kuraka, then, was carried out by a distant subdivision of Collana and the ayllu of Saulli; Choquevilca's Collana neighbors in the Thatuka Valley apparently did not join in. Whether these instigators from "Collana Visicsa" (as Ventura Pinto referred to them in his confession [ANB EC 1781, no. 61:fol. 27r]) were a self-conscious grouping before the day of the assassination (as they were afterward), or whether this was previously merely a geographic designation within the ayllu, is not possible to specify at present.

Pinto, the man who flung the first stone at Choquevilca, tried to exculpate himself by describing the violent acts committed by Choquevilca against him. All that he describes may have been completely true, but abuses by a kuraka that would have been tolerated in the past were now unthinkable in the context of a widespread rebellion and the messianic hope of throwing off the strictures of the Spanish regime. Yet those in Yura who managed to act on their desire for revenge against the coercion of the authorities were precisely those who were in a "structurally appropriate" position to do so.

Urinsaya was too distant from Choquevilca; they had their own hereditary kuraka, and their main dealings with the Spanish state would have been through him. The Collanas of the south, especially those of the Thatuka Valley, were apparently too close. They may have suffered from the kuraka's actions, but they would have shared a great deal with him, such as common kinship, residence, and hamlet-centered ritual activities. The agents for destroying the old order were ayllu members of Anansaya who were subject to Choquevilca but who were removed from him in terms of both proximity and interaction. The rebellion was thus carried out by those of Saulli and the distant Collana Wisijsa rancho, led by a man who was almost an outsider (while still a Collana) from the northern border area of Huatacchi.

For all practical purposes the death of Choquevilca brought an end to hereditary rule for life for the kurakas of Yura. The dispersion of his wealth in animals—over a hundred names appear on the list of people who received llamas and mules in the expropriation and distribution of his herds after his death (ANB EC 1781, no. 61:fols. 21r–22v)—must have had a permanent impact on the material resources of the elite Collana families. Nor was there a successor who could take up the kurakaship, since Choquevilca's three sons were killed along with him.

The Rebellion's Aftermath and Authority in Yura

That these events were truly a turning point is revealed in another court record, this one from 1797, still almost three decades before Bolivia finally gained its independence from Spain. While royal officials had abolished the hereditary kurakaship in most areas after the rebellions of the 1780s (Rowe [1954] 1976:52) and were using other forms of recruitment to the kurakaship by then (such as natural leadership ability, expressed loyalty, and financial resources) (Larson 1979:235), the idea of hereditary succession was still strong among the Andean population. This is apparent in the 1797 record from Yura.

In it, three "poor and starving Indians from the town of Yura" (all from the Anansaya moiety) went to the authorities of the Audiencia in La Plata to denounce a Spaniard named Marcos Mariaca.

They argued that Mariaca had thrust himself into the position of "interim cacique" to the detriment of the proprietor of the role, don Juan Choquevilca, "to whom it legitimately corresponds by right of bloodline" (ANB EC 1797, no. 14:fol. 1r). The three reported that Mariaca was abusive to common folk and indigenous authorities alike, forcing people to work in servile positions without pay. Testimony revealed that Juan Choquevilca was the grandson of the assassinated Pablo, son of the eldest son Lucas. Only five years old in 1781, Juan escaped the violence visited on his father, uncles, and grandfather (fol. 9r). Yet as the testimony proceeded it became clear that young Choquevilca was not himself interested in taking on the post that had been held by his ancestors. All seven witnesses reported that Juan, when counseled that he should pursue his rights, insisted that he was too young and too poor to do so (he was only twenty-one at the time) (fols. 9r, 9v, 10v, 11r, 11v, 12v, 13v).

Since Choquevilca refused to claim the post and no other legitimate candidates stepped forward, Mariaca was confirmed in his position of tribute collector. He was instructed to drop the title of cacique and to avoid involvement in activities peculiar to kurakas. Nor should he burden the Indians with more than his proper share of personal services. It was also decided that Choquevilca could, if he so chose, renew his claim to the kurakaship at a later date (fol. 14r). There is no indication that he did so.

What are the implications of this turn of events? First, in spite of the absence of a hereditary kuraka over the repartimiento, the state still required the payment of its exactions. It was willing to confirm anyone in the role of tax collector who could successfully gather them, regardless of his relation to the community. The presence of Mariaca in such a post—in which a non-Yura, backed by the power of the state, forced the payment of taxes—provided a model for the republican arrangement, the form of state control which is still in existence today.

Juan Choquevilca, for his part, seemed to recognize the futility of the role of principal kuraka. As we have seen, for centuries the kurakas had been torn between their "internal" role as symbolic, ritual, and redistributive head of Anansaya and of the entire group, and their "interstitial" role as expropriator of resources and labor for the state. The wealth and the power that the post brought with it, as well as what may have been a noblesse oblige sense of duty to serve, made a long line of kurakas willing to accept the contradictions. Nonetheless, the conflicts remained, only to be "resolved" through violent political action in the beheading of Pablo Choquevilca and the murder of his sons. The grandson, stripped of his patrimony and without the years of close observation of a predecessor, was simply unwilling to shoulder those contradictions.

While hereditary succession was ended by 1792, the overall arrangement of authority roles seems little changed from the way it appeared in 1764. Ayllu Collana had its governing kuraka, although he was now no longer a kuraka by blood, potentially holding the post for life. Saulli and Capacanaca each had their principal, a person in charge of collecting tribute and presumably with festival duties similar to those of today. Urinsaya was still governed by its own hereditary leader, although his line's automatic claim to the post seems to have disappeared soon afterward as well.[3] This leader ruled over the combined Corca–Manaya Chacti, while another authority was placed over Checochi–Araya Chacti.

Except for reversing the order of the ayllu names in Urinsaya (highlighting the present-day names of the two groupings), ayllu organization at the end of the eighteenth century also differed little from the past. The changes that had occurred were to be found in the continued abolition of the higher levels, the positions over the moieties and over the entire repartimiento of Yura. At the lower-level ayllus there are suggestions that for some time the posts had been taken on for a limited period, shared among the members of the ayllu itself. In 1679, for instance, some witnesses said that they had been (but were not now) *cobrador de tasa* (collector of the tasa) or *enterador de la mita* (mobilizer of the mita). The lower-level posts (such as the heads of the localized ayllu segments) may have always been temporary and rotational.

The abolition of the principal kuraka and the further leveling of community stratification presented the Yuras with the problem of how to continue to meet the demands of the state and yet retain a certain control over their own affairs.[4] Their solution was to employ the same rotational principle already used at the lower levels for the higher posts as well. Taking on the more prominent authority roles, which was once a right of birth and position, now became an obligation that could theoretically be required of all community members. This became the normal pattern for the kuraqkuna of Yura in the nineteenth century. The system was modified on occasion, as we shall see, when people and groups attempted to redefine themselves in more positive terms. Nonetheless, ayllu organization and a similar system of ayllu authorities continued as a conceptual bedrock.

The Nineteenth Century to the Present

Yet the struggles of the 1780s did not leave Yura ayllu organization untouched, as is evident from the first revisitas made in the nineteenth century. In a census from 1820 (ANB Revisitas, book 235) and in a more detailed accounting from 1831 (ANB, Revisitas, book 237a), the split in ayllu Collana which had become apparent in the assassination of Pablo Choquevilca became institutionalized. There were now four ayllus of originarios (full tribute payers) in Anansaya: Collana Tatuca, Capacanaca (now called "Capacana"), Collana Huicicsa (i.e., Qullana Wisijsa), and Saulli. Ayllu Collana had thus been partitioned into two segments, one centered on the Thatuka area (home of the Choquevilcas) and the other on Wisijsa (the focus of the 1781 insurrection). Figure 6.2 summarizes these changes.

As for the structure of authority in 1831, we find in the preeminent position of governing kuraka for Collana Tatuca one Eugenio Herrera, a mestizo (ANB, Revisitas, book 237a:fol. 149r). Serving with him are an alcalde and a principal (who by this time is clearly similar to the jilaqata of today). Capacanaca, which follows in the record, has its own principal and alcalde (fol. 151v), as does the large group of agregado households attached to these ayllus (fol. 153r). Collana Huicicsa also has a governing kuraka, a principal, and an alcalde (fol. 154v). Saulli, appearing next in the census, is governed by an alcalde and a principal. Attached to the entire moiety are a number of forastero households, with their own kuraka and alcalde (fol. 159r).

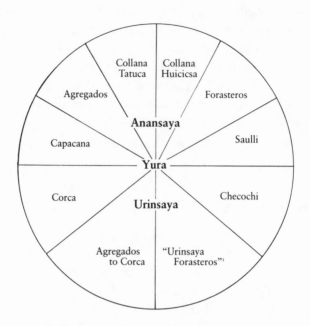

1. Later known as "Agregados to Checochi," then "Sulca Checochi."

Figure 6.2 Ayllus of Yura in 1831

In Urinsaya, ayllu Corca is governed by the same three officials: kuraka, principal, and alcalde (fol. 160v); a group of agregados is linked to Corca under the authority of their own alcalde and principal. Ayllu Checochi lists the same leadership posts as the originarios of Corca. Following Checochi is a roll of forasteros who are linked to the Lower Moiety. Interestingly, by this time the Chacti portion of the names of these two major Urinsaya ayllus has been lost.

In 1831 there were six couples identified as kurakas, eight as principales, and ten as alcaldes. This large number of authorities does not take into account the two groups of yanaconas in the haciendas of Yauricoya and Corincho, each with their own kuraka and alcalde in 1818 (ANB, Revisitas, book 235:fols. 52r, 54r). What this suggests is a considerable growth in the total number of authorities, due perhaps to the attempt to share the burdens of office among as

Table 6.2 Yura Population by Ayllu in 1831

Ayllu	Tributarios	Total population
Anansaya		
Collana Tatuca	57	217
Capacana	23	91
Agregados of these ayllus[a]	(45)	162
Collana Huicicsa	58	216
Saulli	47	148
Anansaya forasteros		
without lands[a]	(22)	90
Urinsaya		
Corca	63	222
Agregados to Corca[a]	(13)	47
Checochi	67	260
Forasteros of Urinsaya[a]	(18)	78
Total	413 (315)	1,531

a. Those listed as agregados and forasteros paid an annual tax of seven pesos;
all the rest listed are originarios, who paid ten pesos yearly. In the 1831 census
the yanaconas of Corincho and Yauricoya were not recorded.
Source: ANB, Revisitas, book 237a.

many as possible. Conversely, this may simply reflect a more careful
recording of the posts than in the last colonial revisita available to
us. The arrangement of kurakas and other authorities also seems to
indicate the existence of the distinction between major and minor
ayllus that is seen in the Yura of today.

The population continued the increased rate of growth first noted
in the second half of the eighteenth century (see table 6.2). There
were now 315 originario contribuyentes, as tribute payers were eu-
phemistically called after independence from Spain. Another 98
agregados forasteros of tribute age were also counted. The total
population had grown to 1,525 among originarios and forasteros
(ANB, Revisitas, book 235:fol. 168r; my calculations give 1,531).
While we do not have the yanacona figures from 1831, thirteen
years before there were some 44 male taxpayers in this category
and some 123 persons in all (ANB, Revisitas, book 235: fol. 55v).

Although the mita had finally been abolished in 1812 (ANB, Mano de Obra catalog SG2186a), it is worth noting that after Bolivia's independence, and for most of the nineteenth century, the indigenous *contribución indigenal* (that is, the old tasa, the tribute paid by all Andean peoples) made up a significant portion of the national budget of Bolivia. Bonilla, quoting Grieshaber, shows that in 1827 the head tax provided 41 percent of the total government revenues, while throughout that decade tribute was never less than 31 percent of income (Bonilla 1980:118). Furthermore, the bulk of these monies came from independent Andean communities well into the last quarter of the century (Bonilla 1980:143–44), in spite of an overall population decline in many Altiplano indigenous communities (Grieshaber 1980). It was not until the renewed expansion of silver mining and then of the growth of the tin-mining industry late in the century—accompanied by the assault on indigenous communities that came about with the expansion of the haciendas after 1865 (Rivera 1984)—that the central administration's reliance on taxes from indigenous communities began to decline as a proportion of the total national budget. Careful attention was therefore paid to the revisitas of rural populations, since the new republican government relied as heavily on indigenous labor and products (converted to cash for the payment of the "contribution") as the colonial government before it had. Also as before, the state turned to the indigenous leaders—the new rotational system of kurakas and jilaqatas—to act as their agents in the extraction of those resources.

As the decades passed, however, it seems that the rotational authorities could not, or would not, work as passionately to ensure the fulfillment of tax burdens as had the hereditary kurakas, who perhaps identified more completely with the authority of the state. Further research is necessary to explore the details of these events. Nevertheless, the fact that a man identified as a mestizo occupied the kurakaship of ayllu Collana Tatuca in 1831 recalls to mind the suit of 1797 to remove another outsider from the same post.

By at least 1855 (and probably considerably before this) a new official appeared on the local scene in Yura, the *corregidor* (ANB, Revisitas, book 243). The title is, of course, not a new one. In colonial

times the corregidor, as we have seen, was a powerful and exploitative Spanish official who had served as the chief administrator at
the provincial level. The post had finally been abolished late in the
colonial period due to the many abuses associated with the reparto
de efectos. However, with the creation of the Republic of Bolivia
after 1825, an office of the same name but with a more delimited
range of authority was reestablished at the level of the doctrina or
the repartimiento (or the *cantón,* as doctrinas were called by 1830).
Thereafter the corregidor became the primary agent for the state
on the local level. Chosen from the growing mestizo class of the
villages and towns, this official would not only identify with, but
would consider himself part of, the state apparatus.

This move represented a filling of the gap in the structure of authority, a gap that had been left empty since the abolition of the
post of the principal kuraka. The individual ayllu members filling
the now rotational roles of kuraka or jilaqata would be reluctant to
apply stiff sanctions to the fellow ayllu member who refused to pay
his contribution. The corregidor, drawn from the mestizo (or vecino) group and who distinguished himself from the Yura by means
of his identification with the urban classes, would not suffer from
the same scruples. For Yura, as well as for the bureaucrats of the
state, this arrangement solved the contradictory demands formerly
placed on the hereditary kuraka, who, as we saw, had to fill the
roles both of the egalitarian communal leader (at least symbolically
in the festival cycle) and of the exploitative master of state exactions. Consequently, in the nineteenth century a division of labor
developed that distinguished between these conflicting aspects of
the authority roles, a separation of functions which, as we saw in
chapter 4, continues up to the present. The corregidor, although he
did not directly take over the collection of the republican tribute,
nevertheless acted as a permanent reminder for kurakas and jilaqatas of the state's presence and its demands (as well as being the
direct taskmaster of the alcaldes). Whereas abuses were previously
charged to the principal kuraka, it now became the corregidor who
applied physical force to gain his ends. This, too, is a pattern that
continues to the present day.

We also see changes in participation in the ayllus in this period.

In spite of the burden of taxation, there is a curious "playing" with the fiscal categories of originario, agregado forastero (the forasteros of previous centuries), and forasteros without land (the colonial yanaconas) during the nineteenth century. As was true in colonial times, these categories continued to pay their tribute at three different rates. In 1845 originarios in Yura each year paid ten pesos per *contribuyente* (contributor, the new term for tribute payer); agregados (some were termed forasteros with lands) paid seven, and the two groups on haciendas paid a little over three pesos per tribute payer (ANB, Revisitas, book 241a). The amounts paid by these categories remained the same throughout the century. What becomes apparent, however, is a movement of individuals and whole groups from lower to higher categories, a process which eventually blurred the differential placement of entire groups into the inferior ranks.

For example, the revisita of 1841 provides a model of organization similar to that of 1831. The population continued to grow (it was then 1,825, excluding the former yanaconas, versus the 1,531 people counted ten years before). The same groupings and same arrangement of indigenous authorities appear. However, there is one small but significant difference: those groups of forasteros who in both censuses are attached to Anansaya and Urinsaya were said to be "without lands" in 1831 (ANB, Revisitas, book 237a), while they were "with lands" in 1841 (ANB, Revisitas, book 241). Although they may have all actually obtained title to land in the interim, it is more likely that the census taker has simply recognized a condition that was already in existence before, perhaps for decades.

Up to 1841 there is still no mention in the records of the "sullk'a" ayllus that exist today, Sullk'a Qullana, Sullk'a Qhurqa, and Sullk'a Chiquchi. By 1855, however, an intriguing change had occurred which reveals how one such "younger" ayllu came into being. Ten years before, a particular set of households had been classed as landed forasteros attached to ayllu Checochi. These households, which even in 1831 (when they were called Urinsaya forasteros [ANB, Revisitas, book 237a:fol. 166v]) had their own kuraka and alcalde, had become in 1855 the newly recognized "Aillo Sulca Checochi." Four of their number had moved from the seven-peso forastero category to the higher ten-peso originario status. The rest continued to pay only seven pesos, however, now as agregados within the same Sulca Checochi (ANB, Revisitas, book 243:fol. 116r). In 1867 there were five originarios in Sulca Checochi (ANB, Revisitas, book 246), in 1872 eight (ANB, Revisitas, book 247:fol. 315v), and in 1877 sixteen (ANB, Revisitas, book 248:fol. 179r). A similar process occurred with ayllu "Sulca Tatuca Collana." In both cases former forastero groups were assimilated to full ayllu status, and a number of households within them "became" originarios.

One other innovation occurred in the middle decades of the nineteenth century. The residents of what had been the hacienda of Yauricoya had been under the authority of their own kuraka and principal since colonial times. In 1845, as we just saw, they paid their tasa at the lowest, "yanacona," rate. By 1867 fifteen members of what was now termed the *parcialidad* of Yauricoya paid their tasa at the intermediate agregado or forastero rate of seven pesos, while the rest—some twenty-seven tribute payers—still paid the lower tax (ANB, Revisitas, book 246). By 1877 what is now the "ayllu" of Yauricoya had six originarios and nineteen agregados, with only seventeen forasteros paying the lowest tax rate. Since the lands of present-day Sullk'a Qhurqa are the same lands that once belonged to Yauricoya, it can only be concluded that the residents of the hacienda evolved into ayllu Sullk'a Qhurqa. Interestingly, the same change did not occur in the other yanacona group of Corincho, all of whom continued to pay at the lowest rate in 1877 (ANB, Revisitas, book 248:fol. 180v ff.). In order to continue our review of demographic trends and organizational innovations, table 6.3 gives a summary of three nineteenth-century revisitas.

The attitude of the independent governments of the Andes toward the ayllus was rather complex and changed over time. On one hand, the importance of the tax payments to the overall national budget was one argument in favor of protecting the integrity of the Andean peasant communities. On the other hand, the liberal agenda believed that the advance of the nation would only be possible through the conversion of rural peoples into independent yeoman farmers. As early as 1825 Bolívar issued a decree abolishing the kurakaships and privatizing the land (Rowe [1954] 1976:53; Sánchez-Albornoz

Table 6.3 Yura Population by Ayllu from Three Nineteenth-Century Censuses

Ayllu	Tributarios			Total population		
	1845	1855	1872	1845	1855	1872
Anansaya						
Tatuca Collana	61	81	105	214	214	267
agregados	4			? 4		
Capacana	27	28	35	87	68	87
agregados[1]	50	59	64	152	154	155
Visicsa Collana	63	77	102	189	176	256
forasteros	6	6	7	? 9	9	15
Saulli	46	53	58	146	126	141
agregados	3	2	8	? 4	2	12
Forasteros with land[2]	30	36	4 [or] 37 [agr]	85	84	101
Urinsaya						
Corca	75	84	90	202	199	218
forasteros	18	11	12	41	27	28
Checochi	75	79	96	229	182	238
Sulca Checochi[3]	2	4	8	? 3	11	28
Forasteros with land[4]	30	37	40	73	75	100
Yauricoya[5]	35	42	5 [or] 17 [agr] 19 [for]	96	85	109
Corincho	13	13	15	31	29	31
Total	538	615	722	1,565	1,441	1,786
Originarios	347	406	503			
Agregados	191	206	219[6]			

1. The numbers suggest that the group referred to as forasteros Sulca Tatuca Collana in 1855 were the agregados of Capacana in 1845. By 1872 they are once again listed as agregados of Capacana.
2. This group by 1872 was listed as agregados of the parcialidad of Aransaya; between 1855 and 1872 some had adopted originario status.
3. The group, known as forasteros de Checochi in 1845, are, in 1855 and 1872, termed Sulca Checochi, the name they bear here.
4. In 1845 this group is referred to as forasteros with lands, but by 1855 they are agregados of Sulca Checochi. That continued in 1872.

Table 6.3 Continued

---

5. While the terminology of the fiscal categories is not always consistent, by 1872 originarios continued to pay ten pesos, agregados paid seven, and two small groups of forasteros without lands in Corincho and a portion of Yauricoya paid three pesos, one real.

6. This combines the two categories of forastero and agregado.

Sources: ANB, Revisitas, books 241a, 243, and 247.

1978:203). While the division of lands that the latter would have required was soon rescinded, the ideology of liberalism was a major factor in the insistence on the part of the national elites that the unity of the "backward" Andean ayllus be broken (Platt 1984).

The attack on the ayllus continued throughout the nineteenth century. In 1842 the Bolivian government arbitrarily recast the nature of the legal relationship between the indigenous population and their lands, decreeing that all "Indian" landholdings were in fact the property of the state. In one stroke Andean people—including the originarios—were suddenly defined as nothing more than renters or leaseholders at the pleasure of the government. Their tribute payment, according to this policy, was simply a fee paid to the state for the right to use the land. This assault on the land tenure of the ayllus was the prelude to a series of steps that led inevitably to a concerted and violent program of alienation of ayllu lands (Sánchez-Albornoz 1978:205–07). In 1866 President Melgarejo declared that "state" lands in indigenous hands had to have their titles formalized according to new legal canons; if not, they would be sold. The native population was given sixty days to carry out the orders; most did not. This soon had a drastic impact on the ability of native communities to retain control of their land base, especially in the departments of La Paz and Cochabamba. In the face of this wholesale effort to destroy the ayllu, Andean groups in many areas rebelled once again from 1869 to 1871, as they had eighty years before. Although the Melgarejan decrees were finally declared null, most of the lands taken from indigenous communities were not returned (Sánchez-Albornoz 1978:207–10).

Security of land tenure became even more uncertain as the tasa was gradually forgone as the major source of revenue in the national budget (Bonilla 1978:180). Thus, in spite of the retraction of the Melgarejan titling program after the dictator's overthrow, the government again acted in 1874 to encourage the privatization of ayllu lands by officially disestablishing the state's recognition of communal holdings as well as any legal status of the ayllu itself. This policy, the so-called Ley de Exvinculación, was, as Platt (1982) has analyzed it, the first agrarian reform and a forerunner of the parcelist land grants to follow eighty years later after the 1952 revolution. Government authorities continued their efforts to implement the liberal ideal of creating an agrarian capitalism by creating a free market in land that would force native Andeans to accept individualized holdings of their fields and pastures as well as the possibility of selling their lands to larger (and presumably more efficient) landholders, that is, to the growing haciendas. Land taxes were also to be individual.

In rural areas the reaction to this "reform" ranged from passive resistance to organized rebellion. This both confused and angered the governing class, who argued that the Andean peasant was seemingly blind to the fact that the law finally regularized land titles in favor of the rural producer, titles which had been in doubt since the time that the state claimed ownership of all indigenous lands some decades before. In Platt's view, however, Andean communities had never accepted state ownership, although they were willing to enter into a kind of contractual relationship based on a "pact of reciprocity" in which the state guaranteed ayllu control over lands in exchange for a series of traditional services, such as the *postillonaje,* the mita, or other personal services to state officials in provincial capitals. The Ley de Exvinculación broke the pact, and the ayllus (now no longer even able to act as legal entities as far as the state was concerned) struggled with those local officials who attempted to carry out the law through yet another revisita and through the expedition of new titles after the measurement of lands.

The degree of resistance varied, however, apparently according to the ecological zones in question. In the punas of Chayanta and Charcas in the Norte de Potosí, the process of granting new titles ground to a halt in the face of thoroughgoing resistance on the part

of the ayllus; the officials in charge of the revisita argued throughout the period that the measurements and titling could only be
carried out through the force of arms (Platt 1982). In Yura, however, the fragmented landholdings of small, irrigated plots for maize
production had always been held, at least in usufruct, by family
lines; there were no large-scale rotational holdings as are found in
puna areas. While the lands of Yura were, for purposes of the tasa,
thought of as ayllu units, many comunarios held titles to individual
sets of fields long before 1874. Harman quotes the corregidor of
Yura in 1882, who was actively involved in the titling revisita in
Yura of that year: "Land tenure is individual, with the boundaries
of each property clearly set out. There is not a single piece of land,
other than pasture areas, that is owned in common. . . . and it is
not unusual for the kuraka of the ayllu to which a person belongs
barely to know the individual due to the distances that separate
their places of residence" (Harman 1987:144, taken from ANB PD
1798, no. 39 [1882]).[5] For this reason the titling undertaken by
the revisitadores in Yura in 1881–82, attempting to implement the
Ley de Exvinculación, at first ran into less resistance than it did
in the Norte de Potosí, where the threat to ayllu lands was more
obvious. However, even here rumors began to circulate about the
ultimate end of the revisita, and it was finally suspended. By 1886
the kurakas demanded to be made exempt from the revisita; they
argued that since their lands were *tierras de origen,* granted by the
Spanish Crown, they should not be included (ANB PD 2071, no. 6
[1886]). The revisita was never completed.

The other major aspect of the Ley de Exvinculación had to do
with the conversion of the tasa to direct land taxes assessed on
the basis of the new titles to be extended. Yet the decision by the
state to forgo tribute was somewhat mitigated by the resistance to
the new form of landholding and the continuing reliance on the
contribución at the departmental level—and even at the national
level, since departments loaned considerable sums to the central
government in the first decades after the shift in taxation (Platt
1982). The contribución territorial paid by Andean peasants now
became the major source of income for the departmental budget
(Rivera [1984:32–34] has shown how important the contribución

continued to be for the highland departments through at least the first quarter of the twentieth century). Therefore, both the central and departmental governments continued to be preoccupied with indigenous tribute. Even after landless folk were removed from the rolls in 1882[6] the tasa was not easily forgone (Sánchez-Albornoz 1978:211–16).

Thus, while a partial measurement of lands was carried out in 1881 in Yura, the last complete revisita of Yura retained in the Bolivian National Archives was made in 1877 (ANB, Revisitas, book 248). It provides a final, detailed documentary glimpse of Yura before the present. We have already seen some changes in ayllu organization and authorities at that time—in the creation from agregado groups, for example, of the ayllus of Sullk'a Chiquchi and Sullk'a Qullana. Yauricoya, now with its own originarios, was also well on its way to the new status of Sullk'a Qhurqa.

In 1877, then, Anansaya was made up, as today, of six groups: Aillo Tatuca de Collana, Agregados of Tatuca Collana, Capacana, Sullca Collana, Aillo Vicsisa, and Saulli. In Urinsaya we find the ayllus of Corca, Checochi, Sullca Checochi, Yauricoya, and Corincho. In all there were now 540 originarios, 190 agregados, and 33 forasteros. The total population was about 2,100 people. (Table 6.4 summarizes the population figures from 1877.) As was also true in 1831, there were more kuraka posts in 1877 than today, six in all. Tatuca Collana, Visicsa, Sullca Collana, Corca, Checochi, and Yauricoya[7] all had kurakas. Each of these ayllus also had a principal or jilaqata, as did the ayllus of Agregados, Capacana, Saulli, and Sullca Checochi. Unfortunately, the post of alcalde was apparently not well recorded in 1877; but in 1867 (ANB, Revisitas, book 246) the arrangement of alcaldes was essentially the same as it is today. Alcaldes served in Tatuca Collana, Agregados (presumably today's Phajcha alcalde), Collana Visicsa, Corca, and Checochi. Assuming this remained unchanged through 1877, the system of kuraqkuna that existed in that year was identical to that of today, with the exception of the kurakas of Sullca Collana and Yauricoya. One can only assume that as Yauricoya became today's Sullk'a Qhurqa, and Sullca Collana was more completely incorporated into today's Qu-

Table 6.4 Yura Population by Ayllu in 1877

Ayllu	Tributarios	Total population
Anansaya		
Tatuca de Collana	112	285
Agregados[1]	64	196
Capacana	40	85
Collana Vicsisa	108	291
Agregados to Vicsisa	11	55
Saulli	65	170
Agregados to Saulli	8	18
Sullca Collana	6 [orig]	16
Agregados to Sullca Collana	33	81
Urinsaya		
Corca	93	210
Agregados to Corca	12	25
Checochi[2]	110	276
Agregados to Checochi	43	98
Yauricoya, originarios	6	18
agregados	19	40
forasteros	17	40
Corincho	16	83
Total	744	1,987
Originarios	540	
Agregados[3]	204	

1. This group, listed earlier as agregados to Capacana, is in this case placed in the record after ayllu Tatuca de Collana.
2. The originarios of Sulca Checochi have been mixed in this census with those of ayllu Checochi, presumably a mistake on the part of the census taker. Thus, the agregados to Checochi here are those listed previously as the agregados to Sulca Checochi.
3. This figure is the sum of 171 agregados and 33 forasteros.

Source: ANB, Revisitas, book 248:fols. 152r–183v.

llana, the posts were abolished as unnecessary, or even as being in conflict with the kurakas of the two larger ayllus.

The last census gives us a view of Yura that is beyond the direct memory of anyone alive today. It may be for this reason that the former fiscal categories of originario, agregado, and forastero, statuses that seem in the nineteenth century to have been important enough that people voluntarily paid more taxes to move from a lower to a higher category, have been lost. Inheritance and subsequent land divisions have obscured the three-tiered tax system. Today, when officials in Potosí send a notice that fixes tasa amounts according to the three classes, the figures are converted immediately (and seemingly with no further thought) into the Yura tasa rates described in chapter 4. For them, taxation amounts have their origins in the last visita. In a sense they have all become originarios and conceive the varying rates they presently pay to derive from a moment of initial equality.

In the twentieth century the kuraqkuna have retained most of the characteristics that they probably acquired after 1781: the roles are rotational; the kurakas' actions stress the egalitarian nature of ayllu membership and the consensual basis of their own authority; and the corregidor, traditionally of the mestizo or vecino category, represents the coercive element of state control. Thus the role of the principal kuraka, the cacique gobernador of colonial times, has been split between the consensual, egalitarian kuraka—symbolically today the manifestation of ayllu unity—and the hierarchical and frequently arbitrary corregidor—who represents the Yuras' relationship with the central state.

The twentieth century has not been without its shocks to that concept of unity, and the changes that the Yura have confronted in recent decades could, eventually, overwhelm the integrity of group organization in spite of past successes to such challenges. The forced conscription of indigenous men at the time of the War of the Chaco, and the more recent opportunities for wage labor in Argentina and in lowland parts of Bolivia, have both taken large numbers of Yura away from their home territory and placed them, as individuals, in direct contact with other elements of a wider international society. In this the kuraqkuna have had no significant mediating role. The central government's continuing policy of breaking up the ayllus—the 1979 order to convert all tasa lands to individual catastro tax payment and the 1985 tax reform plan for yet another new individualized tax system on native lands are only the latest versions of this ongoing effort—only reinforces the erosion of the kuraqkuna's relevance.

We should not, however, assume that abolition of the kuraq-kuna of Yura is the inevitable outcome of the processes of rural life today. This chapter and the last have demonstrated the profound nature of the challenges to the indigenous authorities in the past. They have endured the mita, the reducción, the drastic decline in population, and the continued exactions of the colonial period. The system itself even survived the murder of the principal authority and the abolition of hereditary succession. The indigenous authorities have become more egalitarian in their actions as the exploitative aspects of the role were left to the state-appointed offices, espe-cially that of corregidor. As the ayllus underwent division, and as those Yura without lands became fully integrated into them, the particular arrangement of the authorities was modified, and modi-fied again, to fit the changing circumstances. The kuraqkuna of Yura have survived it all, over centuries, and have prevailed.

However, the *way* in which they have prevailed would likely have been something of a shock to don Juan Roque Choquevilca, who in 1679 struggled with ayllu members as an autocratic and powerful native leader who came to his post through hereditary succession. For the power they have today seems to lie in a different realm from his control of productive resources, his role in the marketplace in the sale of agricultural and other processed goods, and his identi-fication with and assimilation to the ruling elites. The kuraqkuna's power today is one of cultural construction, not economic produc-tion. The rest of this study will examine that power and along with it the kind of world (especially the kind of symbolic world) they, as a group, create. We will thus turn to the sets of meanings and practices which ground the actions of the contemporary kuraqkuna.

THE KURAQKUNA AND
THE CONSTRUCTION OF THE
YURA SYMBOLIC WORLD

From History to Ethnography:
The Symbolic Dimension

The hereditary kurakas of the past would be shocked to see the kuraqkuna today. From their perspective as powerful lords who mediated between the upper spheres of Spanish colonial society and their own humble subjects, the kurakas would no doubt have felt that the egalitarian kuraqkuna of contemporary Yura had suffered a distressing loss of power. However, their judgment might possibly be less severe than we might imagine, because much of what the kuraqkuna do today would have been familiar to the kurakas of past centuries.

Our understanding of the colonial kurakas and of the early republican ayllu leaders is shaped, naturally, by the historical sources available to us. For study at the local level these include records of court cases relating to land disputes, other court documents and legislation pertaining to the indigenous social strata, census records, and tax ledgers. These documents were produced in large part by the members of the colonial bureaucracy—officers of the courts, provincial administrators, accountants—with their own pragmatic ends in mind. The picture we have of the hereditary kurakas is thus one that highlights their interstitial position between the indigenous peasant population and colonial institutions and which, for the most part, says little about those aspects of the authority role that had to do solely with internal ayllu activities.

This account of the history of the authorities of Yura is incomplete from an anthropological point of view, since the full cultural dimension of the early hereditary kuraka's role is by and large undocumented. In the historical materials we have located concerning Yura there are precious few references to festivals or rituals; and while more is available for other Andean regions, this is likely to be an area where historical research will always be constrained by limitations in the sources.

Earlier we discussed the significance of Indian hispanism among the hereditary Andean elite. The assimilation by the Andean kurakas of the cultural forms of the dominant society might seem to indicate that the role of the kurakas in indigenous cultural life would be limited. We have little information, however, on the topic of the Andean authorities' self-identification with their new rulers. Given the rhetorical and strategic nature of much of the writings about the ladino kurakas, we should be cautious in charging the kurakas with cultural collaboration. In those documented cases where kurakas did assimilate to Spanish ways of life (and yet remained kurakas), it is not easy to specify what the adoption of such cultural forms meant to the individuals involved, even though we can easily demonstrate that many did indeed attend school, learn to read and write in Spanish, and dress in European finery. We should keep in mind that it was the highly assimilated Inka elite, if Rowe's ([1954] 1976) analysis is correct, that was the source of the strong nationalist ideology that permeated the native rebellions of the Cuzco region in the late eighteenth century.

What we still lack is an understanding of the degree to which the native leaders of the colonial period shared a common symbolic world, expressed in ritual and festival life, with the ayllu members over whom they ruled. We know that the kurakas were key figures in the ritual life of the community at the time of the Spanish invasion, even though in most places there was a separate body of priests to administer regional and local shrines. After Spanish domination was established, the kurakas soon realized that in their intermediary position between peasant farmer and colonial authorities they had to support, or appear to support, the religion of the conquerors. To be confirmed in their posts by the Spanish the kurakas necessarily had to accept Catholicism and endorse the priests' efforts to stamp out superstition, paganism, and barbarism, to use the idiom of the day.[1]

Even so there is evidence that, throughout the colonial period, local-level Andean kurakas participated in and protected what the Spaniards called "idolatry," the practice of non-Catholic ritual acts (Duviols 1972:264–65). The frequent references to *borracheras* (drunken binges, sprees) throughout the period give us some indication of the strength of Andean ritual activity. Kurakas who were considered to be devout Catholics permitted sacrifices and other indigenous rites[2] and employed Andean symbolism (or, on occasion, the symbolic vocabulary of related lowland traditions).[3]

No doubt much of the kuraka's role in the sphere of Andean religion went unrecorded or was submerged in interaction with the dominant culture of the European elite. Nonetheless, any system of authority, in order to sustain itself, must be grounded in shared legitimations, in common conceptions of both the nature of the world and acceptable and appropriate ways to act within it. The hereditary kurakas of the past, like the kuraqkuna today, must have participated in the Andean symbolic universe, and that shared conception of the world would have been communicated, then as now, in ritual. The base of shared understandings expressed in symbolic acts no doubt provided a mode of discourse about the ayllus, their internal constitution, and their relation to the state. In ritual, especially in communal festivals (if the present is a good indication), the social order is reconstructed and reflected upon. Symbolic action thus provides a means for the reproduction of social groupings and relationships; but it also, I would argue further, provides a set of resources for conceptual and social change.

In symbolic action, as we saw in our examination of the ayllu, the present provides a key to the past. Just what the role of the principal kuraka was in the complex annual cycle of festivals in Yura in earlier periods is not yet clear. But it is safe to assume, from what we know today of the integrity and complexity of their symbolic world,[4] that the kurakas of Yura must have taken part with their fellow ayllu members in the creation, through ritual, of a shared system of concepts and values. Indeed, it is my belief that such ritual participation was one of the primary ameliorating factors that permitted the hereditary kuraka to unite within his person the contradictory elements described previously. In this sense ritual can be interpreted as an instrument of manipulation, of "false consciousness." On the other hand, the kurakas' participation in ritual in colonial times, like the kuraqkuna's ritual activities today, served to ground Yura identity and organization in an image of society which, through the centuries, provided a conceptual and social unity to the ayllus. This unity has permitted them to retain considerable freedom of action and has even aided them in retaining control of their lands.

In this third section of the book we return to an ethnographic form of discourse to describe the performance aspect of the kuraqkuna's roles—the part they play in ritual action today. As we have seen, the nature of the authority posts has changed greatly through the centuries, with the abolition of the hereditary kurakas and the bifurcation of the contradictory aspects of that position into the modern kuraqkuna and the corregidor. Nonetheless, there are continuities rooted in shared conceptual systems and in social action. The cultural dimension that today dominates the definition of the kuraqkuna's roles has been only barely visible in the historical record. It is, however, in the ritual actions of the kuraqkuna (and especially in their role in public festivals) that the continuing power of the ayllu authorities lies. As we shall see, the socially shared knowledge built into the roles and expressed in the kuraqkuna rituals provides a view of the world which orients the Yuras' relationships both within the group and without.

The Symbolic Mediation of the Kuraqkuna

Part three is thus dedicated to the ritual actions of the kuraqkuna and to the symbolic universe that frames those actions. In the chapters that follow we discuss the festivals that the kuraqkuna sponsor and analyze the wider sets of ideas and values upon which they depend to explain and interpret their world.

Chapter 7 introduces the third section with a brief depiction of the different types of festivities in which the kuraqkuna engage and provides a sketch of the annual festival cycle. In chapter 8 we enter into the festival life of the Yura by means of the detailed description of a single celebration, Reyes. Observed in early January, Reyes is a fiesta hosted by the five ayllu alcaldes. We begin by following a single alcalde couple through their preparations for the festival and through the initial part of the celebration which takes them from their home rancho to the central village of Yura. Once in the village, we follow the ritual actions of all those who come together to celebrate. The structure of the festival is described in this ethnographic account, and the way in which the alcaldes symbolically represent the internal complexity of social groupings within Yura is examined.

Chapter 9 broadens the analysis of Yura ritual action by focusing on the complex of meanings surrounding a key symbol of the kuraqkuna, the *kinsa rey,* or staff of authority. The different contexts in which the kinsa rey appears reveal it to be a symbolic mediator among the ayllus, the kuraqkuna, the natural world, and the divinities of field and mountain peak which the Yura believe guide and control their fate.

Finally, in chapter 10 we build on the array of meanings surrounding the kinsa rey in order to provide a more complete picture of the way that the Yura conceptualize the divinities which are most powerfully linked to the actions of the kuraqkuna. We then focus our attention on the key festival of Carnaval. In the analysis of Carnaval we discover that the kuraqkuna not only represent, but also ritually reconstruct, the ayllu order and the "sacred territory" of the Yura ethnic group. The actions of the kuraqkuna in Carnaval are interpreted as a kind of symbolic dialogue. In the first place, a ritual conversation takes place among the different ayllus which constitute the group. But more important, there is a dialogue between the ayllus and the encompassing state in which the Yura insist on the integrity of their lands and on their right to retain a certain autonomy. It is in this dialogue that the kuraqkuna of Yura today most clearly manifest their continuing significance and power. The study concludes, in chapter 11, with certain considerations about the future of the Yura as an ethnic group.

7

FESTIVALS OF THE KURAQKUNA

Ritual and Festivals

All societies seem to exhibit an alternation in the tenor of social relations between periods when human interaction is at a low, diffuse level and other moments when it is much more intense and concentrated. Such shifts in the intensity of human relations are frequently linked to economic activities, as is apparent, for example, in the contrast between the pressures of planting time and the tranquility after harvest or in winter. But this oscillation also exists in the universal movement between celebration and everyday life; that is, societies contrast those occasions which are set aside as festive and those which are not. The precise nature of such shifts obviously varies from one group to the next, and if all societies have times of "effervescence,"[1] then what they get effervescent about becomes the subject of cultural analysis.

The economic base of a society clearly plays an important role in the temporality of festive life. A group of nomadic hunters and gatherers may well follow an annual round that is bound to the regularity of the harvest of wild plants punctuated by the success of the hunt or the constraints of band movement. In the case of agricultural societies, so directly linked to the changing seasons, the sequence of festivities tends to be even more closely tied to the calendar. While personal or family celebrations may not be determined strictly by the yearly cycle, the great communal events follow the succession of seasons with little variation.

This is certainly the case among the ayllus of Yura. The Yura have a rich festival life, one which occupies them for many weeks of every year. Based on the Catholic arrangement of saints and holy days, the festivals are times of prodigious expenditures of effort and physical resources in which a major portion of the population takes part. The festivals of Yura are high points in the social relations among members of the groups and, as we shall see, provide them with the opportunity to step out of the roles of everyday life in order to examine these roles, as well as their place within the larger society.

The scale of celebrations, the deep commitment that the participants demonstrate to carrying them out, and the activities themselves suggest that terms I have already applied to the festivals of Yura—"cultural performances" and "rituals"—are appropriate. The first was coined by Milton Singer, who argued that the ceremonies and artistic performances that he witnessed in Madras, India, were a valid means by which to understand the cultural or symbolic system maintained by a particular group, in the same way that the observation of social actions was useful for the construction of a model of social structure. For Singer cultural performances were large-scale public enactments given over to content (in the sense of dramatic, aesthetic, or ritual action), and not (at least not only) to such utilitarian ends as productive activities or trade. Characteristic of cultural performances were "a definitely limited time span, a beginning and an end, an organized program of activity, a set of performers, and a place and occasion of performance" (1955:23–26).

The festivals of Yura exhibit all these properties. However, it also seems useful to think of cultural performances as a kind of ritual. Of course for many the term ritual implies a reference to the supernatural. Victor Turner, whose contributions to ritual studies are invaluable, nevertheless adopted such a definition when he defined ritual as "prescribed formal behavior for occasions not given over to technological routine, having reference to mystical beings or powers" (1967:19). The core of the concept, however, lies elsewhere. The fact that festivals in Yura do have reference to mystical beings should not obscure what is common to both rituals and cultural performances: that human groups set aside recurring moments "outside of time" in order to negotiate the premises upon which social life (and a group's particular social arrangements) is based, re-creating and communicating among themselves what they see to be the building blocks of their joint existence.

The way such negotiation and communication occur in ritual is through the use of socially shared symbols. A symbol, simply defined, is "any object, act, event, quality or relation which serves as a vehicle for a conception—the conception is the symbol's 'meaning' " (Geertz 1973:91). Of course all human actions and products that carry significance for another person can be said to be symbolic. Yet it is obvious that some actions and objects can be said to be more symbolic than others.[2] Ritual behavior is symbolic behavior par excellence. It is in essence a concatenation of symbols, while symbols, as Turner has put it, are "the smallest unit of ritual which still retains the specific properties of ritual behavior" (1967:19).

The Festival System of Yura

With these ideas as a base, the aim of this chapter will be to introduce the context in which much of the symbolic language employed by the Yura is expressed; that is, through a series of large-scale rituals in the form of festivals hosted by the kuraqkuna. We begin by distinguishing those festivities sponsored by the indigenous authorities from other kinds of large public celebrations that the Yura carry out. In succeeding pages we will expand on this discussion.

In chapter 4 we drew a conceptual distinction within the category of large public festivals between those hosted by alfereces and those sponsored by the kuraqkuna. This is a distinction that the Yura also explicitly make when they discuss their celebrations. In the alférez fiestas the spotlight is on the ritual activities of the couple who has taken on the obligation to host that one event. They are joined by another couple who serve as the "sponsors-elect," the hosts for the following year. Depending on the festival, and on the couple's own wishes, there are three possible ways that they could have gained the position. First, they may have volunteered to take on the sponsorship. Second, they may have been asked by the previous year's hosts. Finally, they may have been appointed by their ayllu's kuraka. They have no service obligations beyond those entailed in preparing for the fiesta and carrying it out. The main objects of ritual attention during an alférez festival are two: the image of the saint to which the festival is dedicated, and, more directly, the *guión* (banner) which the festival hosts keep with them during the days of the festival.

In the kuraqkuna festivals activities center around the couples who fill one of the various authority roles, be it alcalde, jilaqata, or postillón. As we have seen, festival sponsorship is only one aspect of their duties. Most of these kuraqkuna festivals celebrate the beginning and the end of terms of service. The couples finishing their periods in the various ayllu offices act as hosts, and they are accompanied by their ayllu's kuraka, among many others. The principal ritual events focus on the kuraqkuna's staff of authority, the kinsa rey or rey tata.

The words used to specify the concepts of "sponsoring" a festival or "taking on" a kuraqkuna position are *pasar* in Spanish and the borrowed *pasay* in Quechua. Metaphorically, the concept approximates the idea of "passing through" the statuses, since those who are beginning their service are called "enterers" (*yaykuqkuna*) while those who are completing it are termed "those going out" (*lluqsipuqkuna*).[3] The staff and banner are in fact equated with these concepts in Yura thought. People say that an alférez "passes" with the banner, while the kuraqkuna "pass" with the kinsa rey. The parallel use of staff and banner in sponsoring the festivals points both to the liminality of all these positions (to use Turner's term [1969:95]), as well as to the clearly drawn distinction between the two kinds of festival actions.

Another contrast in these categories of fiestas comes in the named sequence of days. Although festivals typically last the same length of time, the days bear different designations in each category. The alférez festival begins late in the afternoon of the first day with an entrance by the festival sponsors to the plaza of the central village (or, in those not held in Yura, to a central area in the host rancho). This, known as the *víspera* (eve), marks the official inauguration of the celebration. The next day is called the *fiesta dia,* the actual day of the saint celebrated (and the day of maximum participation). The *tinku* (meeting, or confrontation of two) follows on the third day, while the fourth day is known as the *dejame* or, in Quechua, *saqipuy.* The fifth, and now final, day (since there are no longer *octavas,* or eighth-day celebrations) is the *kacharpaya* (send-off) of the festival.

Each day thus has a characteristic activity for which it is named. The tinku, for instance, occurs during the morning of the third day in the houseyard of the host couple. Although the term has many meanings both here and elsewhere in the Andes, in this case it refers to a kind of drinking duel. Friends and relatives of the *pasaqkuna* (the sponsors) and those of the *jap'iqkuna* (the sponsors-elect for the coming year, those "taking hold") offer each other cane alcohol and *aqha* (that is, chicha, or corn beer) until they all are astonishingly drunk. In the tinku those who are on their feet the longest "win," although given the nature of the duel it is frequently difficult to declare an unequivocal victor. In the dejame the hosts' banner is carried with considerable ceremony to the houseyard of the jap'iqkuna and officially turned over to them.

The days of the kuraqkuna festivals bear another set of names. The festivals also begin in the evening of the first day with an *entrada* (entrance). The next day is a *visita dia* (visit day), and the third, a *jatun* or *yapa visita dia* (big or extra visiting day). The fourth is the *kacharpaya* (the farewell), while the fifth is termed the *jatun kacharpaya* (big or grand farewell). Usually both alférez and kuraqkuna festivals will have begun even before the first official day and may extend beyond the fifth day, as long as the corn beer lasts. Participation afterward, while enjoyable, is less socially obligatory.

Although we shall not ignore the festivals hosted by alfereces, it will be those of the kuraqkuna that receive our attention in these pages. The contrast drawn between them serves nevertheless to demonstrate that not only is it possible for us to distinguish the festival roles of the kuraqkuna from those of the alfereces, but also that these are indeed "emic" distinctions that the Yura make themselves.

The Festival Cycle in Yura

In the yearly round of festivals we find that kuraqkuna festivals are interspersed, or in one case combined, with alférez fiestas, creating a complex sequence of ritual activity both in the central village and in the entire territory. Common elements recur in different kuraqkuna festivals throughout the year, yet each emphasizes its own particular theme.

The annual cycle is itself divided into two parts. Almost all of the public festivals, both alférez and kuraqkuna, occur between early December and late June, that is, from a point well into the planting season, through the growth of crops, to the harvest, and the drying and storage of the product. The "big" kuraqkuna festivals all occur in the half-year from Christmas to San Juan (June 24). There are other important ritual observances during the rest of the year but, with few exceptions, they are all familial in nature: rituals that ensure the fertility of one's fields, for example, or the health of one's flocks. Planting, which begins in mid-October and lasts until the end of December, signals the beginning of the period when individuals and households who have spent the cold winter months attending to repairs in rancho and field (or, today, working elsewhere as wage laborers) begin to come together. Planting itself is a festive occasion, and large groups of people work jointly in this task.

All Saints' Day (Todos Santos), November 2, is held in the cemetery in the village of Yura and is the first major gathering in the central village since June. Yet it is not a festival in the typical sense of being hosted by public, recognized sponsors. It is rather a mixture, combining the familial (represented by those persons who have lost a relative to death during the year and who therefore set up an "altar" over the deceased's grave from which they serve food and alcoholic drink) and the public (everyone else who goes to the cemetery to console them and to eat and, especially, to drink).

Todos Santos comes in the heart of the planting season, when pre-occupation about fertility is highest; it is framed by a belief in the return of the dead, who are mystically associated with the power of growth and reproduction (cf. Harris 1982b). This celebration is thus an appropriate beginning to the agricultural year's festivals and serves as a transition between the familial concerns of winter and the communal fiestas to follow.

The first sizable public festival is the alférez fiesta of Santa Bárbara beginning on December 4. This, although it is held in the central village, is restricted in its sponsorship to members of Sullk'a Qhurqa. The octava of this festival is the principal regional ayllu celebration for Qullana, and it takes place in Thatuka, a large rancho in the southwestern part of the territory. As is the rule for all the regional festivals, the kuraqkuna of the host ayllu are expected to be present, but the sponsors are the kuraka-appointed alfereces and mayores.

The next festival *was* that of Nawrar (Navidad, or Christmas), the first kuraqkuna fiesta in the central village. Until a few years ago this was the inauguration festival of the Upper Moiety postillones. Although postillones were abolished, Nawrar was retained and hosted by the jilaqatas. There was a decision to abolish the Christmas festival in 1979; the jilaqatas felt that their sponsorship of Corpus Christi and their participation in other festivals was sufficient. After a brief revival in 1980 and 1981 the festival is no longer celebrated.

The alcalde festival of Reyes follows, starting on January 6. This fiesta will be described in detail in the following pages. On February 2 falls the regional festival of Candelaria in the rancho of Thullta, located in the southeastern part of the zone. Candelaria is hosted on a rotating schedule by members of the Chiquchi, Qhurqa, and Wisijsa ayllus.

Carnaval, which is the high point of the year for kuraqkuna participants, occurs in February or early March. A movable festival, it begins on the Thursday before Ash Wednesday and lasts through the first Sunday in Lent. Carnaval will be described more fully in chapter 10.

The next major fiesta in the annual cycle is Encarnación, dedicated to the patron saint of Yura, Our Lady of the Incarnation. Although the day for Encarnación is March 25, Annunciation, the celebration is postponed to the first Sunday after Easter. This is considered the year's big festival (jatun fiesta) and provides, in a sense, the model by which all other festivals are measured. Both alfereces and kuraqkuna participate. For the Yura, their patron saint, affectionately termed "Mamita," represents (among other things) the fertility of the earth and all that grows in it. The octava of Encarnación is the context for the regional festival of San Ramón in the high southern district of Phajcha. In the past the Phajchas carried their saint the distance to Yura, but in recent years they have celebrated San Ramón in their home rancho of Qaqa Pata.

Corpus Christi, also hosted by the kuraqkuna, is the next celebration, and is one of the year's highlights. Corpus, which usually occurs sometime in the month of June, could be termed the "jilaqata festival." Although the focus is on the jilaqatas of the Upper Moiety, all ten couples participate. Every jilaqata is accompanied by a band of special musicians, called a *jula jula,* whose six members each play both a huge drum and a miniature panpipe. The jilaqata hosts are joined by a jatun alférez appointed by the kurakas according to a system of rotating turns among the four major ayllus.

San Juan follows Corpus on June 24. Once the time when the Lower Moiety postillones entered their posts, this has continued to be celebrated, at least through the early 1980s, with a tinku (in this case a water battle), an event that has always been the main attraction of the festival. Hosted by the alcaldes (who are responsible for transporting the water to the central plaza), the two moieties face off for an uninhibited half-hour battle, members of Qullana against those of Qhurqa, and Wisijsa against Chiquchi. The fight consists of water duels in which two men (often assisted and coached by their wives) pair off amid the general pandemonium and, using special cans and throwing with impressive force, pitch water in each other's face. In recent years the tinku lost many of its participants, since many young men, the most enthusiastic water battlers, have already left Yura by late June to work in the cities or in industrial agriculture elsewhere in the country. The tinku was not celebrated in 1987.

San Juan concludes the cycle begun with Santa Bárbara and Navidad. One other regional festival, Santiago, in the rancho of Thawuru, occurs in the depth of winter; and only one other gathering takes place in the central village of Yura—August 6 (called simply Agustu in Yura), Bolivia's national independence day. This festival is celebrated with events organized not by the Yura but by the rural schoolteachers and their students. The Yuras who participate do so as parents, and although the kuraqkuna are encouraged to attend, they normally do only if they have children in the central school.

But for these two exceptions, then, there is a hiatus from San Juan until December. During this period the focus changes from symbolic reflection on the ayllu organization of the region to a more localized concern with kinship and rancho. Not until the next year's Santa Bárbara will people once again congregate in the central village. Until that time the village of Yura is *ch'in* (silent).

The festivals of Yura, as we have seen, tend to occur at significant points in the agricultural cycle. While not ignoring the realities of the Gregorian calendar, the Yura think of the year as beginning at planting, which ideally starts either in late September or early October. Planting continues for a number of weeks and is largely undisturbed by other celebrations. Even the localized festivals, such as the two versions of Santa Bárbara, do not begin until the corn plants are already past the tender *yura* stage and are growing rapidly.

Navidad and Reyes occur at a time of rapid growth of the crops (and, if it is raining sufficiently, at a time of relative leisure since irrigation canals do not have to be dug and the hard work of weeding and forming the rows is over). Carnaval, as we shall see, ideally occurs at first fruit, when the earliest crops can be eaten. Seven weeks later, Encarnación comes right after the harvest; and Corpus is celebrated when the weather is cold and the fields are barren and dry.

Subsidiary themes of the festivals refer to these points in the agricultural cycle but at the same time they are clearly linked to the astronomical and solar calendars. For instance, the festival of Corpus is linked quite explicitly by the Yura to the fact that the sun (*Amunchis*, "our master, our lord"), the source of warmth and light for crops, animals, and people, is close to its lowest point.[4] It is frequently paired by informants with Encarnación, the latter being *Mamalaqta* (belonging to the mother) while Corpus is said to be *Tatalaqta* (the father's). On each occasion the two objects of veneration are in a diminished state: at Encarnación, identified with the fertility of the earth, the harvest is newly over and the fields are now dormant; while at Corpus the sun is at the solstice. Together, the power of earth and sun are propitiated and celebrated. It is therefore symbolically appropriate that the jilaqatas, with their special ties to the fields, enter their posts during these two postharvest festivals, those of the Lower Moiety first, at Encarnación, then those of the upper at Corpus.

Other festivals also occur at significant points in a wider symbolic whole. Given the real difficulties of life in the arid Andean environment of Yura, first fruits become all the more important as an assurance that there will indeed once again be a harvest. Carnaval is then the most joyful of all festivals, so much so that the very name of the festival in Quechua, *Pujllay*, means "to play." Likewise, the smaller regional festivals—the two Santa Bárbaras on December 2 and 9, Candelaria on February 2, San Ramón the week after Easter, and Santiago on July 25—act to mark off significant moments in the agricultural cycle at the same time they spotlight the different component regions of Yura. One could develop further the way that the yearly round and the fiesta cycle form a coherent symbolic unit in relation to both the solar and the agricultural cycles. But it is no less true that the festivals, especially the kuraqkuna festivals, also operate at another level of discourse, one that refers to social groupings and the social order.

Let us therefore turn to an examination of one such kuraqkuna festival, Reyes. In the course of a discussion of this example, we shall see the way in which a single kuraqkuna celebration illustrates the Yura conception of the structure of their society and the relation of that society to the wider social world.

8

THE FESTIVAL OF REYES

Reyes, which begins on January 6, is a large-scale festival celebrating the investiture of the alcaldes—the five members of the kuraqkuna who serve the vecino corregidor.[1] In the following pages a composite description will be presented of the sequence of events of Reyes, and the form and meaning of festival action will be analyzed. As in all kuraqkuna festivals (with the exception of Carnaval, discussed in chapter 10), the activities of the five principal days of the fiesta take place in the central village of Yura. In this context the canton capital of Yura is more important than its small size or humble position in the governmental hierarchy would indicate. The way that the Yura comunarios think about the village, and the ways they use it, are important factors in the analysis of the ritual itself.

Preparations and Preliminaries

Preparations for Reyes are undertaken weeks, even months, before the festival begins, both in Yura and in the home hamlets of the alcaldes. The *yaykuq* alcaldes (pl., *yaykuqkuna*), the five couples who take up the posts during the festival, provide less food and drink than the five *lluqsiq* couples—those leaving the posts—but even for them preparations begin long before the first week in January.

To contrast the activities of these two categories of participants, let us take a typical example from a single ayllu, Chiquchi. The scenes I will describe for Chiquchi are duplicated throughout the canton by the kuraqkuna of the other three ayllus. We shall call the Chiquchi alcalde couple who are entering the post Juan Mamani and Inisa Chuki, and the couple they are replacing, Bonifacio Kalisaya and María Phurqu.[2] Don Juan and doña Inisa live in a large village called Karaka, located a three-hour walk from the central village of Yura on a ravine off the lower Taru River. They formally asked their ayllu's kuraka to be allowed to serve in the post of alcalde and were then appointed by him. As the yaykuqkuna, the entering alcaldes, they will provide corn beer, alcohol, and some food for those who join them in celebrating.

Don Bonifacio and doña María, the couple leaving the post, live in a river valley two hours' walk to the east of Karaka in the hamlet of Ch'aki Wayq'u. For them, this particular Reyes is the culmination of a year's activities which started the previous January when they were the yaykuq couple to another outgoing Chiquchi alcalde pair. During their year of service they participated in other festivals in Yura and one in Thauru (where the regional fiesta of Santiago requires the Chiquchi alcalde's presence). The husband, Bonifacio, served the corregidor for two and a half months, and both attended meetings in Yura at other times. This festival represents for them a major outlay of resources, money, and labor, but successful completion of their duties at Reyes (successful in the sense that they sponsor it in a way which shows they are neither poverty-stricken nor stingy) will bring with it the esteem of their neighbors and a sense of satisfaction.

María Phurqu went to the central village of Yura before Christmas to oversee the making of corn beer for the festival. She and Bonifacio had already had the vast amount of corn meal needed to make beer prepared for them at a mill in a neighboring valley, and a work party the previous November had brought a large load of firewood to their Yura patio as fuel for brewing the beverage. In all, María had nine wantas, or batches, of corn beer made to serve the guests—one she made herself, while the rest were contributed by eight other women, friends and hamlet mates. All together this would produce a total of some 450 gallons of corn beer. Both she and the yaykuq Mama Alcalde will have yet another batch of corn beer ready at their home settlement to serve before and after the stay in Yura. Corn beer is only one (if undoubtedly the primary) element of conviviality at the kuraqkuna festivals. Both couples will also serve purchased cane alcohol to guests and fellow participants.

As the beginning of the festival approaches, the pace of activities quickens. A day or two before the festival celebration begins in the village of Yura, the *tropas*—the dance troupes which are the primary social units for the duration of the festival—begin to form at the hamlet houseyards of the kuraqkuna. A tropa (*rupa* in Quechua) is the entourage which clusters around each authority couple. The tropa is usually made up of the alcalde couple's hamlet mates and the relatives of both husband and wife who live in other settlements.[3] Godchildren, other ritual kin, friends, and even passers-by may also join in. In fact, any member of the ayllu who wishes to participate can do so. Because of the sheer physical demands of the festival, most members of the entourage are younger people. Age is no barrier, however, and if older men and women decide to take part they are welcomed.

The purpose of the troupe is to provide music and accompaniment for the authority couple throughout the festival. For Reyes, and for Carnaval as well, the men play *flautas*, large, five-holed vertical flutes, and *bombos*, small sheephide drums, while the women dance in a circle around them. Also included in the group are those people whom the alcalde couple formally ask to take on special service positions for the festival. These latter supervise the preparation and distribution of the corn beer, alcohol, and food.

The men who will accompany the alcalde couple get together during the evening of the first day at the couple's home and work out three or four songs, called *wayñus*. Although they bear the same name as the huaynos of Peru, their main similarity lies in the fact that the rhythm in both is based on four beats to the measure. In contrast to the highly developed poetics of huaynos in the Cusco area (see, for example, Mannheim 1979), Yura wayñus have no lyrics; they are either totally instrumental or, at times, the melody is chanted. The songs can be taken from almost any source—marches, songs heard over the radio, or new compositions by Yuras. The songs from outside undergo a process of conversion in tonality and melody that makes them unrecognizable to the uninitiated. Each song is simplified and streamlined, becoming a basic canon that will be repeated over and over again during the days of the fiesta. The musical esthetic favors what is, to our ears, a harsh, raucous sound.

Although the style of playing is shared by all, each group can be recognized by its particular wayñus, which serve as a kind of trademark. From that morning at the alcalde's houseyard when the songs are first devised until the festival is over, the musicians rarely lay down their flutes. Although they do sleep, the younger ones frequently do so for only three or four hours a night.

In the case of Bonifacio Kalisaya and María Phurqu (who with this festival are finishing their service in the alcalde post), fellow "ranchos" and ayllu members begin assembling at their houseyard on the morning of January 5 in anticipation of the *pusarquys*,[4] special ritual visits to the home ranchos of relatives and kin of the kuraqkuna that occur in the days immediately preceding the festival. By noon five young men with flautas and two with bombos are well on the way to composing the wayñus they will play. As the fiesta progresses, more and more people will gradually join the troupe until there may be as many as thirty musicians and fifty dancers in the larger tropas. The core, however, is always the small group that forms at the houseyard of the authority couple.

On the morning of January 6, after the ritual visits to kinfolk, the incumbent alcalde couple and their troupe journey to the home of the couple who will be taking on the alcalde position for the coming year. The kuraka of Chiquchi, Carlos Umana, and his wife, Silwika Kunturi, join the festivities at this point. When the kuraka couple (the Tata Mallku and the Mama T'alla)[5] arrive they are served alcohol from a *telmadera,* a flat silver dish adorned with a llama, and corn beer from a *turu,* a wooden bowl with a carved yoke of oxen in the center. The lluqsiqkuna, the incumbent alcalde couple, are also served from these special vessels on entering the patio. Then all the adults present are served alcohol and beer. After several hours of ritual drinking, pouring of libations, and dancing, the combined entourages will make their way to the central village of Yura, where, on the night of January 6, the celebration of Reyes has its formal beginning.

As the moment to leave for Yura approaches, the authorities prepare for the *aysaqay*. Aysaqay means "to escort ritually," or, more literally, "to pull along." For the aysaqay of the new alcalde the kuraka takes the woven cloth in which the entering alcalde's kinsa rey, his staff of authority, is carried and ties it around him like a sash, over his left shoulder and under his right arm. The kuraka and the yaykuq alcalde then dance, with the kuraka pulling on the cloth (called the *uxanta*) and thus leading the alcalde along. The combined tropas of the new and old alcaldes then join together, follow the authorities out of the patio, and begin the trip to Yura. For the entire length of the journey (which, since nearly everyone is drunk, takes even longer than normal), the kuraka grasps the cloth wrapped around the new alcalde and leads him to the central village, to assume the duties of ayllu leadership.

The Festival

The Entrada

On the evening of January 6, then, each troupe makes a formal entrance to the central village. The troupes usually arrive late, often after dark. They may have struggled along through a downpour and will be tired, footsore, and drunk. Nevertheless, the Entrada in a sense marks the formal beginning of the festival, so the tropas draw on their reserves of energy to display a high level of enthusiasm and festive spirit.

To describe the Entrada to Reyes requires some mention of the nature of the village of Yura itself. The village is generally almost empty, a ceremonial center which fills only at festival times. During most of the year the population is less than a hundred people. At festivals such as Reyes it can swell to a thousand or more. At first sight the village of Yura appears to be set up in the typical hispanic grid pattern, with a central square, two streets running north to south, and three streets east to west; a number of pseudo-urban blocks bounded by these streets are thus formed (see figure 8.1). Yet, after watching how the Yura move through the town, how they occupy it at festivals, and how they talk about it, it becomes

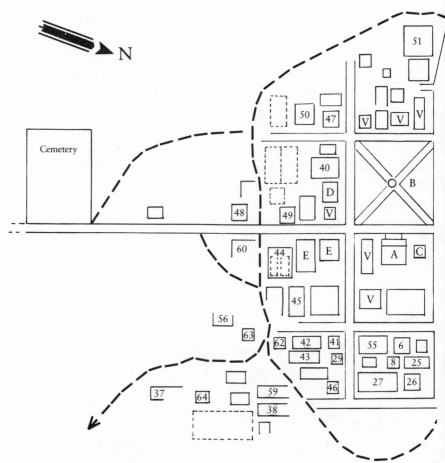

Figure 8.1 The Village of Yura

clear that in fact Yura is in essence a series of patios, open spaces surrounded by one-room stone or adobe houses. Paths connect the patios; some of these follow the streets, while others climb the hills behind them or cut through the center of the blocks. In all, there are more than sixty named patios in Yura. Individuals inherit the right to occupy particular patios and, when sponsoring a festival, the ayllu authorities utilize these patios as home bases for their celebrations.

The Entrada is made in the late afternoon or evening of Janu-

Legend

——— Footpath
A Church
B Central Square
C Corregimiento
D Municipality
E School
V House of a Vecino
Numbered areas are residential patios of
Yura ayllu members

ary 6 and follows a detailed and regular pattern of movement.
The entrance to Yura is made according to the moiety affiliation
of the ayllu that the troupe represents: the Upper Moiety tropas
of Qullana and Wisijsa always enter from the south, while those
from the ayllus of Chiquchi and Qhurqa in the Lower Moiety come
in from the north. At each end of the main north-south street of
the town is a sacred spot, a small shrine called an *alma samana*
(resting place for the dead).[6] All the tropas go to these spots for a
final *ch'allay*, or pouring of libations, before the formal entrance to

the plaza of Yura. After the libations are poured the alcaldes' entourages assemble—the drummers and flutists stand in loose ranks and the women dancers form lines on each side. Behind them come the carriers of the kinsa reyes, the alcalde couple, and their closest family and friends. Others, those in charge of serving drink, bring up the rear, carrying corn beer in a variety of vessels.

Things do not always go as smoothly as in the typical case outlined here, of course. One year when I was present a heavy rain began in the late afternoon of January 6 and lasted until well after dark. Many tropas were caught on the trail. Some sought shelter at the first hamlet they came to. Others trudged on in the rain, braving the rivers, to take refuge in their own patios in Yura. Only well after the rain finally stopped did several troupes make their formal entrances. A number of groups arrived at their patios in Yura after midnight and simply waited until the next morning to make their Entrada.

The Chiquchi kuraqkuna enter the town from the north, move along the principal street into the plaza, and dance up to the entrance of the church. There the musicians stop playing their wayñus, and the members of the troupe, moving into a loose semicircle, all kneel down in respectful silence. Then, with flutes and drums sounding again, they move to the northwest corner of the plaza. The musicians and dancers form concentric circles; the kinsa rey is held off to one side and the kuraqkuna couples dance in the center of the circle—usually by themselves, holding each other's hands. Guests and passers-by are offered corn beer to pour libations at the corner and to the kinsa rey. Then the circles break and the groups move on to the next corner. They continue around the periphery of the square, pausing only briefly at the other corners. Passing again in front of the church, the tropas move from the outer edge into the center of the plaza, to encircle the Rollo.

The Rollo is a red stone cylinder standing some three meters tall and built on a square base of the same material. Although apparently a common construction in Spanish reducción towns dating from the sixteenth century, such monuments play a role in ritual in the Andes which suggests that they may have been identified with the *ushnu* of Inka times,[7] the structure found in the center of many Inka cities which may have served as a dais or an altar.

At the Entrada, then, the troupes end their dance sequence in formation around the Rollo; the musicians remain in the center enclosed by the women dancers. They continue like this for some time, even as other tropas come into the plaza and perform their Entradas. As more groups move to the Rollo—all playing their own wayñus—the first tropas to arrive move off to one side and reestablish their circles on the edges of the plaza, continuing to dance well into the night. The groups finally leave the plaza hours later, going out through the same corner by which they entered. The tropas retire to their authority's patio to rest briefly before beginning anew.

Day Two: The Juramento

The second day of the festival, January 7, begins early. The more energetic young musicians are often playing by first light. The troupes of the yaykuq and the lluqsiq both pay visits to the kuraka's patio. The kuraka's wife, the Mama T'alla, has her own corn beer ready and ceremonially serves the guests. After several rounds of drinks the kuraka and his wife allow themselves to be escorted back to the patio of the entering alcalde. Here the kuraka couple is served three bowls of cane alcohol and one of corn beer. These initial toasts to the kuraka mark the opening of the day's festive activities.

Before nine o'clock that morning the different troupes set off toward the patio of the vecino corregidor for the *juramento* (the swearing-in ceremony) of the yaykuqkuna. Each entering alcalde is accompanied by his kuraka. All ten alcalde couples are obliged to present the corregidor with a large container of corn beer and a pitcher of cane alcohol drink, which he then distributes as he wishes.[8] The lluqsiq alcaldes are adorned with colored paper flowers, while the yaykuq can be identified by the pink-and-orange tufts of wool that have been attached to their hats since the "pulling-along" ceremony the day before. The corregidor stands behind a table which has been converted to a *sink'a llijlla*.

A Kuraka at the
Juramento of Reyes

The sink'a llijlla is a ritual space created by placing a carrying cloth (a *llijlla*) either on a box or small table or simply by laying it on the ground. Coca leaves, ritually referred to as *sink'a*, are enclosed in a small woven square, an *unkuña*, and placed in the center of the cloth. Coca leaves are the defining element of this ritual space, although other items shape it depending on the context. The creation of this ritual table, elsewhere called a *mesa*, is a widespread practice in the Andes; it is always set up for certain symbolic manipulations, such as in curing or divination (cf. Tschopik 1951; Bolton and Douglas 1976; Joralemon 1985). In Yura, a sink'a llijlla is established any time people gather together for festive or ritual ends. At the swearing-in ceremony the sink'a llijlla bears, in addition to the unkuña of coca leaves, a crucifix, the silver drinking cups that each alcalde has brought, and ten kinsa reyes—five from the yaykuqkuna and five from the lluqsiqkuna.

Although the swearing-in ceremony is held at an early hour in the hope that the festival participants will still be sober, this is frequently a vain expectation. The mutual serving and drinking has already been going on since dawn. Both the lluqsiq and the yaykuq are the object of such vehement invitations to drink by the members of their entourage that it is impossible for them to avoid consuming large quantities of corn beer and alcohol before the mid-morning ceremony. The juramento thus tends to be a rather boisterous affair.

The setting for the juramento takes shape as each of the ten tropas dances into the patio of the corregidor, forms a circle, and goes through its repertoire of wayñus. By the time all have arrived a sizable crowd has managed to squeeze into the patio. In addition to the corregidor, other vecino notables are present—the mayor, the civil registrar, and the rest of the self-termed "good people" (*gente buena*) of Yura who feel their presence is appropriate.

Speaking in "vecino Quechua,"[9] the corregidor delivers a homily on the responsibilities of the position that the alcaldes are undertaking and on the dangers of drink. The inebriated audience responds with vigorous exclamations of agreement. Then the corregidor asks each yaykuq to make the sign of the cross with thumb and forefinger and administers the oath in Spanish. After the swearing-in is over, the corregidor may call a public meeting. In 1979, for instance, the kurakas outlined their arguments for abolishing several festival celebrations.[10] The recommendations, which had already been informally discussed at length among ayllu members before that day, were accepted.

After the meeting ends the primary activity of Reyes begins— the *visitas* (visits). These visits are the major preoccupation of the tropas for the better part of the next four days. Each alcalde troupe carries out a sequence of ritual visits to the patios of all the other participating authorities. On entering a patio the dance group forms concentric circles. The carrier of the kinsa rey lays the staff of authority on the ritual table set up by one wall of the patio. The hosts (or their servers) immediately offer the kuraqkuna visitors corn beer and alcohol. The troupe, still playing its entrance wayñu, moves to the right (*pañaman*) until it finishes that song. The direction is then changed to move clockwise, *lluq'iman,* for the second wayñu. The patio servers put a pot of corn beer in the center of the two circles; as the musicians play, one of their number serves the others. On the third song the circles move once again to the right. This is the concluding piece of the visit, and at some point in the song the musicians will turn to leave, breaking through the ring of dancers. The "traveling order" of the tropa—male instrumentalists in the center, women on the sides—takes form again as they move out of the patio. During the last wayñu a designated assistant gathers up the kinsa rey, and he and the kuraqkuna couple join the dancers as they leave.

This pattern of visits is followed closely throughout the days of the festival; one visit differs little from another. The visits constitute a basic ritual unit in Reyes in the sense that they are repeated time and time again, day after day. Every tropa sets out each morning to visit the other tropas in a continuous to-and-fro movement from patio to patio, throughout the town. The order in which they are carried out, as we shall see, also has its significance.

Day Three: The Runa Enteray

On the morning of January 8 another ritual transfer of authority takes place which confirms the swearing-in of the new alcaldes that occurred the previous day. This event, known as the *runa enteray* (to hand over the people),[11] is a ceremony involving just ayllu authorities and members, not the corregidor. It graphically marks the assumption of responsibility by the new alcalde in each ayllu. For the runa enteray the kuraka and the lluqsiq alcalde visit the patio of the couple who is taking on the alcaldeship. The lluqsiq alcalde arrives with his tropa and his kinsa rey, as well as with a special burden: around him has been tied a carrying cloth which contains a small woven bag holding loose grains of corn. These are the grains, mentioned previously in the discussion of the jilaqata, which represent the households of the ayllus. In the case of the alcaldes, strict accounting is less important than for the jilaqatas, and the numbers are conventional. Although in theory each grain, referred to as a *lilantiru*, [12] represents an ayllu household, the number of grains does not correspond exactly to the household count.

This ritual of "delivering the people" occurs in a festive manner; it begins with the lluqsiq alcalde dancing in the center of his tropa's circle of musicians. After the dance is over, the lluqsiq removes the cloth he is carrying and places it on the new alcalde's table. The carrying cloth (llijlla) is untied, the bag of corn carefully removed, and the grains poured out. Participants crowd around as the grains are counted. The tally is then checked with the number that was recorded the previous year. The participants pour libations to the corn grains as conversation becomes general and interest shifts back to the dancing. The musicians move into place and begin a wayñu while the corn is placed back in its bag and wrapped up in the carrying cloth. The companions of the entering alcalde tie the bundle around him and he is then joined by his wife, the new Mama Alcalde. The two move to the center of the musicians' circle and dance. With these ritual actions the yaykuq couple formally accepts the "burden" of the ayllu. The llijlla containing the corn grains will remain in their possession until the following year. After an hour or so of dancing and ritual drinking, the bundle is removed and stored in the new alcalde's patio house. Festive visits to the patios of the other participating ayllu authorities begin at this point and continue throughout the day.

Day Four: The Kacharpaya

After the usual early-morning visits to the kurakas in their patios and the necessary ritual libations, the alcalde tropas set out on their round of visitas. But today another element is added: after the visits to the patios of all the ayllu authorities are concluded the dance groups make formal entrances to the plaza, following the same sequence of movements as in the Entrada on the first day of the festival. After saluting the church, the groups then proceed systematically around the periphery of the square, clockwise or counterclockwise, depending on their moiety affiliation. They again end up circling the Rollo, where they dance for a time before returning to their patios.

A Dance Troupe Visita at Reyes

This trip around the plaza is called the Kacharpaya, and it constitutes a preliminary leave-taking, the first formal farewell to the festival experience. With the Kacharpaya the level of festival participation increases. On this day many more women join in, so that the average number of women dancing with each tropa increases from around twenty to forty.

All the participants are dressed in special clothing. The women wear their finest outfits and put on long chains of old coins and medallions, precious family heirlooms made up mostly of silver pieces from the nineteenth century. At the top of each chain is a silver disk (*ch'aska*, or star); the most highly prized of these chains, pinned shoulder-high with large silver needles (*tupus*), extend down to the feet. These ornaments are worn only on this one day, the Kacharpaya of Reyes. The men serving in the kuraqkuna roles also mark the Kacharpaya by dressing in the *unku*, the traditional clothing worn by Yura men that has been largely abandoned as daily wear in the last few years.

The kacharpayas themselves, the farewell trips around the plaza

Women Dancers Wearing Their Ch'askas

performed by the various troupes, begin in late afternoon and last until dark. By this time other troupes have already begun to return to the plaza for the final element in Reyes: the nightly dancing around the Rollo.

"Rollo-Dancing" at Night

Starting on the first full day of the festival, the tropas regroup in their patios every night after dusk and dance to the plaza. There, after passing by the corner associated with their ayllu, they move to the Rollo, encircle it, and dance. Each night this rollo-dancing becomes more elaborate until, by the third and fourth evenings, there may be, after nightfall, as many as eight to ten tropas in the plaza at once, each group of musicians playing their wayñus with great enthusiasm, and each set of dancers moving to the music with intense concentration. Four or five groups may be clustered at once around the Rollo, each playing against the other, while more groups form subsidiary rings on each side of the monument.

As many as three huge concentric circles of dancers may surround the musicians grouped at the Rollo, and in these several hundred women coming from different tropas are dancing. The musicians play at the greatest volume they can manage, trying to drown out the other groups present with the vigor of their own music.

Competition builds as the groups play on; one group may prevent another from approaching the Rollo by refusing to let anyone pass through its circles. A tropa may succeed in playing so loudly that another loses the beat of its wayñu and has to quit playing. Everyone present interprets this as a defeat for the latter group, and its members feel humiliated. Eventually, in a context in which many are drunk, tempers flare and fights may start. This sometimes breaks down into disputes between whole tropas until friends, relatives, and *compadres* come to pull the contenders apart.[13]

Many aspects of the festival of Reyes are arresting sights for the novice observer. A dozen alcalde entourages moving through the patios and paths of Yura, itself totally given over to the festival, are a remarkable spectacle. To take part in the festive visits and the ritual drinking leaves a deep imprint in the memory. I would argue, however, that none of these things is as thoroughly impressive as the dancing at night around the Rollo. Here hundreds of young men and women strive to outdo each other, to dance with more enthusiasm and to play with more devotion than all the rest. The cacophony created is like nothing else ever heard. The dancers, expressing their fervor with the vigorous stamping of feet, create clouds of dust that swirl up past the lone light bulb illuminating the scene and into the night sky. The music and dancing last for hours, creating for the participants a kind of "peak experience," a powerful climax to each day's activities.

The Jatun Kacharpaya

The final day of the festival of Reyes occurs on January 10 and is termed the Jatun Kacharpaya (the grand farewell). The couples entering the alcalde posts have by this point fulfilled their obligations as festival hosts; but the lluqsiq alcaldes continue for an additional day in the role of festival stewards, providing food, beer, and alcohol to the tropas that accompany them. Many members of the tropas of the new alcaldes join the entourages of the lluqsiq-kuna and participate in this second day of farewell. The entering alcalde couples themselves often accompany their predecessors, the lluqsiq, on their visits and their trips around the plaza. The tropas of the lluqsiqkuna are now at their greatest strength.

The Jatun Kacharpaya repeats the movements of the day before, with all the participating entourages making formal yet spirited processions around the corners of the plaza. Although the young women dance without their chains of coins, they exhibit even greater dedication and intensity than the day before, and the Jatun Kacharpaya unfolds at an even higher energy level. Virtually all the participants are drunk; many of the older people, after almost a week of continual heavy drinking, look exhausted and spent. As the key performers in this final ritual, however, they demonstrate a resolve that "the show must go on," and the Jatun Kacharpaya is carried out with a final burst of enthusiasm.

Each of the lluqsiq alcalde troupes, now at the height of their size and strength, dances around the square with great fervor. All are aware that the Jatun Kacharpaya marks the end of the festival, and the young, especially, are reluctant to relinquish the festive experience. Groups confront each other in the plaza, vie with each other in a competitive spirit, and attempt to demonstrate once again their superior skill and dedication to the music and the dance. As during the previous days of celebration, the carrier of the kinsa rey is the only one sure to be *ch'aki sunqu,* sober. He follows the musicians in the Jatun Kacharpaya, standing off to the side when the circles form at the corners and mounting the base of the Rollo when the tropa moves to encircle it. The troupes finally retire to their patios for a rest, but return once more to the plaza for a final climactic session of rollo-dancing. The frenetic quality displayed earlier is redoubled. The dancing lasts late into the evening. As the last moment of celebration, it must surpass all that has gone before it in sound, in dance, and in the desire to excel.

The Days Afterward

The festival is over. The farewells have been made, and the energy of celebration expended. The day after is one of recovery and of attending to the preparations for returning home. The serving of alcohol, however, continues, although at a greatly reduced level. Some musicians keep playing their wayñus, but quietly, in the patios, now a memory of the themes of the festival. At mid-morning some tropas set out for home. They gather together one last time, with the musicians at the front, flanked by the dancers, with the alcalde couple and the kinsa rey at the rear. Others will spend the afternoon in Yura, returning the next day to their hamlets.

One last act related to the festival remains to be carried out by the new alcaldes after their return to their home settlement. Each alcalde is required to keep two kinsa reyes in his possession while serving in the post. One of these is always carried with him while the other remains at home. In a ceremony called the *tianuqachiy*, the staff, along with its cloth covering, is hung on the wall in the spot where it will be left during the year. The new alcalde couple and their companions pour a libation of corn beer, and then one of alcohol, to the kinsa rey. With the completion of this final act of their installation as ayllu authorities, they embark on their year of service.

Analyzing the Celebration of Reyes

The foregoing pages have provided many of the details of Yura festive life. Although there is inherent value in describing a major ritual from a little-known area of the Andes, we can go beyond description to offer some interpretations of the social and cultural significance of this particular kuraqkuna ritual. First, we should direct our attention to the importance of the canton capital as the ritual center. I have already hinted at the significance of the social organization of space in Yura. This ritualization of space is a fundamental theme underlying the entire festival.

Let us begin with a consideration of the central square of Yura. The four corners of the square are, in ritual contexts, shrines (*altares*) to the four major ayllus. (See figure 8.2.) The sides of the

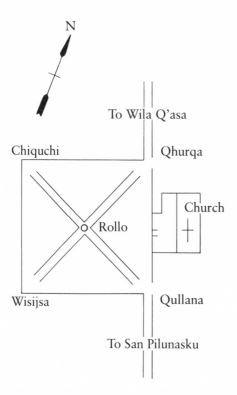

Figure 8.2 The Central Square

central plaza are oriented, approximately, to the cardinal directions. The altars of the Upper Moiety therefore face north, with the southeastern corner identified as the altar of ayllu Qullana, and the shrine of Wisijsa on the southwest corner. The Lower Moiety altares face south; Qhurqa is on the northeast corner and Chiquchi is on the northwest.[14] The upper halves within the moieties (that is, Qullana and Qhurqa) are identified with the east, and the lower halves with the west. The plaza thus presents in miniature a kind of conceptual map of the organization of the canton.

The model making inherent in the village of Yura does not stop at the plaza. In the same way that the lands of the ayllus cluster in the valleys of Yura by cardinal direction, the patios in the village

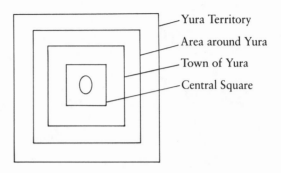

Figure 8.3 Yura as "Concentric Squares"

tend to be grouped in relation to the ayllu altars of the central square.[15] Most Qullana patios are located in the south and southeast sections of the village, along with numerous Wisijsa houseyards. The Phajcha patios (part of Qullana) are also located on the south, largely set apart from the rest. In the northwest are the Sullk'a Chiquchi patios; the bulk of the Chiquchi patios are to be found in the northern part of the village. Qhurqa patios are for the most part in the north and northeast.

Interestingly, the socialization of space according to the ayllus' geographic relation to the center is a principle adopted by the vecinos. The vecinos have chosen to occupy the central area of the region, namely the canton capital and the nearby town of Punutuma. This pattern is reinforced within the village of Yura, where most of the vecinos reside on or close to the central square. They thus occupy the center both geographically and in terms of economic and political power.

This arrangement leads me to suggest that Yura can be pictured as a series of concentric squares.[16] (See figure 8.3.) The central plaza itself summarizes Yura organization by assigning each of the four corners to a major ayllu. At a level beyond that, quadrilateral organization is reflected in the location of ayllu patios within the town, as described above. The concentric squares concept can be extended as well beyond the boundaries of the town, since lands from all four ayllus "happen" to come together in the hamlets around the central village. At a higher conceptual level there also exists the notion that the lands of the major ayllus ideally correspond to the four directions. Thus we see that the Yura have taken a broken topography of steep slopes, narrow valleys, and dispersed ayllu lands and, conceptually at least, "squared it off," assigning an organizational meaning to place.

Ritual Action in "Socialized" Space

The structuring of space according to the principles of ayllu organization forms a stage for the ritual performance of the festival of Reyes. As we have seen, the kuraqkuna's festival troupes become identified with the ayllus they represent. Their movement through the ordered universe of village and plaza comes to be a syntactical statement of the principles of ayllu organization. First, let us consider the ritual visiting. Since patio location is not random, the way a tropa moves through the town to carry out its visits is likely to have an operational concept behind it. This is indeed what occurs: the order of visits differs according to the ayllu affiliation of each tropa.[17] A glance at figures 3.2 and 8.1 will facilitate the reader's comprehension of the structural relationships among the ayllus as well as the organization of the central village.

The visits, which start on the second day of the festival immediately after the swearing-in ceremony, begin with a visit to the lluqsiq alcalde called the *originario*. Until recently this was always the Qullana alcalde, which means that the alcalde representing the upper half of the Upper Moiety was visited first. The originario designation is now rotated among the alcaldes of the four major ayllus; however, during one year when I observed the celebration of Reyes, a Qullana alcalde couple happened to hold the originario position, which meant that all tropas began their rounds in the Qullana patio. The Chiquchi and Qhurqa groups which I accompanied that year went from the Qullana lluqsiq alcalde's patio to the surrounding Qullana patios, almost all of which are located in the southeast part of the town. Next, the tropas moved to the southern extremity of the village, where the Phajcha patios are located. Here are usually lodged the Phajcha alcaldes, both yaykuq and lluqsiq, as well as the

Ariaw jilaqata—all members of the major ayllu Qullana. The Chi-quchi and Qhurqa tropas then moved north to a section of the town where there are a number of Wisijsa and Qhurqa patios. The patios of the Wisijsa and Sawlli jilaqatas, the Wisijsa yaykuq and lluqsiq alcaldes, and the Sullk'a Qhurqa jilaqata are often located here. Moving north and west, the tropas come to a large clustering of Chiquchi and Qhurqa patios where they find the four jilaqatas as well as the two yaykuq and the two lluqsiq alcaldes of the Lower Moiety. These are visited last.

The Upper Moiety tropas of Qullana and Wisijsa follow a reverse order of visits. After beginning their sequence with the originario, they march across town to the patios of the Qhurqa lluqsiq and yaykuq alcaldes and the two jilaqatas from that ayllu. They then go to the Chiquchi patios. Qullana dance troupes normally visit the different Wisijsa patios before returning to the Phajcha sector of town and then on to their own. The Wisijsas follow a similar pattern but visit the Qullanas (including the Phajchas) before returning to their home patios.

The specifics of movement vary with each year's festival, as the exact locations of the patios of the ayllu representatives differ from year to year. Nevertheless, the general scheme for the first day of visiting is to begin with the originario, then visit all the represen-tatives of the opposite moiety, move on to the major and minor ayllu representatives of the other ayllus in one's own moiety, and end with visits to all the representatives of one's own major and minor ayllu. This sequence is followed on the first day of visiting; on the third day, Kacharpaya, the order of visits is reversed. On the second and fourth days the visitas are theoretically restricted (after beginning at the originario's) to the authorities within one's own moiety.

The order of festival visits among the ayllu authorities and their tropas shows how each grouping conceives of its relation to the others in terms of relative social proximity. Each time the troupes leave their patios to carry out their visits they are redrawing the lines of Yura social organization. In the visiting at Reyes, ritual space becomes elaborated through a principle of temporal succession. The festival visitas, which act as symbolic recognition and confirmation of ayllu identity, are necessarily sequential. The order they exhibit serves to remove ayllu organization from a simple two-dimensional plane by creating complex hierarchies of relationships. The order of visits are, in fact, ayllu-specific chains in which both geographic and social or organizational postulates are at work in fashioning the individual links. The social construction of space combined with the temporality of the succession of visits serve to reaffirm and crystallize Yura ideas of social order.

There are many other elements in Reyes which would add the flesh of content to the structural skeleton I am emphasizing here, such as an analysis of the ch'allay or of the kinsa rey, but I will postpone discussion of these until later. There is one theme, however, that is repeatedly evident in Reyes and that adds an important element of symbolic power to the events of the festival; this is the representation of male and female complementarity.[18] Before returning one last time to the question of ritual space, then, a brief comment on that issue will be useful for our analysis.

Male-female complementarity is apparent in innumerable aspects of the ritual. For example, in the construction of the ritual tables mentioned previously, one designated as "male" serves as the site for the kinsa rey, while women pour libations at a separate sink'a llijlla, viewed as "female," which is placed on the ground.[19] The very requirement that couples, rather than individuals, must always fill the kuraqkuna posts reinforces the male-female complementarity basic to Yura ritual. Furthermore, I would suggest that an analysis of the contexts of ritual action shows this complementarity to be expressed in symbols linked to physiological processes, even though the Yura themselves do not explicitly make such an interpretation.

I am referring here to the arrangement of participants in the troupes as they move about the village in the visits. As figure 8.4 shows, two lines of female dancers flank the male musicians. The dancers are "potentially available" young women as well as some older women past the age of childbearing. The dancers form a female "sheath" around a male interior, most of whom, it might be added, are playing "phallic" vertical flutes. The sexual aspect is perhaps clearest when the tropas arrive at a patio for a visit. The procession moves into the houseyard with the young woman join-

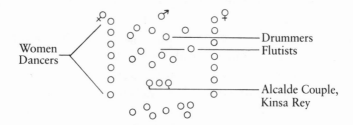

Figure 8.4 The Dance Troupe

ing hands to form a vaginal U-shape enclosing the male musicians. Once in the houseyard, the "U" is transformed into one large enveloping circle, and the longitudinal image becomes a cross-section. The circle remains closed until the drummers break through it as they lead the troupe out of the patio and on to the succeeding visits.

If the sexual image just described seems an exaggeration, let me once again call to mind the nightly dancing around the Rollo. This monument, in its form and its position, is strongly male and phallic in ritual contexts. The same spatial ordering—males in the interior, females on the outside—is again in evidence, magnified. It is also notable that as young, "novice" girls dance around this upright stone cylinder, a certain relaxation of sexual restrictions occurs, and new amorous relationships are formed.

The variable positions during the festival visits of the alcalde couple suggest that the sexual identification of the pair is ambiguous. The Tata Alcalde and the accompanying kuraqkuna are, except by special invitation, the only males who join the women dancers. The other men must play an instrument if they wish to take part in the dance troupe. In the visits the alcalde couple always dance and are served together, in contrast to the functional segregation of all other men and women. As the couple moves with the kinsa reyes in the procession from one patio to another, they take the "male" position behind the musicians. Once in the patios, however, they may join the circle of women dancers, or, alternatively, they may move to the very center of the two concentric circles. The kuraqkuna couple thus represent in their dance position the unity of male and female, appropriate here in this context of the explicit depiction of sexual complementarity manifest in the form of the tropa. In the symbolic actions of the festival dance, the stark portrayal of physical sexual complementarity is placed side by side with an image of male and female as a unitary social and ritual entity.

It should not surprise us that conspicuously sexual references occur in what seems to be an extended dialogue about social groupings. If, as we shall see, a single dominant symbol can be said to possess the property of "polarity of meaning" (Turner 1967:28), then the same property can be found in the sequence of ritual acts in a key cultural performance like Reyes. Although the symbolism may work at a level below the conscious mind, the physiological reference acts as a powerful backdrop to the more organizational themes brought to the fore through the order of visits in structured space.

Let me conclude this discussion of Reyes by turning once again to the two moments that bracket the events in the central village, the Entrada and the Jatun Kacharpaya. These two events in the plaza of Yura signal the beginning and end of the principal actions of the cultural performance. They mark a shift in the mode of thinking about Yura as well, from picturing it as a small, dusty canton capital to a view of it as an elaborate ritual complex, a microcosm of Yura and, it might be added, even as the center of the world.

In the Entrada and the Jatun Kacharpaya, the tropas of all the ayllus, major and minor, move toward the plaza from their "moiety chapel," the ritual stopping points on the northern and southern edges of town. The tropas enter through the "senior members" of the moiety, and all groups pour libations there. As the tropas begin their trip around the plaza they next encounter the altar of the lower half of their own moiety. Finally, the tropas move into the "territory" of the opposing moiety; although the dancing circles form briefly at the two altars, libations are not usually poured. In every case the troupes outline once again—both as prelude and postlude—the conceptual social order of Yura according to principles of precedence and structural proximity. Each ayllu is re-created ritually in the pouring of libations at its altar; and its ties to the other ayllus are sketched in the movements of the dance around the plaza.

At each Entrada and Kacharpaya the groups reaffirm their vision of the Yura social order.

These festival sequences highlight ritually the various levels of social grouping—moiety, major ayllu, and minor ayllu. The peregrinations of the dance troupes around the plaza end with the groups encircling the Rollo. The pillar becomes at this moment a symbol of unity. The Rollo, as the tropas join around it, represents the oneness of the maximal ayllu over and above the multiplicity of its component segments.

This unity is not unambiguous, however, for certain aspects of the Entrada and the Kacharpaya refer to social relationships beyond the maximal ayllu. It will be recalled that the first step of the Entrada is the formal paying of respects at the door to the church. This act may well have had its origin long ago as a pragmatic response to the demands of oppressive Catholic priests. But many years have passed in which no priests have resided in Yura, and it is unlikely that any have attempted to shape Yura ritual practices for decades (except, perhaps, to suggest that they all be abandoned as pagan). By now this gesture of obeisance to an outside ritual institution has become, in Yura terms, an appropriate way to begin the festive event: it makes sense to Yuras in terms of their own logic.[20]

The unity that the Rollo symbolizes is made even more complex by the ideas associated with the monument itself. Its significance as a potent symbol for the Yura maximal ayllu is clear in the ritual action oriented toward it. We will consider the Rollo in more detail in chapter 10. Let it be said now, however, that its symbolic associations accompany the notion of colonial domination. The focus on the Rollo in the last moments of the Entrada and the Jatun Kacharpaya ends both these ritual events in an inconclusive way. They affirm Yura organization and its ultimate unity, yet leave the question of the relationship to the wider society unresolved. In addition to the overwhelming stress on internal organization, there is an unarticulated ritual recognition of a reality beyond the boundaries of the Yura meaning-world.

In the preceding pages we have examined the kuraqkuna's participation in festival ritual. We have recounted the elements of the fiestas, however, as a series of acts with little attention to the ideas and values which give them meaning. In chapter 9 we will turn to the conceptual level in order to analyze certain aspects of the Yuras' worldview which underlie their ritual actions. I hope to demonstrate that one important factor which motivates the Yuras to continue to take on the kuraqkuna posts is the role they play in constructing and making manifest the Yura symbolic universe.

9

THE SYMBOLIC WORLD
OF THE KURAQKUNA
The Staff of Authority

The reproduction of relations of power and subordination occurs in the interaction of social persons in daily life, as individuals learn and then act out their social roles. But in Yura, as in most traditional agrarian societies, the practice of egalitarian social relationships within the group, as well as the nature of power relations among group members and other social strata, are reflected upon in ritual. In ritual, Yuras objectify a particular view of the world; at the same time they attempt to comprehend (or perhaps to mystify) the implications for social action of the norms they profess to live by, and which are communicated in the ritual act. One of the functions of ritual is this process of social reproduction in that it presents the rudiments of social arrangements in the context of symbolic action and provides the means by which these are passed on to the next generation.[1] We have just seen how the festival of Reyes does that, involving the participants in a dramaturgical sequence of events which refer to and re-create the Yura conception of the social order.

However, a narration of the different steps of the festivals is not sufficient to fully comprehend them, for it fails to explicate the wider context of thought that underlies the kuraqkuna's actions. In this chapter and the next, therefore, we shall focus on the symbolic references that occur in ritual in order to place actions and objects with which we are already familiar into the context of a wider set of beliefs and values. In this chapter we concentrate on one key symbol, the kinsa rey, or staff of authority. In chapter 10 we will broaden the analysis to include other conceptions of spiritual power before we turn to an examination of one last festival, Carnaval, in which all the symbolic forms to be discussed are conjoined in an elaborate cultural performance.

An Approach to the Analysis of Symbolism

Much has been written in the last two decades under the rubric of symbolic anthropology. These studies have expanded our understanding of the ways in which cultural forms motivate persons to act as members of society, and of the ways these forms can be manipulated for individual and group ends. The best of the symbolic studies have attempted to address the issue of the relationship between symbolic form, power, and social hierarchy.[2]

After more than twenty years, Victor Turner's 1967 article, "Symbols in Ndembu Ritual," is still an essential guide for symbolic analysis. Turner focused on what he termed "dominant symbols"— encompassing, synthetic symbolic forms around which important group rituals are oriented (and from which they are constructed). According to Turner, dominant symbols possess three principal properties: condensation ("many things and actions are represented in a single formation"); the "unification of disparate significata" (the referents included within the range of meanings of the symbol can derive from widely diverse domains); and the polarization of meaning (the observation that referents tend to cluster at two poles, the "sensory," and the "normative" or "ideological"). The sensory pole, with its links to such human biological phenomena as sexual acts or organs, blood, and excrement, seems to provide, at a deep psychological level, much of the emotional power of the symbols. The ideological pole, on the other hand, includes references to social principles, the "norms and values that guide and control persons as members of social groups and categories" (Turner 1967:28). The three overall characteristics of symbols outlined here—condensation, unification, and polarization of meanings—are summed up by Turner in the concept of *multivocality*.

While Turner's work with the essentially unstratified Ndembu did not lead him to make this point, we might add that, in class societies, the meanings carried at this ideological pole may well reflect contention among groups to impose their conflicting images of the social order on others. Those groups at the bottom of the class hierarchy are faced with a struggle for definitional primacy between the social situation in which they live and the hegemonic ends of the dominant classes; this point is especially relevant to the situation of the Yuras.

In the same discussion Turner analyzes the properties of a dominant or synthetic symbol through the use of three kinds of data: its external form; the interpretations offered by specialized and "lay" informants; and its contextual placement. In the third set of data there is a dual aspect: first, in the examination of the symbol's placement within a system of symbols; and second, in an operational analysis which focuses on how people use or interact with the symbol, where social action in relation to the symbol is seen to disclose general attitudes toward it which might not otherwise be revealed. These latter understandings are "largely worked out by the anthropologist" and may conflict with the conscious interpretations held by the members of the social groups (Turner 1967:20–22).

Symbols do not occur in isolation. Rather, they are elements in the construction of ritual. Rituals—and here we use the term in a broad way to include any culturally regularized, compressed symbolic performance—"reveal," as Wilson once argued, "values at their deepest level. . . . Men express in ritual what moves them most, and since the form of expression is conventionalized and obligatory, it is the values of the group that are revealed" (1954:241).

The importance of both the reflexivity and communicative aspects of ritual suggests that it can usefully be seen as a performance, or, as one writer put it, as a "transformative performance revealing major classifications, categories, and contradictions of cultural processes" (and social principles, it must be added) (Grimes 1976, quoted in Turner and Turner 1978:244). Clifford Geertz's culturalist framework makes a similar point. He argues that dominant symbols bring about social transformation by providing actors both with a cognitive construction of how the world is at its most fundamental (the symbol's "models-of" character) and with a normative and hortatory assertion of how social beings should act and how the world should be (its "models-for" aspect). Ritual is the major locus of the "traffic in symbols" that brings about such a linkage (1973:93–94). If, as Burke (1973:9) has written, symbols embody attitudes (or, as his more dynamic phrasing has it, "the symbolic act is the *dancing* of an attitude" [his emphasis]), then ritual is the means by which values and ideas embodied in the system of symbols are expressed. From the phenomenological perspective of Berger and Luckmann (1967), ritual is a socially bracketed moment in which the shared symbols that underlie the overarching symbolic universe (which is itself historically created in the ongoing process of the formation of social institutions from the "flux of everyday life") are brought to conscious consideration by the participants. In this way ritual renews the unifying meaning-world—which theoretically integrates competing principles of social life—and endows that meaning-world with (at least momentary) power and veracity.

It would be a mistake, however, to assume that ritual is an unchanging, rigid performance that only serves to bring straying individuals back into society's fold or to reconcile competing factions into an idealized Platonic world of cultural absolutes. Ritual and symbols can be creatively altered by group members to reflect new social arrangements and new understandings of the world. Or, as we suggested is the case with class societies, ritual symbols can serve a conflicting role in the struggle for power and against oppression. On one hand, they may provide the means for group mobilization and self-identification, as Cohen has amply demonstrated (1969, 1976, 1981). This aspect of symbolic action is relevant in the present context in terms of recent studies of the ideologies of peasant resistance, the many cases where Third World peasants have rallied around key sets of symbols—peasant ideologies—to act at some level as a coherent and powerful political force (Kahn 1985).

On the other hand, a major aspect of the power of dominant elites in class societies is their control of the means of symbolic production, especially in the mass media and the schools, and in the control of state-level celebrations such as national holidays. The elite's efforts to impose a hegemonic set of symbols are in many cases successful, and the lower social classes may subscribe to the dominant framework provided for them from above. In such cases the symbols become means of manipulation of the powerless to prevent or postpone the formation of a shared consciousness of class.

None of these symbolic processes takes place in a simple, unambiguous way. The multivocality of symbols ensures the flexibility of meanings that are socially assigned to key symbols.[3] Through lived experience, or through manipulation by a subgroup or class, the symbolic center of a ritual symbol can be shifted through time such that it acquires new referents. This can occur with no overt rejection of the symbol, so that appeals to the legitimacy of tradition (that is, the idea that what is "valid is that which has always been" [Weber 1978:36]) can be maintained in the face of dramatic reformulations in symbolic praxis.

A multicausal view of society and culture insists that systems of symbols can act as a stimulus to new social arrangements as well. While we may want to give a place of prominence to the social forces underlying economic production, symbolic processes also have a dynamic of their own.[4] Turner's (1969) discussion of the phenomenon of communitas is instructive in this regard. He identifies communitas as that experience typical of the liminal phase of rites of passage when human equality is stressed over hierarchy, and when the common, shared humanity of ritual participants is emphasized over their normal structured statuses. Communitas can be, he argues, a source for creativity in ritual; for if this experience balances life in structure and thus serves to reinforce it, communitas is also a moment in which the inherent creativity of symbolic formulations can lead to structural innovations.

Thus a model that focuses on social process is necessary to analyze the relationship between ritual and social action. Ritual is a kind of "social drama" (Turner 1974:23–59)—it describes social relations and constructs the central meanings that orient a group's actions; but it also transforms in the very process of description, reformulating those meanings in such a way that social relations may be fundamentally altered. By unifying (or by effecting an exchange between) the poles of meanings of the dominant symbols, the ritual attempts to create an image "in which society's members cannot see any fundamental conflict between themselves as individuals and society" (Turner 1974:55–56).

Yet where real conflict and struggle exist, and where groups must attempt to maintain coherence and autonomy in the face of exploitation and the imposition of arbitrary political power by an alien elite, rituals cannot simply ignore these social realities but must somehow reflect upon them. Ritual may then be structured to guide participants through a sequence of steps that express the conflicts and inconsistencies of social life, yet which may provide a renewed vision of society in which these conflicts are seen to be part of a larger, necessary whole. On the other hand, the images discussed in the ritual context may refer to the contradictions inherent in the group's situation through a complex, ambivalent reference both to group goals and to the realities of power and control. In either case the ritual attempts to impose meaning on the chaos of event.

It is in terms of this perspective that I would like to turn to a description and analysis of one dominant symbol, the kuraqkuna's staff of authority. An examination of the kinsa rey provides an entrée into many of the themes discussed in an abstract way in the preceding pages, themes which underlie the role of the kuraqkuna in sustaining the Yura vision of the world.

The Staff of Authority

The kuraqkuna carry with them a staff of authority, the kinsa rey, or rey tata, during the festivals and when fulfilling official functions. At the most superficial level we can say that this is their token of office; the couple who display it at festivals are signifying that they have taken on and are currently serving in one of the kuraqkuna posts. But the kinsa rey is much more than a simple sheriff's badge. It is in fact the dominant symbol on which rests the entire complex of meanings sustaining the institution of the kuraqkuna. An examination of these layers of referents permits us to enter more deeply into the meaning-world of the kuraqkuna.

The historical origins of the staff of authority are lost to us, although it is quite likely that this is one case where Andean and

European symbolism overlapped. In Andean iconography the use of a cane or staff as a symbol of power and authority is quite ancient, going back at least to the Early Horizon of Chavín, nearly three thousand years ago. In what is today Bolivia, the best-known example of the staff image may be the so-called staff god carved in the Gateway of the Sun at Tiahuanaco; this archaeological site dates from the Middle Horizon, between A.D. 600 and 1000 (Orlove 1985:46–47). On the other hand, the *vara,* or staff, was also an emblem of political power in Spain and her colonies. For instance, the ordinances of the viceroy Toledo ([1575] 1925), promulgated at the time of the creation of the reducciones, specified that native authorities should carry a wooden staff as a sign of political office. The use of the staff today, which is still widespread throughout the rural Andes, has this dual historical grounding.

In appearance the kinsa rey is not particularly imposing. It consists of a narrow rod, usually about thirty inches (eighty cm) long, made of a dark, heavy tropical hardwood called *chunta.* A silversmith polishes the wood to a sheen, then decorates it with metal rings placed along its length. He crowns it with a silver cap to which is affixed a saint's medal on a chain (San Miguel, the Archangel Michael, is the most popular figure in this connection). Another cap is attached to the bottom. As we saw in the discussion of Reyes, each kinsa rey has a scarf associated with it, its *uxanta* or *pañurimanis.* Woven from rare vicuña wool, it is considered an integral part of the staff and is always found either wrapped around it or nearby. Since each staff is made as a work of art by individual craftsmen, no two are identical and each is readily distinguished by its owner. Yet all share these general characteristics.

The kinsa reyes are owned by individual men, inherited from their forebears. Although it is possible to buy them (and they are sold both by rural silversmiths—one resides in the central village of Yura—and in the market in Potosí), the owners I knew had inherited theirs. Most staffs give the appearance of considerable age. Women do not inherit or own kinsa reyes; the staffs are passed from father to sons. If a man has no male heir, he may leave it to his daughter's husband. Lacking children, he gives it to a nephew.

In any hamlet only one or two persons will own a kinsa rey.

A Jiliqata of Jatun
Qullana Holds His
Kinsa Rey

However, a few *kinsa reyniywaq* (possessors of kinsa reyes) owned
two of them, and two men I met owned three. Men in Chakilla,
the neighboring ex-hacienda of herders, expressed a cultural ideal
to own three kinsa reyes, a short one and two of normal size.[5] If
this was once the case in Yura, it is not a goal held today. All the
informants of whom I asked this question (some fifteen owners
in all) said one could own as many staffs as he could afford and
desired. The two men in Yura who followed the Chakilla pattern
of owning a miniature staff and two full-sized ones joined the other
informants in denying any special significance to this.

Nevertheless, these triplets fall into the logic of the name applied
to the staffs—"three kings"—and in their explanation of the origin of that name. We would naturally suppose that there was some

connection to the three kings of the Epiphany. Most Yuras make no such link and have no explanation at all for the name. One informant gave a typical response when he said: "Unaymanta nisqa, unaymanta chay suti kasqa. Ajinapuni a. Mana kanchu kwintu chaymanta." (From olden days, it is said, from olden days that name is said to be. It was always that way. There are [however] no stories about that.) However, another made reference to the biblical kings when he said: "Unaymantapuni rey karqa, rey kasqa, nin. Rey Melchor, Rey Baltazar, Rey Gaspar. Chaymanta chay." (A long time ago, there was a king, they say there was a king, King Melchor, King Baltazar, King Gaspar. That comes from that.) Yet neither could this man recall any explanatory stories. A third informant who listed the same three biblical names said he had seen a story in the Bristol Almanac about the kings, while no one else mentioned the names in this way or ventured any other account of the origin of the kings.

If the idea was once more widespread that the three kings of Bethlehem were commemorated in the staff of authority (perhaps when the church catechism was known more widely than today), it has been lost for most people. The names continue to be applied and remembered by some, but the connection with the Christian origins has been broken.

Still, all kinsa reyes have titles and names. In ritual circumstances they can be referred to by the title "Wayna Wiraqucha" (something like Young Gentleman).[6] Each kinsa rey also has its own personal name. The three kings' names of Gaspar, Melchor, and Baltazar are used (and not only by those who own all three, for a man may inherit a single kinsa rey whose name is Gaspar or Melchor). But other names are more common: Wayna P'aquchu (Little Blond Youth [the -chu being a Yura diminutive]), Wayna Wayq'u (Youth of the Ravine), and Wayna Maquti (Maquti is the name of a peak). One was named after an ayllu (Juan Qullana), and several were given a local surname (Juan Eusebio). Some Spanish titles are heard, such as "Jiniru" (in Spanish, género, genus, but also cloth) and "Urganu" (órgano, organ). One was named Muthu Chupa (Blunt Tail). My impression is that the names are used affectionately and their humor appreciated; the staffs are not necessarily referred to solemnly or with veneration in all contexts.

This does not mean, however, that the kinsa rey itself can be treated lightly, for in spite of a sometimes whimsical name, the rey tata is considered a locus of the divine. It is a powerful object that must be treated with respect. As we saw in chapter 4, this is plain in the Yuras' ritual interaction with the staff. It is also expressed, although less explicitly, in the way they talk about the kinsa rey.

The going gets somewhat difficult here, because the Yura do not express their beliefs in terms of tightly reasoned logical arguments. Part of this lack of theorizing derives from the absence of a group of specialists set aside to elaborate and record the symbolic formulations they hold (such as a literate priesthood), a result of conquest by a foreign culture. The *awkis*, the local curers and diviners,[7] do acquire a more esoteric knowledge of the complexities of the supernatural than most, but they are, in a sense, private operators—more on the model of shamans than priests—who have no special public role in the rituals involving the kuraqkuna, nor do they see themselves, at least at present, as "codifiers." The Catholic priests, who also participate in the festival actions of the kuraqkuna, do so from their perspective as Europeans with a vision of the Catholic church greatly influenced by the Second Vatican Council, Medellín, and Puebla. The Yura worldview, and their relationship to it, confronts these Spanish priests with painful dilemmas. They are clearly not codifiers of the intellectual aspects of the Yura symbolic world but are rather the representatives of a powerful alternative to it.

However, there is another factor involved in the degree to which Yuras express, or do not express, their beliefs in language, the result, in my opinion, of a kind of cultural emphasis. One way to phrase this would be to draw a line representing a continuum in which one end would be labeled "language alone" and the other "symbolic action alone." On this line we would then situate social groups by their relative cultural tendencies to elaborate either the linguistic or the dramaturgical "action" aspects of ritual. No real culture (that is to say, the symbolic universe of no real social group) would be placed directly over the poles of this continuum. Yet most social groups, societies, or subcultures[8] would lie closer to one end of the continuum than to the other. The Panamanian Cunas's great orators (Sherzer 1974) clearly stress language to a high degree, while anthropological tradition has it that the Zuni of the American Southwest emphasize symbolic action. This continuum can be illustrated even within a symbolic framework which is at some level widely shared, such as Euro-American Christianity. It is evident that Quakers focus on language to an extraordinary degree and would be close to the "language alone" end (Bauman 1974). Fundamentalists and Calvinist-derived denominations also emphasize language, although they would lie somewhat closer to the center. Lutherans, Episcopalians, and post–Vatican II Catholics attempt to balance more closely language and symbolic action (or, in their terms, word and sacrament). Medieval Christianity and Lefebvrian Catholicism stress symbolic action at the expense of the word.

The Yura fall into this last category. Although Yuras obviously express themselves with the subtlety of any other group of human beings, they are not encouraged by their traditions to become, for example, great orators.[9] The communication of deeply held values and of ideas about the order of things is accomplished by preference in ritual acts, that is, in symbolic action and not verbally.[10]

Nevertheless, the Yura do of course talk about the kinsa reyes. When asked, many stated that the staff was *santu jina*, "like a saint." This statement requires some comment, however. Their concept of saint is, not surprisingly, quite distinct from that of theologians or educated Catholics. The Catholic Encyclopedia represents the latter's view when it defines saint as "a title properly given to those human members of Christ recognized by the Church . . . as being in heaven and thus worthy of honor" (XII:852).

The use of the term *santu* in Yura is closer to the idea as expressed in the popular peasant belief in Europe (e.g., Christian 1972), where the saint is thought to be more than a respected soul in heaven. Rather, the saints are at least active intercessors, and may even be conceived to have their own supernatural abilities to act on behalf of their devotees. I do not wish to enter into theological questions beyond the scope of this work or my expertise, but in Yura, the saints' images are treated as if spiritual power inheres in the image, or in the place with which it is associated (though it might be added that the "place" can be either specifically geographic or it might also be a grouping in the social order as well as a location in space).

It is in this sense that Yuras speak when they say that the kinsa rey is like a saint. One young man, who had recently attended catechism classes held by one of the Spanish priests, volunteered the notion that "Jesus Christ was inside" the kinsa rey. References to Jesus Christ in Yura were very rare and no one else ever repeated those words. Nevertheless, they are not wholly idiosyncratic in that they reinforce the conclusion that the kinsa rey is thought to be, in itself, an object in which supernatural power resides.

The actions of the kinsa rey are experienced in one's fortunes in everyday life. The staff, like Pacha Mama (Earth Mother) and her manifestations, is said to be *phiña*, which can be roughly translated as "bad-tempered," "quick to take offense," or even "angry." If certain ritual acts are not carried out (the description of which we shall turn to presently), the kinsa rey will punish (*kastigay*, borrowed from Spanish) those responsible for the failure, whether it be the couple who has borrowed the staff or the staff's owners. The nature of the punishment can vary, but it centers either on the persons who failed to provide the offerings or on their animals. In humans the symptoms may be shortness of breath, severe constipation, or the inability to stand up correctly. In animals an epidemic will attack the sheep or llamas and they simply die off. The kinsa rey will not cause illness in children (although certain other spiritual entities will), and I am under the impression that it visits illness only on the male half of the authority couple, and not on the wife.

In the normal course of things it is usually not immediately obvious what the origin of such an illness might be. Those afflicted go to an awki and ask him to determine the cause of their problems. By divining with coca leaves, he is able to advise the questioner whether the kinsa rey or some other spirit is at fault.[11] When it has been decided that the kinsa rey is the source of the illness, then it is necessary to "ask the pardon" (*perdunta mañay* or *perdunakuy*) of the staff by conducting a rite in which incense is burned and oblations are poured to it. When this is done, Yuras assert that the disease will subside (*thañipullanqa*).

If the human owners fail to perform the necessary rituals, misfortune may not follow immediately. The kinsa rey may first attempt to remind the owners of their duties by appearing to the man in a dream in the form of a *wiraqucha,* a tall, light-skinned European ("something like you," one informant told me). When the dreamer awakes, he realizes that the figure he saw was the kinsa rey, which had appeared to draw his attention to the necessity of making the offerings. We see here a first indication of the kinsa rey, a key symbol in Yura self-definition, associated with an image of outside power and identity.

According to the opinions of some Yuras, the kinsa rey can be offended in a way that the perdunta mañay will not erase. One elderly informant, who lived in a hamlet not far from the central village, recalled that he had loaned his kinsa rey to a man in Layk'u, far to the south, when the latter served as jilaqata. At the end of the year the kinsa rey was returned without its vicuña scarf. It had been lost at some point during the festivities of the year and was never seen again. The man apologized and the owner had another scarf woven. Soon afterward, however, the ex-jilaqata went blind and never recovered his sight. The owner told me he felt that if the man from Layk'u had only been able to find the lost scarf, his vision would have been restored.

Another man, who had reportedly been something of a misfit in the past, became an *evangelista* (fundamentalist Protestant). I am not certain of the circumstances of this conversion, although it seems to have occurred when he was working as a wage laborer outside Yura.[12] In any case, he decided on his return that his kinsa rey was against the tenets of his new faith, and he broke it in two and threw it in the river. According to everyone who related this story, his Qhurqa hamlet was soon struck by a series of hailstorms, destructive not only of his fields but also those of his innocent neighbors. The storms finally subsided, although it was not reported what actions he may have taken, if any, for that to occur. This man has more or less abandoned any special evangelista observances since then.

The kinsa rey, then, requires of its owners (or of those who have borrowed it while they are filling one of the kuraqkuna posts) a number of specific acts. A state of obligation exists between the human owner[13] and the staff (a point that Gow [1976] has also made). Primary among these duties is the regular offering of incense, corn beer, and alcohol, which should be made, when possible, on Thursdays and Saturdays. This small ceremony can be performed just among family members, although frequently one's hamlet mates may be invited. The kinsa rey is hung at a specially designated place on the interior wall of the house, its vicuña wool scarf draped around it. Incense is sprinkled on embers held in a potsherd. As the smoke begins to waft up, first the husband, then the wife, kneel in front of the kinsa rey. They may say a conventional phrase, such as this one that I recorded: "Reyes Tata, Mallku, ama phiñakunkichu, ama phutikunkichu, Kuntur Mamani" (Father Reyes, Male Condor, don't grow angry, don't grow sad, Condor Eagle).[14] Then the staff is sprinkled with alcohol and corn beer by the couple and by the others present.

Although such a ceremony could be carried out weekly, it is normally done less often, perhaps once a month for those serving in a kuraqkuna post and even more infrequently for those who own a kinsa rey not being used. One obstacle to more ch'allays, as such libations are known, is the need to have corn beer available. The great labor involved in making the drink means that often none is on hand.

Beyond these occasional offerings the owners must also celebrate the kinsa reyes' "birthday" or name day on January 6, which is also the Entrada of the festival of Reyes. On that day all the kinsa reyes of the canton are brought out into the house patios and placed on a ritual table, where they are cleaned with alcohol. The staff is held upright on a metal plate and alcohol is poured over it while it is swabbed with cotton. The alcohol that runs off collects in the plate; a few drops of this are poured as a ch'allay, and the rest is drunk by the assembled men.

The most important obligations that humans have toward the kinsa rey, however, are the two acts termed *misachiy* and *yawarchay*. Where a kinsa rey has been loaned, the borrowers usually perform them a few weeks after leaving their post and then return the kinsa rey to its owner. An owner who has not loaned his kinsa rey will do the misachiy and the yawarchay himself. Although no fixed date is set for this, the two actions should be carried out at least every other year. Some felt the misachiy, at least, should be done yearly.

The *misachiy* (to do a mass) means simply to take the kinsa rey to "hear" mass. This action is thought to bring about a transfer of spiritual power to the staff. When the manufacture of new kinsa reyes was discussed, it was said that any competent silversmith could make a new kinsa rey, but it would remain ineffective, a mere object, until a mass had been dedicated to it. One older man said, "Mana valornin kanchu, mana kastiganchu misachinanchiskama" (It has no energy, it does not punish, until we take it to the mass).[15] Once the mass is carried out, then "*reypacha,*" it changes from a decorated stick into a kinsa rey.

However, hearing the mass is not a one-time affair. It must be offered regularly, yearly or biennially. If the mass is not given the rey tata may remind its owners by its punishments. Once the kinsa rey has received spiritual power in the first mass, it requires its owners to expose it again and again to that power.

The procedure itself is fairly straightforward. On the morning of the mass the kinsa rey is taken into the church. Before the mass begins the priest is usually standing in the chancel, prepared to receive requests for dedications of the mass. In Yura today the priest fills out a slip which bears the sponsor's name and states to whom the dedication is directed. The *recibo,* the receipt given, is considered by most Yuras to be an essential material representation of the act. Some priests are understandably somewhat reluctant to write "kinsa reyes" on the slip, so they may compromise by writing "Cristo Rey" (Christ the King), such that the staff owner's duty is performed without violating the priest's ideas of propriety. The curate may bless the staff and it is placed on the main altar, where it remains during mass. After the mass is over, the owner reclaims his kinsa rey and, before leaving, awaits the aspersion of holy water.

The misachiy can be done at any church, although the church in Yura or one in Potosí is usually chosen. Mass has not always been frequent in Yura, since for many years no priest resided regularly in the canton. Even today most Yuras bring their kinsa rey to the central village only for festivals, the time when most masses are celebrated. For several years the Spanish priests assigned to Yura did not want to issue a receipt for the staff and refused to allow them to be placed on the altar. Those who wanted their kinsa rey to partake in the ceremony were only allowed to hold it with them in the pew. Some Yuras reluctantly agreed to that, but many others felt it was inadequate. These joined the Yuras who already made the trip to Potosí with their kinsa rey, carrying it along when they went to buy supplies or sell apples.[16] The priests now serving in Yura have since relented, feeling that "popular religiosity" has its place in the church, and the staffs are once again being placed on the altar.

After the misa the kinsa rey is taken back to the family's house-yard, usually in the home hamlet but sometimes to the patio in Yura. At the least the kinsa rey is made the object of a special libation; it is placed on the sink'a llijlla, the ritual table of carrying cloth and coca leaf which is set up along one wall of the patio. Libations are then made to the staff and to Pacha Mama. In every ch'allay throughout the year the vicuña scarf is usually left with the staff on the table and it becomes spattered, stained, and eventually quite filthy. Although it is washed from time to time, the state of the scarf often brought a smile to the lips of Yuras whenever it was mentioned: there was almost a sense of pride in the degree of be-dragglement of the scarf. After the libations are poured the kinsa rey is formally returned to its place on the interior house wall while incense is burned and more libations are poured.

Every few years, however, a much more complete rite should be carried out, the *yawarchay* (sacrifice or, as a verb, to bathe in blood). Again, no fixed date is established for this ritual; people do it whenever they can after the misachiy, almost always in the house-yard. Although the exact order of events varies slightly according to different informants, the following is a composite of some fifteen descriptions of it by different people among whom there was considerable agreement in the details.[17] This description applies to those kinsa reyes that are *uwijaywaq*, that is, they require the warm blood of a sacrificed animal. Other staffs are only *ch'aki* (dry), and to these the offering of *k'ichira* is made. K'ichira is created when small chunks of flesh—pieces from the tongue, eyelid, lip, heart, lungs, kidney, and other organs—are cut from an animal sacrificed for some other purpose. Indeed, k'ichira is always taken from a sacrificed animal; the difference lies in the fact that the ch'aki kinsa rey does not require warm blood—k'ichira which has been collected previously suffices. The uwijaywaq kinsa rey is offered k'ichira taken from an animal sacrificed for that purpose. Why some kinsa reyes require the blood of an animal killed at that very moment and others do not is unclear to me; Yuras always answer that question with the conventional "Ajinapuni" (It has always been that way).

Although I did not conduct a census, my impression is that most staffs require blood. When it is time for the yawarchay the neighbors and relatives are invited to the houseyard, where the kinsa rey has been brought out and placed on a ritual table. As people arrive they are invited to pour libations to the staff, and the men are served alcohol in the staff's *wasu* (from Spanish *vaso*, a miniature metal cup) as well as in the large *qulqi wasus* (silver cups).

The hour arrives to kill the sheep; from this moment, the men act as primary participants. The animal is led outside the patio to a convenient spot close to the entrance. One man holds the sheep while another plunges a knife into its throat. Blood spurts out as the arteries are pierced, and this is caught in a basin. The carcass is then butchered. While one person cuts up the animal, another prepares k'ichira. He also removes the heart and places it on a metal plate.

The heart and the blood are carried into the patio and placed on the ritual table that has been set up—again, a box covered with a woven carrying cloth on which is placed another small weaving holding coca leaves. The staff is then held vertically on the plate, its bottom tip thrust into the heart. The men pour and smear the blood onto the staff, saying such phrases as "Qampaj, Rey Tata, Mallku" (For you, King Father, Male Condor). The blood that runs onto the plate—or at least part of it—is then drunk by the men, either raw or made into a *yawar kaldu*, a "blood soup." The men also eat at least some bits of the raw heart. As one man, who was later a kuraka of one of the ayllus, told me in reference to the heart, "Y después se lo comen, también, pues, así puro, crudo no más. Más alimento, no?" (And afterward, well, one eats it too, like that, pure, just raw. It's more nutritious, isn't it?) He added a statement that will prove significant in the later analysis of these practices, saying, "El condor nunca no muere cuando está con eso. . . . El condor come, pues, la carne cruda" (The condor never dies when he's with that [the heart]. . . . The condor, you know, eats raw meat).

After the kinsa rey has been covered with blood it is once again cleaned with pure alcohol, as it was before being taken to the misachiy. This alcohol, like the blood, is also drunk by the men participating. Only a small portion of the heart is eaten, however, and the rest, along with the k'ichira, is then offered in a *mijtachiy,* a burnt offering. For this a quantity of hot coals from the cooking fire is placed in the base of a broken pot. The owners then kneel in front of it and the husband and wife burn incense over the coals. Making an invocation, the husband scrapes the k'ichira (including the heart) from a plate onto the embers. He will probably also add *q'uwa,* the redolent shrub that is almost always burned to the deities, as well as other objects.

Once the k'ichira has been consumed, the hosts serve all those present a *kumpiru* (Spanish *compero,* or festive meal). The kumpiru begins with mounds of mut'i and *quesillo* (farmer's cheese) if the season is right. This is followed by a soup in which the mutton from the sacrifice is cooked. As the meal ends, both men and women pour libations of corn beer and alcohol over the kinsa rey and the ritual table it lies on.

That, then, is the yawarchay. This and the misachiy are the two sine qua non for possession of the kinsa rey. If they are not performed, it is thought that the spiritual power that resides in the kinsa rey may act to the detriment of its owners. It is also clear that these rituals are both costly and exacting. One could ask why anyone would want to own such a thing, if in the end it required continual expense and could lead to serious misfortune if it were treated incorrectly.

One argument that could be advanced to explain why Yuras want to possess a kinsa rey would be a universalistic one, that it is a manifestation of some desire or drive on the part of human beings in general to transcend their everyday reality, regardless of how uninviting that transcendent reality may be conceived to be. Yet this is a weak position from which to argue, for the explanation becomes tautological: the Yura want to keep kinsa reyes because something inside them makes them want to keep them.

There may be, of course, some who inherit a kinsa rey and are faced with its facticity against their wishes. No one ever suggested that, however. Indeed, the owners seemed to feel honored and proud to possess the kinsa rey in spite of the fact that it was both burdensome and potentially dangerous. For this apparent contradiction I have no easy solution. I offer here my own interpretation (although no one ever expressed it in this way to me) simply as a provisional explanation until further research can either confirm or rebut it. I believe it to be consistent with Yura thought.

Within a commonsense view of everyday life, we Euro-Americans tend to take much for granted. If we are not at the moment visited by misfortune, then good health, moderate prosperity, and a roof over our heads strike us as right and proper, a reflection of the nature of things. This is not to imply that we always, or all of us, share this view, even in unreflective moments. Obviously, in the context of social analysis or of religious thought this seems a false view. Nevertheless, when our attention is not focused on the basic facts of our existence, most of us assume that a neutral world will continue to be such.

The Yura view, I suggest, is more conditional and cautious. The Yura, too, naturally share a taken-for-granted reality: they assume that day will follow night and expect the house that was standing when they fell asleep to be there when they awaken. But the Yura are especially conscious that they live in a world of change, in which most changes lead only to difficulties and pain. One hesitates to suggest a simple cause for such an outlook on life; but we can point to the fact that they do, indeed, live in a very marginal ecological situation in which material conditions of life are extremely arduous. In bad years people know hunger. Furthermore, death is a continual reality, a much greater presence than it is for most Americans. It strikes all ages, but especially children. These factors, if they are not causes, are at least of one piece with an underlying sense of life as a dangerous enterprise. The power of the kinsa rey, as with other Yura formulations of divinity, lies in its active strength to uphold life, animal fertility, and health (among other things) in the face of disease and death. The good things of life are fleeting and require the continuous energy of the divinities to be sustained.

The Yura establish a kind of relationship of reciprocal exchanges between themselves and the kinsa rey. That is, they adopt this cultural principle for organizing social ties and use it as a model for their ties to the gods. When those who possess a staff fail to carry out the duties that they owe it, then the kinsa rey is thought correspondingly to withdraw its underlying spiritual power from some aspect of the realm it controls, and misfortune occurs. To possess a kinsa rey, then, is to enter into an active association with its sustaining power. That tie bears its risks, but it also holds out the hope of protection from some of the trials of life. This same kind of thinking, I would argue, also underlies Yura relationships with the divinities, which I will discuss in the next chapter.

Reprise: The Kinsa Rey as a Key Symbol

In the preceding pages we have gradually built up an image of the layerings of meanings surrounding the kinsa rey using three sorts of data: a description of the staff itself, reports of how people conceptualize it and its powers, and sketches (based both on observation and on interviews) of several ritual acts centering on the rey tata. From this we can make the following preliminary statements about the kinsa rey: It is conceived as a powerful locus of the divine with a special link to animals and to health. Its nature is to be *phiña*, "capricious"; it therefore must be treated with affectionate respect and, at times, even with fear. The practices of naming and reference show that it is seen as both a generic and a highly individualized power. Rules for ownership and inheritance show that it bears a special relationship to males, and especially to the kuraqkuna; its phallic form reinforces these masculine attributes. Finally, acts carried out during the blood sacrifice reveal that the kinsa rey is also joined conceptually to the image of the male condor.

Many of the meanings surrounding the staff make certain ambiguous allusions to the dominant society. Its power seemingly derives from the offerings made to it; yet one of the central offerings which empowers the staff is linked with an institution—the Catholic church—which is associated with the nationally oriented classes and which has its center of authority outside Yura. Further, the staff appears in dreams as a white European.

While the complex of meanings centered on the kinsa rey leads to a number of possible interpretations of the kuraqkuna's participation in ritual, reference to the staff alone reveals only partially the beliefs and values that the Yura use to guide their actions. In the next chapter we shall, without losing sight of the significance of the kinsa rey, attempt to link these ideas to others which situate the Yura in a broader world beyond the confines of their territory.

10

A SYMBOLIC DIALOGUE
The Spirit World,
Carnaval,
and the State

In chapter 9 the Yura formulation of a symbolic universe was addressed by means of a focus on the kinsa rey, the staff of authority the kuraqkuna retain as an insignia of office during their term of service. We were led to consider animal sacrifice, the role of "outside" spiritual powers, and the relationship between Yura peasant farmers and the difficult physical world they inhabit in order to begin to assess the range of meanings the staff encompasses. The kinsa rey, however, is only one of a number of supernatural entities that shape the Yuras' understanding of their place in the world. Here we will place that key symbol into a broader context of thought and action by examining two other representations of supernatural power, *Pacha Mama* (Earth Mother) and the *jach'aranas* (the lords of the mountain peaks). We will then link Yura thinking about these spiritual agents to the actions of the kurakas, the paramount posts within the four major ayllus, and then consider the role of all the kuraqkuna in a major festival of the annual cycle, Carnaval.

Pacha Mama and the Jach'aranas

We have already mentioned Pacha Mama a number of times, but a description of Yura beliefs about her nature has been left until now. Due to the very generality of action attributed to her, Earth

Mother is perhaps the most difficult divinity to describe. While many students of Andean civilization have written about Pacha Mama, perhaps the study by Mariscotti de Görlitz (1978), who also reviews earlier efforts, is the most comprehensive work on indigenous ideas about the deity as they are found in Andean culture. While her perspective is more folkloric than anthropological, her ethnographic observations suggest that the Yuras' understanding of Earth Mother is shared quite widely by other Andean peoples. In the present discussion, however, we shall not attempt either an exhaustive review of those generalized beliefs or a complete analysis of the full array of Yura ideas about Pacha Mama. Rather, we will restrict ourselves to sketching those characteristics most relevant to the ritual actions of the kuraqkuna.

The Yura conceive of Pacha Mama as the most comprehensive of the deities. She is, in fact, described as one-in-many; her powers and the degree of interest she demonstrates in human affairs vary depending on the context of reference and on the particular ritual situation. Pacha Mama is primordially identified with the earth. At the most inclusive level in the hierarchy of her multiplicity, she represents the physical world, paired with (and in a certain opposition to) the sun, which is termed "Dyusninchis" (Our god) or "Amunchis" (Our lord, our master). In this context the earth is conceived to be feminine while the power of the sun resides in his masculine ability to inseminate the earth and make life possible.

Thus everything on earth and in it "is," or is sustained by, Pacha Mama. At this high level of abstraction, any offering made to any place- or earth-associated deity, as well as to any created object, is also an offering to Pacha Mama.[1] Nonetheless, Pacha Mama is especially associated with fields and cultivated spaces. In the Yura ritual vocabulary, Pacha Mama is commonly termed the *virgin de la tierra* (Spanish, virgin of the earth). The adoption of Spanish phrases for important concepts is not at all unusual, since the language has considerable prestige even among those who do not speak it; this particular usage is widespread throughout rural Bolivia. In the same way, fields in Yura are respectfully called, in the Quechua pronunciation, *wirjinkuna* or *wirjinis* (virgins). For example, a person, when describing what he planted in a particular field, might say,

"*Chay wirjimpi tarpuni yuraq sarallata*" (I only planted white corn in that field).

This is not just a lexical substitution for the common word for field, *chajra*. The fields, as a source of the sustenance of all, are believed to benefit from offerings by humans in order that there be abundant harvests. That is, they too have an element of the divine in them with which human beings can interact. This is most clearly manifest in the oblations that women perform in the fields in the winter, as when, in August, women "feed" Pacha Mama by burning offerings of herbs and, in their best field, a llama fetus. This identification with the divine is also evident in the terms themselves. A young married woman put it bluntly: "*Wirjinpa 'Pacha Mama' sutin*" (The name of the "virgin" is "Pacha Mama").

All fields together, thought of as a unity, are thus the Virgin or Pacha Mama. But specific fields and places are also *wirjinkuna*, that is, individualized aspects of Earth Mother. One can speak, therefore, of the virgin of a particular field or of a cluster of fields. One man referred to a field grouping on a small plain by the Yura River (a place called Wayt'uki) as the "Wayt'uki virgin." But these more localized aspects of Pacha Mama are not restricted only to cultivated plots, for Yuras also speak of the virgins, the spiritual aspects, of ravines and other natural locales.

As with the kinsa reyes, all these wirjinis can be capricious, or *phiña*. It was thought, for example, that the virgin of one ravine where four people had committed suicide over the years was especially phiña and required frequent offerings of blood. The virgin of another ravine was said to be fierce because of the accidents that occurred on the narrow mountain path running through the spot.

Manifestations of Earth Mother also protect populated places: hamlets, larger settlements, and the central village of Yura. These are also called wirjinis or *mamitas* (mothers) and are associated with the female images of chapels and churches. While this conception of the wirjin takes on a form that appears familiar in traditional Catholicism, the Yura interact with these wirjinis of populated places in essentially the same way that they do with the aspects of Pacha Mama of the fields. The same offerings of corn beer and alcohol are made, although candles and incense are also considered appropriate as gifts for the images of the village wirjinis. As was discussed in chapter 9, the Yura concept of the saint's image is to view it not as a historical figure but as a center of supernatural power that has present control over the fortunes of human beings— their wealth and health, their products, and their flocks. As Gross has written in reference to such Andean concepts: "The peasants of the Andes fetishize the earth as an animate thing which gives and withholds its fruits (both vegetable and mineral) in reciprocal exchanges with humans, hence the necessity of propitiation" (1983:696).

In Yura the principal and most powerful refraction of Pacha Mama is that of the Virgin of the Incarnation, the patron saint of the central village. This representation of supernatural power is ultimately linked to all Yuras in the same way that they all think of themselves as belonging to a single unitary ayllu. Yet both regional and ayllu-specific mamitas serve to create other allegiances and other specific obligations for individuals in different structural situations within the whole group. At the lower end of this scale are the "house saints," which oversee very small hamlets. Between these two extremes are the mamitas of the larger ranchos, such as Santa Wara Wara (Santa Bárbara) of Sullk'a Qhurqa or of the rancho of Thatuka. As an example of Yura thought about such virgins, the Virgin of Thatuka is renowned for being particularly phiña. Those who sponsor the annual fiesta in Thatuka must be especially careful to fulfill the correct ritual obligations to her or suffer her punishment. In accounting for the death of one sponsor during the days of the festival in 1978, one informant said, "*Chay wirjin runata mikhun. Yachan yawarchayta runa yawarwan*" (That virgin eats people. She has the custom of making a sacrifice with human blood). A virgin can therefore be capricious as well as nurturing. The right relationship must be maintained.

Pacha Mama and her manifestations as guardian spirit of field and valley, sustainer of humankind, and protector of settled places, contrast with another Yura formulation of divinity, that of the spiritual powers associated with the mountain peaks. These are called the *apus* or the *jach'aranas* (or, less often, *sach'aranas*).[2] These lords of the mountain peaks have special control of and responsibility for the animals, who in fact spend much of the year grazing on their slopes away from human habitation.

Yura concepts of the jach'aranas are most clearly expressed in an elaborate ritual of propitiation of the spirits of the mountains called the *q'uway*. Always carried out in *Chiraw*, or "winter" (when the fertility of the fields is dormant), this family rite usually begins with the sacrifice of a sheep and culminates in an offering to the principal mountain lords, performed on a peak at dawn. Twelve prepared plates and several vessels containing (among other things) coca, corn beer, alcohol, corn meal, llama fat, k'ichira, and three llama fetuses, are consumed in a fire, given to the "twelve sanctuaries" of the mountain peaks. The jach'aranas, like the manifestations of the Virgin and the kinsa rey, are also thought to be phiña—unpredictable and potentially bad tempered. Similarly, they require the human beings with whom they have a relationship to provide them with the "food" of oblations for which, in turn, the jach'aranas shelter and protect them. The lords of the mountains are thought to be hungry, to "crave" the offerings. As the officiant at the q'uway dumps the offering plates into the fire, he tells the mountain peaks, "You wanted this, you craved it, you asked us for it."

The kinds of conceptual oppositions that intrigue structuralists are at work in Yura beliefs about the mountain spirits. The jach'aranas are said to keep flocks of animals that graze close to the peaks at night. For every domesticated animal or cultural artifact that humans have, the jach'aranas have a corresponding natural one. Thus, instead of dogs, the jach'aranas own foxes; for burros, they have *wisk'achas;*[3] and for llamas, vicuñas. The vicuñas are especially important, for many of the mountain spirits are placed in a special category called *abonadores* (fertilizers). The abonadores have great wealth hidden within their slopes; it is they who have kept the great mine in Potosí producing during all these centuries. They do this by sending the silver from within their own "bodies" to Potosí on vicuña caravans at night, to replace the ore that the miners take out each day.

The Yura concept of the jach'aranas as lords of the mountains and protectors of the herds is similar to the idea of the *wamanis* or the *apus* of southern Peru (as described, for example, by

Allen 1981; Arguedas 1956:197–200; Favre 1967; Fuenzalida 1980; Marzal 1970:250–53; and Núñez del Prado 1985:247–49). Perhaps most relevant for the analysis here is the link conceived to exist in the southern Andes between the image of the wamanis, their "human" form, and the condor. In rural Ayachucho the link is quite explicit: the wamanis transform themselves into condors as well as into "tall, white, bearded males who dress elaborately in western dress" (Isbell 1978:59, 151–55). In Apurímac the apus are thought to be "large, blonde, blue-eyed men, dressed in fancy clothes and riding boots" (Gose 1986:299). Bastien found a strong symbolic identification between the condor and the mountain peaks of the Charazani area of Bolivia (Bastien 1978:63). García (1983) recounts a séance conducted by a native healer who was able to speak with the mountain peaks; the arrival of the *apu* was signaled by the sound of a vigorous flapping of wings because the spiritual being had arrived, according to the ritual specialist, in the form of a condor.

In Yura, the condor—which is linked semantically, as we have seen, to the kinsa rey—is also conceptually joined, according to informants, with a representation of the mountain peaks. At one level such links are associational in experience: one sees the condors circling high above the summits, and the flocks, which are subject to the protection of the capricious jach'arana, are frequently attacked through its condor agents, acting, in Yura thinking, as the emissaries of the mountain peak.

However (and in apparent contrast to the understanding of most of the Peruvian researchers), although the realm of the jach'aranas is at one level set in opposition to that of Pacha Mama and is thus spoken of as if it were masculine, the overarching relevance of the male-female metaphor in Yura thought seems to dictate that mountain peaks, and the spirits of the mountains, must also be categorized as masculine and feminine. The male peaks are referred to as *mallkus* and the females as *t'allas*. In Yura, certain peaks are especially responsible for fertility and for the health of animals; these are addressed in the invocations of the q'uway propitiation for the flocks in a way that identifies them as either male or female jach'aranas: "Lakachiri Mallku, Lakachira T'alla! Tarachaku Mallku, Mama Chikupaya!" One informant said that the t'allas are the smaller mountains, the lower peaks, while the male mallkus are the high, overarching summits of the zone. Each high crest is then linked with a lower one in the vicinity into a male-female pair. Another man made the contrast by referring to the mallkus as *urqus* and the t'allas as *cerros*. This use is not universal, and cerro in Spanish can be roughly translated into the Quechua *urqu*, for they both can mean "hill" or "mountain."[4] But urqu has the additional meaning in Quechua of "male," as in *urqu llama,* "male llama." This lexical fact serves to emphasize the gender categories that are conceived to exist.

Even with this short sketch of the mountain spirits, a number of common themes linking the jach'aranas and the kinsa rey can be seen. The lords of the mountain peaks (the male ones, termed mallkus or male condors) watch over and sustain the herd animals. The kinsa rey, which in invocations is addressed as "Tata Mallku," and in the yawarchay is closely identified with the condor (as are its male owners and handlers), may seek retribution by attacking the herds if it is not properly propitiated. The staff of authority must always wear a "poncho" from the wool of the vicuña, an animal that serves as the special beast of burden of the jach'aranas. The kinsa rey may be manifest in dreams as a wiraqucha, while the jach'aranas are conceived to be powerful beings who control great wealth (and while the image of a European for the mountain spirits was not mentioned in Yura, it clearly exists elsewhere in the southern Andes). Furthermore, blood sacrifices are made to both, while such sacrifices are normally not made to Pacha Mama alone.[5] The kinsa rey, the jach'aranas, and the condor are joined together in a triad of mutual references.

The Kuraka as Symbolic Nexus

It is thus evident that the Yura have created a series of interrelated concepts which place the kinsa rey into a wider context of thought than a discussion of the object in isolation revealed. The range of meanings can now once again be tied to the kuraqkuna, especially to the chief role, the kurakaship.

As we have seen, just as the jach'aranas are termed "mallkus" and "t'allas," the kuraka couples of the four ayllus are addressed in respectful terms as "Tata Mallku" and "Mama T'alla."[6] The kuraka *qhariwarmi*,[7] or couple, stands, it will be remembered, in a special relationship to the ayllu. First, they sponsor no particular festival in their term of office, yet are always expected to be present to accompany the rest of the kuraqkuna as the latter carry out their festival duties. The Mama T'alla receives no help in direct reciprocity or ayni in her work as the other women kuraqkuna do from relatives and friends. Indeed, the kurakas stand, in a sense, above the normal patterns of mutual assistance that are the norm for all other Yuras in daily life.

This seems to derive from the view that the kurakas are, metaphorically, the mother and father of the ayllu. The same respectful behavior that is ideally shown to parents should also be shown to the kurakas. When the kurakas pay ritual visits to their ayllu households (as they formerly did during the festival of Guadalupe and as they still do at Carnaval), they are said to be visiting their "children." This idea was most clearly expressed in the past, when couples went to the kuraka couple during festivals to ask to be selected to fill a kuraqkuna post in the future. All informants who commented on this topic pointed out that the formal request they made was identical in essential aspects to the ceremony in which a young man asks the parents of his beloved for her hand in marriage. Intriguingly, this rite is called the *kuntur* (the condor). In the kuntur the expectant couple would go to visit the kurakas in the middle of the night. They took alcohol and invited the kuraka couple to drink as they made the formal request. They begged on their knees to be chosen for the post, as the prospective son-in-law will beg his lover's parents.

The kuraka couple, in their role as mother and father of the ayllu, do not enter into the normal "record-keeping" relationships of direct, equivalent exchange between ayllu members, just as an individual's ties to his parents are exempted from such strict accounting: you do not expect the children whom you raise to repay your every action as a parent in strict reciprocity.[8] The special position of the kurakas—reflected in the importance attached to their presence and participation at all the other festivals of the kuraq-kuna—goes beyond a representation of them as parents. What is created is a complex layering of identifications which ground the kurakas (and, because they share many of the same characteristics, the other kuraqkuna) in basic concepts of world order and value. The foregoing descriptions of ritual and belief have pointed to many of those concepts; what remains is to join those ideas more explicitly to the kuraqkuna themselves.

Many of these conceptual linkages lie, once again, with the kinsa rey. The staff of authority is identified with the kuraka, more precisely the male half of the kuraka pair. This identification is apparent in several ways. The kurakas (and the other male incumbents of the kuraqkuna posts) wear a folded poncho on their shoulders as a sign of office during their term; no one else wears the poncho in this way. Likewise, the kinsa rey must always be wrapped in its poncho, the vicuña scarf. This male emphasis is strengthened by the fact that the kinsa rey, beyond being owned only by men, can be touched and carried only by men as well. Again, in the same way that the kuraka is the Tata Mallku, the kinsa rey is properly addressed as "Mallku." During festivals the kinsa rey and the kuraka (and, again, by extension the alcaldes and the jilaqatas) are always together in the same tropa. The kinsa rey becomes the kuraka "sacralized," while the kuraka becomes, in a sense, the kinsa rey in human form.

However, the kinsa rey is also linked with—and as Turner would argue, derives much of its affective power from—certain "gross" physiological referents at its sensual pole. Although no Yura said as much to me directly, its physical form, and certain joking references they made, indicate that the kinsa rey is at one level conceived to be a phallus, one so filled with potency that women cannot approach it. At the yawarchay it is bathed in blood, for the gods are thought to assuage their hunger by consuming the blood spilled; this combines aspects both of death and of food and fertility. The staff is then cleaned with alcohol, which along with corn beer is the primary agent for the transformation of everyday experience to "festive" consciousness, alcoholic inebriation. As the object of libations, the staff, and especially the vicuña scarf, become impreg-

nated with corn beer and other drink. In this way the kinsa rey
reaches the same degree of "personal abandonment" that the Yura
seek in festivals when they drink, as many do, through the stages of
increasing drunkenness to unconsciousness. The kinsa rey, which
represents symbolically the person in the authority role, also comes
to incorporate the physical characteristics of blood, the penis, and
vomit.

As we have seen, however, it is also identified with—or is an
aspect of—those most powerful of spirits, the lords of the mountains, which are themselves linked to the condor, the high-flying
bird which never dies. Again, the idea of the "mallku" is the key
here, uniting a whole series of concepts: the mountain peaks, the
kurakas, condors, the kinsa rey, and the wiraqucha. The kinsa
rey and the Tata Mallku (the kuraka) both participate explicitly
in the spiritual power of the mountain peaks. Furthermore, the
jach'aranas of the peaks are, at a higher level of generality, themselves incorporated into the most inclusive of deities, Pacha Mama.
This is demonstrated ritually in festivals when the kinsa rey is
placed on the ritual table of the hosts in each patio. Informants
agree that this table, the miniature, structured ritual space we discussed previously, is in fact a representation of Pacha Mama. Libations poured to the kinsa rey as it lies on the ritual table are
simultaneously, Yuras affirm, libations poured to Pacha Mama. The
conjunction of these two representations of divinity, one submerged
in the other, makes the ch'allay, the libation, an offering to the
deities which sustain all life.

Thus, in ritual action the kuraqkuna are identified with the powerful lords of the mountain peaks, the condor, and the staff of
authority. These associations place the kuraqkuna in a mediating position between the people of the ayllus who have delegated
to them their authority and the spiritual powers that are thought
to determine the fortunes and the welfare of men. This continues
a centuries-long tradition whereby the kuraqkuna represent their
ayllu to "higher" forces. Yet this interposition has now become a
symbolic act involving a conception of supernatural entities rather
than a direct struggle with the agents of an encompassing state. It

also takes a form that seems peculiarly and thoroughly Andean, as if the centuries of subjugation to a colonial structure of extraction and exploitation had been forgotten.

However, the social reality of subjugation has not been erased, even in the symbolic formulations and acts of the kuraqkuna. A number of references to outside powers and forces reveal a wider conceptual universe within which the symbolic acts take place. For example, the characteristics of the wiraqucha introduce a note of ironic paradox to this otherwise seemingly pure Andean world-view. Our sketch of the history of the kuraqkuna leads us to have expected this, of course, for the fact remains that the Yura and their ancestors have never been free from attempts at external domination, before or after the Spanish invasion. Whatever may have been the ultimate origin in pre-Columbian times of the concept of a white-skinned creator god, every Yura is well aware that today people who approximately fit that description—hispanic Bolivians and foreigners—control the central government and possess the wealth of the cities. This is reflected ambiguously in their conception of the jach'aranas. The mallkus of the peaks transport their silver to Potosí at night to keep the mine flowing; but the wealth, everyone knows, goes not to the peasant or the miner, but to those who control the state. In a similar vein, the kinsa rey is, in a sense, a Yura deity, sharing its power with the kuraqkuna. Yet if it does not have a mass dedicated to it, presided over by an urban (frequently foreign) priest, the staff is nothing but a lifeless stick.

The images linking the kuraqkuna, the kinsa rey, and the mountain spirits contain this ambivalence. The authority that the kinsa rey embodies, while rooted in the supernatural order and related to the existential realities of Yura life, is linked, however implicitly, to the wider domain of society. This perhaps becomes clearest in the festival of Carnaval, the one celebration in the annual cycle in which all the kuraqkuna are, jointly, the hosts. Let us conclude our study of the symbolic world of the kuraqkuna by examining this, the crowning fiesta of the Yura indigenous authorities, first describing the sequence of events of the festival, then interpreting the actions and key symbols in light of the preceding ideas.

The Fiesta of Carnaval

As is true wherever Mardi Gras or Carnival is celebrated, Carnaval in Yura occurs in the last week before Lent. While in the northern hemisphere the festival is traditionally associated with the impending end of winter, in Yura it falls in late summer, about the time when the crops are beginning to ripen. The Yura think of Carnaval, then, as a first-fruits celebration, and their satisfaction at the end of the threat of hunger adds to the significance of the event. Indeed, the most common Quechua name for the festival is Pujllay, "to play." [9] The sense of fertility fulfilled is an underlying theme of Carnaval.

As we saw when we described the busy ritual calendar of kuraqkuna festivals, activities related to these celebrations occupy the attention of a major proportion of the population for weeks of each year. Most of the fiestas of the kuraqkuna, like those sponsored by alfereces, take place in the central village of Yura and are characterized by at least two days of mutual visits from houseyard to houseyard by the troupes of dancers and musicians who accompany the authority couple.

Although at Carnaval no kuraqkuna celebrate the beginning or end of their term of service, all of them—kurakas, alcaldes, jilaqatas, and, formerly, the postillones of the Upper Moiety [10]—actively take part. Indeed, Carnaval is, as we shall see, a kuraqkuna festival par excellence, the apotheosis of the fiestas based on mutual visits. Given the symbolic implications of these visits for the construction of social identity and social groupings, Carnaval is the most insistent of all the celebrations in its emphasis on Yura concepts of internal organization and external relations.

As was evident in the discussion of Reyes, a common theme of the kuraqkuna festivals is the ritualization of concepts of space and geography. All the festivals sponsored by the kuraqkuna not only emphasize the structure of ayllus but also link the multiple groupings of the social order to a conception of their physical territory. This sacralization and "socialization" of space is an aspect of ritual language quite widespread in the Andes (cf. Allen 1981; Rappaport 1985; Urton 1984; Zuidema 1978). In most kuraqkuna festivals this ritual reference to territory takes place largely in the context of festive activities restricted to the central village of Yura. In Carnaval, however, such reference is taken out of the microcosm of Yura and expanded into an elaborate movement of groups throughout the entire territory.

The festival gets under way on a small scale on the Thursday before Ash Wednesday, a day set aside in Bolivia to celebrate the spiritual kinship ties established between women at the baptism of children and in other life-crisis rituals. Although one or two of the authority couples may call together their followers in the central village of Yura, most choose their home hamlets as the starting point for their participation. That afternoon young men and women who are the *ranchos* (hamlet coresidents), relatives, and ritual kin of the kuraqkuna couple begin to arrive at their home, singly or in small groups. As in Reyes, this group will form the core of the tropa; the men once again compose the three or four wayñus that they will play for the female dancers during the next week. Such groups are gathering at the dispersed house compounds of all the kuraqkuna officeholders, in what could be as many as nineteen places in the canton since one such troupe can, potentially, form around each of the nineteen different posts that the Yura maintain within the kuraqkuna system. As in all Yura festivals both *aqha* (corn beer) and cane alcohol flow freely from the very beginning. The events described in the following pages all take place in the context of a thoroughgoing consumption of alcoholic drink.

The Journey to the Edge

The participants spend the first night in the houseyards of the various kuraqkuna sponsors they have decided to accompany. Friday morning, soon after dawn, the celebration begins—again, as in Reyes, the young men pick up their instruments to play, and the women hold hands and dance in a circle around them. The small numbers of dancers and musicians that start out this first morning will swell greatly in the days to come. After all have eaten and drunk, the troupe sets off together, dancing along the rough paths and rocky riverbeds of canton Yura to the wayñus of the flute and drum. Each troupe carries with it, in a place of honor, its authority's kinsa rey.

However, rather than dancing to the pueblo of Yura, the various troupes set out to visit all the dispersed households of their ayllu, one by one, over a period of five to six days. Every authority couple has a traditional route which takes them from their home hamlet to a standard beginning point. They then move from there in an unvarying geographic sequence to the ayllu boundaries, the point where their ayllu meets the very edge of Yura territory, before they turn back toward the center (always by a path distinct from the one they followed out).[11] Sometimes journeying through long stretches of uninhabited, arid valleys or along solitary mountain trails, the troupe travels from hamlet to hamlet, playing their wayñus and dancing; the visits never stop.

At each houseyard the visit is carried out in essentially the same way. Each householder, aware that the troupe is arriving, has prepared a sink'a llijlla in the center of their house patio. The visit begins as the troupe enters the houseyard with flutists and drummers playing and women dancers shuffling in step to the music. The bearer of the kinsa rey follows them in and lays it, loosely wrapped in its vicuña scarf, on the sink'a llijlla. The householders see to it that the kuraqkuna couple are served corn beer and alcohol and set down a pot of beer in the center of the circle formed by the musicians. The hosts then bring out a potsherd filled with hot coals in order to offer incense to the kinsa rey. As in the visits to the ayllu houseyards in Yura during Reyes, the musicians and dancers form concentric circles and continue to play and dance; the men are on the inside, while the women, holding hands, surround them. The householder couple waits until the musicians finish their song and the dancing stops. Then the husband, followed by the wife, pour libations of corn beer and alcohol to the staff; they also both sprinkle coca leaf over the staff, and most kneel and offer it incense. The musicians stand silently until these acts are completed, then they take up their song again. After circling for a few minutes, and without missing a beat, the troupe breaks its circle and files out through the houseyard door. They move on to the next house and repeat the performance.

The specific route followed by the authority couple in the days of visits depends on the post they hold. The top two officials of each of the four major ayllus—the kuraka and the alcalde—follow the same circuit; if the two happen to be from the same group of hamlets their followers may join together to form a single troupe. The jilaqatas of the preeminent minor ayllu segments (which are, as we saw in figure 3.2, the jilaqatas of ayllus Jatun Qullana, Jatun Qhurqa, Jatun Chiquchi, and Wisijsa Qullana) also follow the routes of the major ayllu authorities and thus visit the same houses as the kuraka. The jilaqatas of Sullk'a Qhurqa,[12] Sullk'a Chiquchi, and Sallwi each have their own routes. Although the Qullana authorities pass through the area of Phajcha, a herding zone in the far south of Yura territory, the Phajcha alcalde[13] begins his route there and visits households in the southernmost reaches of the area, ranchos that are also visited by the Agregado jilaqata of Qullana and, in most years, by the Qullana Qhapaqa jilaqata as well. The Sullk'a Qullana jilaqata normally accompanies the jilaqata of Jatun Qullana.

The details of these journeys—which route each troupe takes and whom they visit—would weigh heavily even on readers quite familiar with the diverse geography of Yura canton, so I will not go into them here. The general goal of all the troupes is the same, however: to follow the kuraqkuna couple and their staff of authority through the ayllu's communities out to the *mojones,* the mountain peaks which mark the boundaries of the entire ethnic region. As we saw in chapter 5, early sources have revealed that these mojones were established soon after the foundation of the reducción of Yura in 1575 and have remained unchanged ever since.[14] At the base of these peaks, down in the river valleys, are rock cairns that serve as boundary markers. Certain of these peaks are the traditionally designated termini on the outward journey of the kuraqkuna troupes.

After several days of visits and travel, then, the troupes arrive at the boundary. As the culmination of the first half of the pilgrimage, this is seen as a moment of special significance. The members of the troupe make any repairs that are needed on the stacked rocks of the boundary cairn. A ritual table is set up and the kinsa rey placed on it. The authority couple then leads the troupe in pouring libations and burning incense to the kinsa rey and the cairn, an offering made simultaneously to the staff and the peak.

The Journey Back to the Center

The libations at the distant mojones mark only the halfway mark on the journey. The troupes then turn inward, toward the center, and continue to visit more ayllu households, drinking, dancing, and taking the kinsa rey to each house for the offerings it will receive there. As the days pass the festival builds in intensity, and the dances become more elaborate. Many of the young men put on spectacular condor and puma costumes over the traditional male dress, the unku. Some have also constructed an object called a *kuntur uma* (condor head), made of a framework of four thin poles covered either with skeins of colorful yarn or with the yarn woven into a pattern. It may stand three meters tall and is topped with the dried head of a condor.[15] The costumed men, including those who carry the kuntur uma, begin to dance along with the women. The women have tied their best carrying cloth on their backs and bear their finest weavings within it; most carry brightly colored flags as they dance. The dancers form lines and dance in a braid, the lines weaving in and out, as they visit the houseyards and pass through the hamlets and villages on their route.

By Tuesday, the day before Ash Wednesday, the different troupes have already covered a considerable portion of their routes. Many of them join together in several of the larger settlements for a ritual feast of cheese, cooked corn grains, and meat. These feasts take place according to ayllus, such that the higher levels of Yura organization—the major ayllus, even the moieties—are made socially visible. Most of the Qullana groups join together at the large village of Thatuka, the Wisijsa authorities meet at Charquyu, and several of the Qhurqa and Chiquchi groups meet in Thauru. Sullk'a Chiquchi celebrates its feast in Ch'ujñi Uqu, and the Phajcha alcaldes

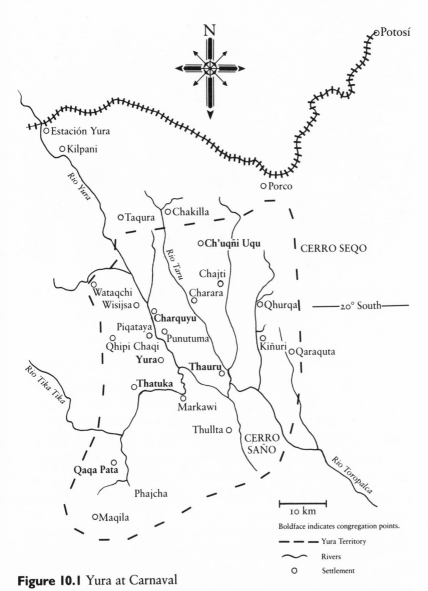

Figure 10.1 Yura at Carnaval

meet in Qaqa Pata, the main hamlet of that area (places that are highlighted in the accompanying map of Yura, figure 10.1). All of these ranchos have either chapels or *calvarios* (shrines), and the special meal is preceded by dancing and "braiding" in the yard in front of the sacred image housed in each. As is common when

Entering Yura at Carnaval

dance troupes of different ayllus come together, there is a sense of challenge and competition in the volume of their music and the vigorousness of the dance as they confront each other.

On the morning of Ash Wednesday each troupe moves toward the core village of Yura, visiting the ranchos of their ayllus closest to the center. During the afternoon all the groups enter the village and come together in its plaza, the principal meeting-place and dance ground for the Yura unitary ayllu, where they put on an elaborate display of music and dance.

As we saw earlier in Reyes, the central plaza of Yura is transformed into a kind of microcosm of Yura canton; each of the four corners of the central square becomes an "altar" of one of the four major ayllus, Qullana and Wisijsa in the south and Qhurqa and Chiquchi in the north (see figure 8.2). In the center stands the Rollo, a red stone pillar located at the intersection of the four rock walkways which begin in each of the four corners. As occurs in the Entrada of the festival of Reyes, the troupes enter the square according to their moiety affiliation, group by group. Every troupe stops and pours libations at each of the four corners—that is, at

Carnaval: The Dance around the Central Plaza

the four altars of the ayllus—as they dance their way around the outside edge of the plaza. Again, they stop for a longer time for libations at the corner which is the altar of their own major ayllu. Once the circuit around the plaza is complete, the dancers turn to the interior of the square. The musicians form a circle around the Rollo. The dancers, maintaining their files for dancing in braids, undertake an elaborate sequence of movements which takes them to the sides and corners of the square. As they arrive at the edge of the square, their outward movement is reversed as they interweave in the braid and return to the center; the condors and pumas lead and the flag-bearing women follow behind. The kinsa rey, which was carried in the vanguard of the troupe in the initial movement around the square, is held by a designated participant at the base of the Rollo, where he remains standing during the time the troupe is in the plaza. As the dancers finally join the circle around the Rollo, the stone pillar, according to informants, serves to represent the joining together of all the component groups into the total unity of the maximal Yura ayllu.

The formal entrance on Ash Wednesday is the prelude to a short stay in Yura. On Thursday morning patio visits like those that have already occurred throughout the canton continue. Most of the people present in town, of course, are the troupes of the authorities themselves. But participants do not restrict their movements to the other authorities alone, for they also visit the houses of the few mestizo residents of Yura, starting with the corregidor and the intendente, or town mayor. Many members of this group, the vecinos, are now reluctant to provide the corn beer and alcohol necessary to serve the visitors, and thus plan to be away from home that morning to prevent the troupes from entering their houseyards; for even the vecinos feel obliged to fête the celebrants. Yura informants report that in the past the vecinos participated more fully.

Thursday afternoon the troupes enter the plaza one last time before they leave the central village. The same complex dance patterns that were used the previous day are repeated. Interestingly, this last dance in the plaza, which in Reyes and all other kuraqkuna festivals is the kacharpaya, the farewell to the festival, is not termed that on this occasion. Rather, people simply say that they "go home" (the Quechua term used is *lluqsipuy*, to leave or go out). Although visits are still made by some troupes as they travel to their home villages, and Carnaval continues informally in the hamlets until the following Sunday (Domingo de Tentación, when most Yuras set up a ritual table in their houseyard and pour libations to the first of the maturing crops), the central events of the festival culminate on this day, when the troupes perform their "going out." Given this sequence of events, then, let us turn to an analysis of the symbolic context.

Carnaval and Symbolic Ambiguity

The festival of Carnaval is a succession of ritual acts in which the persons filling the ayllu authority roles accompany the symbolically powerful kinsa rey, the staff of authority, through the individual constituent households of the ayllus out to the boundary markers. The movement begins in an outward direction, from the central, "human" home areas to the solitary, uninhabited extreme points at the periphery of the integrated territory. Here the kinsa rey and

Carnaval Dancers

the boundary shrine (both of which represent and are linked to the powerful lords of the mountains) receive the offerings of their human "children." Then the troupes turn back inward, and the accumulated expression of ayllu membership and participation builds as the groups gradually join together at higher levels of organization. Finally, all the ayllus and all Yura join together in one moment of union in the plaza of the central village.[16]

Carnaval thus provides the Yura with a clear means to reflect upon, and to reconstitute, their ayllus. The ayllu (embodied as it is in the sponsoring authority's troupe) directly reincorporates each household into its "body" through the ritual visits. The libations poured and the incense burned at every household's ritual table in honor of the principal symbol of the ayllu—the kinsa rey—serve to reintegrate that family into the social unit. Their affiliation with the ayllu is thereby affirmed.

The hierarchy of ayllus—minor, major, moiety, and unitary—becomes more evident as the troupes move through the territory, outward and then inward, coming together at the feasts in the larger settlements and finally in the central plaza of Yura. In an oppositional and yet complementary fashion the boundaries among groups and their territories are made manifest. In the process the kuraq-kuna have not only reasserted the integrity of their conception of social geography, but they have also proceeded to unite the ayllus into ever larger groups at higher levels of abstraction. As they do this they draw a schematic map of Yura social organization. In the end they proclaim the unity and indivisibility of the whole area, dancing around the Rollo in Yura.

These actions are more than socially symbolic, however, for they refer explicitly to a conception of divinity that links the movement of groups through a territory with spiritual entities which oversee the well-being of all within that territory—the people, their fields, and their flocks. At one level this is evident in the generalized ine-briation that is a social prerequisite for participation. The drunk-enness that results from consuming vast quantities of corn beer and alcohol is the essential state of consciousness for festive interaction. Allen argues it is more than that, though, when she says: "The purpose of ritual drinking and the ensuing intoxication is to open channels of communication with other categories of being, particu-larly with sacred places" (Allen 1984:164). But the particularities of this conception of the sacred will become clearer if we attempt to synthesize the roles of four central symbols of the festival: the ch'allay (the pouring of libations at the ritual tables); the kinsa rey; the mojones (the rock cairn at the boundary of the territory); and the central plaza's stone pillar, the Rollo.

The pouring of libations in an ayllu member's houseyard that takes place in the course of Carnaval has a dual end: first, of ensur-ing a right relation with Pacha Mama[17] (recalling that all ch'allays are, at one level, directed to this conception of the fertility of the earth), and, second, of appeasing and enlisting the power of the kinsa rey. The kinsa rey represents the power and authority of the group to which the libation pourer or incense burner is assert-ing a claim; through these acts the householders place themselves in the care of, and under the authority of, the kuraqkuna who carry the staff. In this sense the ch'allays have an eminently social goal.

As for the kinsa rey, two primary foci of meaning come to the fore during Carnaval: its semantic links with the corporateness of the ayllus and its links with the spiritual power of the jach'aranas, the lords of the mountain peaks. The identification of the kinsa rey with the kuraqkuna, especially with the kuraka, is at the core of this first conceptual focus. At Carnaval, by means of the movements of the various kuraqkuna troupes through the ayllu's households, the kinsa rey becomes increasingly united, in a direct, physical way, with the entire ayllu. While this embodiment of the ayllu is suggested in other kuraqkuna festivals such as Reyes, it is acted out in Carnaval as family after family offer incense to the staff while it lies in their houseyards on the ritual tables they have constructed.

But the kinsa rey also combines with that the uncertain and potentially dangerous power of the condor and the jach'aranas, who are in Yura thinking a source of wealth and power. The jach'aranas are, again, an ambiguous and often capricious force in the world; they must be treated correctly in ritual in order to ensure that they will act benevolently toward humans. Yet, if propitiated properly, the jach'aranas share their spiritual power with humans, a power expressed in the fecundity of the flocks. Indeed, the identification made between humans and llamas in a number of ritual contexts [18] suggests that proper relations with the jach'aranas will ensure not only material rewards but human fertility and reproduction as well.

This dimension of the staff's power is most evident when the troupes arrive at the boundary markers of their territory, the mojones, to pour libations for the ayllu as a whole. The kinsa rey's symbolic identification with the male condor, the mallku, the "bird that never dies," as well as with the jach'aranas, the lords of the mountain peaks, is at play. The high summits at the boundary of Yura territory are perhaps the most powerful peaks of all—those that surround, enclose, and protect the lands and people within them. It is therefore not surprising that in the offerings at the boundary marker the kinsa rey, this paramount symbol of the social group which has become embued with the ayllu in the days of the outward movement (but which also has direct links in belief to the gods of the mountains) is brought into contact with the point of maximum power of the jach'aranas. Here the accumulated offerings of the ayllu households are joined to the power of the mojón, the representation of the lord of the mountain peak which, as the boundary of the Yura ethnic group, can be seen to envelop and protect the ayllu. The kinsa rey, a primary manifestation of ayllu authority, is thus joined to the most peripheral geographic point which the Yura proclaim to be under their ayllus' control. The edges are again fixed, really and in ritual, and the assertion is made that human society—the Yura ayllu—extends up to this point. This act reaffirms the continuing validity of their conception of their territory.

The trip to the boundary thus is designed to bring the power of the kinsa rey, a symbol combining the supremely social and the thoroughly cultural, face to face with the edge of culture and society. In the offerings of incense, corn beer, coca, and alcohol made at the rock cairn to the mojón mountain peak and to the staff, social groups (themselves intimately linked to the specific geography of Yura territory) are confirmed in their process of reconstruction. Symbolically, these acts seem to deny the forces of chaos in society and nature, and to renew a single, particular construction of reality. The tenuous and fleeting institutions and sets of meanings that a people—situated at a particular time and in a particular place—create and maintain are imposed (once again) on nonhuman reality at the "edge" of the world, an end accomplished largely by sacralizing it. Our own society's unrelenting imposition of meaning on the nonhuman world is so thorough that this dramaturgical act by the Yura may seem paltry by comparison. Nevertheless, in the desert valleys of the southern Andes, where wrenching a bare subsistence from the land is a central and preoccupying focus of human life, the ritual at the mojón borders on the audacious.

As the troupe leaves the mojón and returns toward the center, men, who in other contexts rarely dance in kuraqkuna festivals without musical instruments, now take up condor wings, the condor head, and puma costumes. All three reflect the contact with the jach'aranas, the first two as aspects of the representation of the lords of the mountains, and the third closely identified with them.[19]

All of this symbolic complex—ritual tables in each house, the offering of corn beer to spiritual entities identified with the boundary mountain peaks, the focus on the re-creation of the ayllu in their hierarchical arrangement, the music and the dance—could be analyzed in terms of a strictly Andean cultural tradition. These ritual actions seemingly relate to internal preoccupations with organization and to indigenous conceptions of spiritual power and efficacy. That this indigenousness of the festival is not merely an imposition of the observer is confirmed by the fact that women carry their best weavings in a bundle on their backs and the men return to the unku, a dress style that they or, in many cases today, their fathers, have otherwise abandoned. The wearing of the unku was a basic indicator of indigenous identity in the past, while the weaving of textiles is for women a definitional symbol of their own productivity and creativity, demonstrating their mastery of a skill which mestiza women in the central village and urban women do not possess.

However, this careful elaboration of the "Andean" leads us to question why such an emphasis is perceived to be necessary. This indigenousness is all the more interesting when we recall the intense involvement four centuries ago of the Yura in the mining metropolis that was Potosí. As we have also seen, the Yura ethnic identity itself is a creation with roots in colonial administrative mechanisms established long after the Spanish invasion; the use of the name as an ethnic label does not appear in the record for many decades. Indeed, Yura as a separate entity developed only after the gradual fragmentation of a larger ethnic grouping during the first century after the establishment of the reducciones. The account of their ethnogenesis has only recently become available to the Yura, however, and could not be a factor in the cultivated folklorism of Carnaval.

The symbolic role of the kuraqkuna should be highlighted in this context, especially since Carnaval is the one kuraqkuna festival in which all participate. Although the kuraqkuna are charged, in the course of their service, with extensive ritual sponsorship throughout an elaborate annual cycle, the entire authority role structure has until quite recently continued to bear the primary responsibility of bargaining with the state, of acting as an intermediary between the ayllus and the structures of the dominant society. The kuraqkuna's goal has been to ensure relative autonomy and continued access to lands by providing the state and its representatives with a series of services. As we saw in chapter 4, each post has specialized in the performance of some activity related to ayllu-state relations. To summarize, the alcalde is an assistant to the corregidor, the local Bolivian official residing in the canton capital. The corregidor has been, since the beginning of the republican period after 1825, an outsider bringing state authority (and, very frequently, oppressive forms of state extraction) into the heart of the local-level ethnic group.

The abolished post of postillón served as a courier and mail carrier, a service carried out for the state, its officials, and class representatives. Most of the correspondence was not, of course, from one illiterate Quechua-speaking ayllu member to another, but was rather related to business or governmental ends or to the personal needs of the vecino local elite. Finally, the jilaqata was perhaps most clearly linked to the ayllus' response to state impositions, for beyond festival sponsorship the jilaqatas were responsible for collecting the tasa, the collective head tax, from the members of the minor ayllus. The tasa is still collected in Potosí and paid by the ayllus of Yura.

The ayllus themselves have been structured, albeit unintentionally, according to state interests in the effort to keep track of the taxable population; the wealth of census and tax records that we have reviewed from 1595 to 1889 demonstrate considerable concern with the details of ayllu structure. At times, such as in the early nineteenth century when a major part of state revenues came from the indigenous head tax, the state was greatly concerned about the maintenance of ayllu integrity—although at other times the state has attempted, as it does today, to destroy ayllu unity through the privatization of lands. But even when the state no longer cared whether or not these Andean social groupings continued to exist, ayllus were retained by indigenous populations largely as a strategy consistent with their conception of the relationship with the state, based on the idea that the payment of the ayllu tasa would ensure their continued autonomy and access to resources.[20] That is, the Yura still invest considerable effort in both the symbolic and real re-creation of the ayllu because, according to Yura informants' thinking, only by paying the tasa as a group do they fulfill their side of what they perceive to be a semi-reciprocal relationship with the state which allows them to retain control of their lands.[21]

Carnaval: A Dialogue between the Ayllu and the State

Carnaval thus provides the context for a series of symbolic acts which stress in ritual terms the kuraqkuna's historically mediating and shielding role. The festive troupes that form around the authorities come to embody the various levels of ayllu organization; the visits they carry out demarcate and reconfirm the social and geographic reality of the ayllu units. The kinsa rey, the Yura leader's staff of office, symbolically refers to generative power, to the authority of the kuraqkuna, and—in the context of the libations poured at each household—to the corporate nature of the group. As the ritual sequence continues, the staff also becomes identified with the territorial boundary markers and with a sacralized embodiment of these, the jach'aranas, the lords of the mountain peaks.

This layering of meanings becomes more complex, however, as these supernatural conceptions make reference to powers beyond the local level. For instance, the jach'aranas, which guard the territorial unity of Yura, are seen as controlling the wealth of the mines. Given the history of the Potosí region, the control of the mines by Spaniards and labor in the mines by Andeans is in local folklore a kind of essential representation of exploitation and the extraction of wealth (cf. Rasnake 1988). The kinsa rey and the jach'aranas are also both conceived in certain contexts to take the form of tall, light-skinned Europeans. Thus the act of pouring libations to the staffs and the boundary markers, which can be seen as a confirmation of group identity and of ayllu boundaries, has as well a strong element of propitiation of outside supernatural powers in order to ensure the integrity of those lands and boundaries; and these powers are represented in a form peculiarly similar to the national dominant classes. The libations poured at the boundary marker thus seem to carry out in symbolic form an act parallel to the ayllu members' careful collection of the land tax, the goal of which is also to ensure that the state will respect the ayllus' control of lands.

Once the boundaries are confirmed and the propitiation to the outside powers made, the troupes then return toward the center, gradually demarcating in sequential order the higher levels of the ayllu order until they join together in the central village. Once there, the symbolic dialogue with the state continues as the troupes dance in the village. The festival ends with final visits paid to vecino households and mestizo authorities[22] and with the culminating dance around the Rollo.

The Rollo is by far the most ambiguous of the symbols of Carnaval. On one hand, the ritual action occurring at the entrance of the troupes into the central plaza at Carnaval, as is also true of such entrances from the town patios in other kuraqkuna festivals, demonstrates that the Rollo serves as a symbol for the overall unity of Yura. The design of the plaza, in which the four stone walkways have been built like the spokes of a square wheel (one from each ayllu shrine to the Rollo) confirms our conclusion that the Rollo serves as a symbol for the overall unity of Yura. But there is an important note of ambivalence in the Yura conception of the Rollo, reflected in ideas about its origins. Their oral tradition ascribes its construction to the Spaniards of the colonial period. The 1679 document described in chapter 5 states that the Rollo was the place where Choquevilca and the other hereditary rulers, acting for their Spanish overlords, carried out punishments; those who were convicted of crimes were tied to the pillar when they were flogged (ANB EC 1679, no. 22:fol. 4r). One present-day informant claims that the head of Juan Pablo Choquevilca, the last officially recognized Yura governing kuraka, who was murdered in 1781 for his support of the Spanish Crown, is buried at the foot of the Rollo. The ambiguity of the Rollo is underscored by that fact that many Yura say today that the monument is also properly called the *kawiltu* or *cabildo*,[23] a remnant of the name of the form of government that Spanish policy imposed on indigenous groupings over four centuries ago.

Located in the very heart of the microcosm of the Yura social order created in the central plaza, the Rollo is thus a hybrid monument. Its phallic power is simultaneously an image of the totality of the Yura ethnic group and of the imposition of state power. Dancing around the Rollo, with the kinsa rey held at its base and with men dressed as figures of condors and pumas, the obelisk becomes for the Yura an evocative vehicle to synthesize the contradictions that arise from group autonomy and state control, by providing a conceptual means to unite the power inherent in the two.

In the ritual action of Carnaval, then, the people of Yura symbolically define state control as an inevitable element of social life. The logic of the relationship with this state is not unlike that with other sources of power: the state is potentially dangerous, capable of inexplicable acts, and demanding of correct propitiation. If proper offerings are made in services and money, then the state, like the jach'aranas, will permit the Yura to live in peace and, perhaps, to flourish. The Yura, for their part, are concerned with the never-ending need to ensure access to and control of their fields and pasturelands. The cultural performance of Carnaval, with its sacralization of land and territorial boundaries, with its identification of spiritual power with the ayllu order and its authorities, and with the ambivalent propitiation of the symbols of outside power, serves to accomplish that.

ll

CONCLUSION
Symbolic Power and
Cultural Resistance

The urban traveler who climbs aboard a truck in Potosí for the fifteen-hour trip to the isolated railhead of Uyuni cannot help but note the distinctiveness of the indigenous people as he enters Yura territory about halfway through his journey. As the truck bounces across the high plain of Chakilla and skirts a long ravine leading to the hamlet of Wisijsa, the first thing our traveler may note is the singular uniformity of the women's dress: the peculiar, round felt hat; the dark overskirt, tied tightly with a heavy woven belt about the waist; the striking fineness of the weave of the homespun cloth. He may also see some older men dressed in similar fashion, wearing the same hat and a voluminous shirt woven like the overskirt, worn over knee-length pants. If he listens to a conversation between two people, the traveler may note that they, like others along the road, do not speak the Spanish of the city but rather prefer to speak Quechua. He may be intrigued by the large stone houses he sees in Yura (many built on multiple levels to take advantage of the valley slopes), and by the terraced fields that make it possible for the desert valleys to bloom.

What the traveler who merely passes through this region will not be aware of, however, is the complex arrangement of groupings into which the Yura organize themselves. Nor would he know of their commitment to their festivals, or the coherence of their ritual as an expression of their worldview and values, or, perhaps most important, the sense that the Yura possess of themselves as a social entity.

Many factors have contributed to this capacity of the Yura to retain their sense of group identity, exemplified by the structure of the ayllus and by the great public rituals. It has been my contention in these pages, however, that one key element in the foundation of their unity and cultural distinctiveness has been the institution of the indigenous authorities, the kuraqkuna.

Let us review what we have attempted to accomplish in this study. We began with a description of the ecology of the Yura region and a discussion of its people. We then turned, in chapter 3, to a consideration of Yura social organization. Here we saw that in spite of the confusing dispersal of houseyard and hamlet along the rocky, arid valleys of the zone, the Yura organize themselves into various sorts of social groups—minor and major ayllus, Upper and Lower Moieties, and an inclusive unitary ayllu which incorporates all the Yuras of the entire region within definite, traditional boundaries. We then portrayed in some detail the ayllu authorities —jilaqatas, alcaldes, and kurakas. In the course of examining these various topics it became evident that in Yura we are speaking of a self-conscious group with a shared ethnic identity and with a set of leadership roles which administer certain public functions within a fixed territory. The Yura maintain a complex internal organization which unites them into a single entity vis-à-vis neighboring ethnic groups and the urban-oriented mestizos who live in the town center.

Some might argue that this sense of ethnic identity and the corresponding continued existence of the kuraqkuna, while an interesting ethnographic phenomenon, can simply be attributed to social isolation, to the difficulty of the mountainous terrain, and to the distance from the cities. Perhaps these rural folk hold on to their quaint customs because they are, and always have been, cut off from the great currents of urban life and Western culture. Perhaps ayllus and jilaqatas are nothing more than ghosts of a dead past, a relic of the utter remoteness of these valleys.

However, our examination of the kuraqkuna's past in chapters 5 and 6 challenged the idea that the Yura and their ancestors have been, through the centuries, segregated socially from the wider society. Indeed, studies of the historical sources available for the region reveal that they have never been cut off, from the time of the Spanish invasion or before, from involvement in broader processes and entities outside their territory, especially in the mining economy and the state. The sixteenth-century Wisijsas moved about a large territory to farm their dispersed lands and to care for their flocks within the vertical archipelago they controlled. Their hereditary leaders visited the Inka capital of Cuzco and their men served in the Inkas' armies in what is today Ecuador.

Soon after the arrival of the Spaniards, the Wisijsas and their contemporaries were forced to mobilize great amounts of resources to pay the heavy tribute imposed on them. Long before the viceroy Toledo regularized the mita, they were working in the mines for Spaniards (Zavala 1978:27, 28). As the Wisijsas became fragmented through time into smaller groupings such as the Yuras, they were still governed by their own hereditary leaders, who found themselves in an intermediary position between the Spanish elite and the state on the one hand, and the ayllus on the other. There is little indication in the sources, then, that the Yura were isolated, or saw themselves as isolated, in their high Andean valleys. The Yura did not see themselves as beyond the reach of the state in 1679 when some of them complained to Spanish authorities about the abuses of the kurakas; nor were they unaware of their relationship to higher authorities in the 1720s when they asked the colonial regime to lower their tribute payments due to epidemics and lobbied for reforms in the mita; nor were they isolated in 1781 when they joined the widespread revolt against the colonial regime and its agents.

Finally, even after the abolition of the Potosí mita in the early nineteenth century, the Yura can hardly be said to have been living in isolation, set apart from the larger society, as they continued to form part of the indigenous base of the population which financed the Bolivian state through their taxes. We also see the Yura using fiscal categories that were imposed on them by state taxation policies to raise their relative status within the group. In the twentieth century the Yura accepted the Huanchaca Company's electric plant in Punutuma, began to journey to Pulacayo to sell their goods and to work, and continued to go, as they always have, to Potosí. Fighting in the War of the Chaco and traveling to Argentina and the lowland areas of Bolivia for seasonal work have only served to broaden their contacts with other regions and with the state. Isolation from the mainstream is no explanation for the cultural continuities we have observed.

Yet research into the history of the kuraqkuna reveals much more than the Yuras' involvement through time in a wide spectrum of social relationships. Most important, we saw that in the eighteenth century the nature of indigenous leadership changed in a significant way. Andean authorities in Yura, formerly powerful hereditary lords who identified with the Spanish elite and who ruled (more often than not) with an iron hand, have today become egalitarian. Today's ayllu leaders serve on a rotational basis, enunciating communal decisions that have been reached through practical consensus. In comparison with the kurakas of old, they wield little power to coerce and to punish.

This shift from the dominant local indigenous leaders of the past to the communitarian authorities of the present was a general process throughout the region that has become Bolivia. We now understand more, however, about the specifics of the transformation. In Yura, the 1781 rebellion is the key event. As we saw, Choquevilca's assassination was a dramatic reaction to the real contradictions of the principal kuraka role; it resolved what had been an unresolvable conflict between the kuraka as a symbol of unity for the ayllu and the kuraka as a procurator through which the state carried out its extractive goals. The adoption of a system whereby the authority roles were rotational, drawn from the ayllu at large, and egalitarian in nature meant applying to the higher-level kurakas an arrangement that presumably was already in use for the jilaqatas.

At first this new system was apparently less effective in squeezing out the tribute required by the colonial and republican regimes, for in both 1797 and 1830 the chief kuraka, from ayllu Qullana, was a mestizo. Soon the post of corregidor was established within the canton and filled from the growing group of vecinos—that urban-oriented population with direct ties to the European elite—whose ties to the ayllus were either attenuated or nonexistent. The corregidor, not bound to the ayllus through links of reciprocity and kinship (as are the kurakas and the rest of the kuraqkuna), could carry out with fewer qualms the demands of the central government. What had taken place, then, was a leveling of the ayllu authority roles, accompanied by a shift in the structure of power from an internal hierarchy to an external one. The inequality that existed between ayllu members and their own ethnic kurakas was transformed into stratification between the ayllus (represented by their rotational authorities) and the vecinos in the central village, who identify themselves wholeheartedly with the urban classes and, ultimately, with the state.

It might be argued that these changes through the centuries—the breakup of the Wisijsa ethnic group, the shift from hereditary leadership to rotational roles—have been so fundamental that it is misleading to speak of continuities at all. However, the case for using this term derives from the real and identifiable retention of Andean cultural elements in a wide range of social forms and practices. Beyond the fact that the human population is continuous over the years, we find, for example, the same major ayllus and the same ranchos today that appeared in the earliest records. Ayllu organization, in spite of its reduction in scale, has also remained quite similar; Qullana is still the principal ayllu of the Upper Moiety, and the Lower Moiety is still composed of Qhurqa and Chiquchi, now merged with the former Araya Chacti and Manaya Chacti. Furthermore, the weight of evidence supports the conclusion that the system of symbols utilized by the Yura, discussed in chapters 8–10, is largely derived from the Andean past.

It should not be thought, however, that continuity implies stasis. When it is argued that certain peasant groups in the Andes have retained elements from their past, it would be foolish to conclude that change—often significant change—has not occurred. One can only wonder, rather, why the severe impositions of the Spanish colonial state did not completely destroy the people and their culture. Yet the Yura and many other groups responded creatively to the changing power situation by applying certain enduring principles and concepts to new contexts. One example of this we have just discussed —the emergence in Yura at the end of the eighteenth century of a rotational, egalitarian kuraka. As a result, the traditional functions of the hereditary kuraka thus were split between the kuraqkuna of the ayllus and the post of canton corregidor.

If, however, this model of the bifurcation of the hereditary kuraka role is accurate, with what are the kuraqkuna left? Perhaps one way to address this question is to examine certain key terms which have underlain the discussion from the beginning but have not been addressed explicitly—the ideas of power and of authority. While the sources indicate that the hereditary kurakas had power —for example, the power to make certain decisions for the group, to resolve disputes and to punish, and to mobilize resources and human labor—it is rather more difficult to specify the nature of the power that today's kuraqkuna enjoy. Given this fact, is it even appropriate to term them "authorities"?

The concepts of power and authority are always linked in social analysis, even though satisfactory definitions of both terms have not been easy to achieve.[1] The most widely accepted formulation of these concepts is perhaps that of Max Weber, who defines power as "the possibility of imposing one's will upon the behavior of other persons" (1978:942). Weber feels that power is too broad a term to be useful for sociological research, however; he goes on to develop the concept of "domination" (as his *Herrschaft* is usually translated)—power resulting from a socially recognized position of leadership. Two aspects basic to this concept, according to Bendix's exegesis (1977:292), are the necessity of "compliance with a command" as well as "evidence of the subjective acceptance of commands by the ruled." The reasons why a social group accepts a particular system of domination vary, according to Weber: such motives as self-interest, emotional attachment, convention, response to coercion, or the recognition of economic power may be at work. Yet when individuals uphold an order because of their belief in the legitimacy of the system, that is, when leaders exercise their domination legitimately, then the leaders have "authority." Authority, then, is legitimate domination (Weber 1978:31–38).

When Weber turns to why social actors ascribe legitimacy to the existing order he is most interested in distinguishing legal and rational modes from tradition and emotional attachment. This lack of curiosity about the complexity of the so-called "traditional" makes this part of his definitional exercise less valuable. As Weber himself recognized, all systems of authority have complex and mixed bases of legitimacy, and even the most rationally constructed legal system can acquire a weight of meaning that leads us into the realm of symbolic analysis.

Weber's reluctance to consider more profoundly the ways that traditional forms of legitimacy are maintained in social action can be attributed largely to two factors: his greater interest in the power of charismatic authority to effect change; and his focus on the move in Europe toward a rationalization of systems of domination in legal and bureaucratic forms. This was accompanied by an emphasis on Western forms of power and authority which are based on centralized control and the imposition of decisions and orders. This approach does not deal well with those cases in which decision-making is either more fragmented or more consensual than it is in the feudal, absolutist, or bureaucratic models he was developing. Even in situations where there is an elaborate concept of authority vested in particular offices, the nature of that authority may not be rooted in the ability to command obedience.

Such is, as we have seen, the case in Yura today. As we have just argued, the native authorities of the sixteenth century did indeed have power, the ability to control the actions of others and to demand that their subjects obey them. Our sources also suggest that they had authority; that is, their domination was accepted as legitimate. It was grounded in a series of factors including hereditary succession, the greater control of productive resources and human labor, wealth, and the ability to employ coercive power, as well as in the presumed symbolic dimensions of their position, that is, their identification with the deities.

Reviewing the historical development of the kurakas in terms of these concepts, we see that the bases of legitimacy of the native lords were challenged by the Spanish invasion and the creation of the Spanish colonial regime. The kurakas became the primary intermediaries for the extraction of surplus and labor, most notably in the demands for workers in the Potosí mines and for the payment of the head tax. The ayllu order was confirmed, yet distorted and fragmented, by the process of colonial consolidation. The kurakas themselves vacillated in their roles between identification with the Spanish overlords and efforts to maintain the cohesion and the few prerogatives of the Andean groups beneath their control; they struggled to be both the Andean native lords who protected their people by interacting with the spirit world and the state, and the arm of the oppressive alien world that was working to impose a new order.

The bases of legitimacy finally gave way in the revolutionary events of 1781. The native authorities, at least as they had previously been constituted, ceased to exist. But, in the debris of that defeat, the two necessary functions of the roles—the imposition of state demands, and the formulation and maintenance of group identity and cohesion—were separated and reassigned to new protagonists.

What, then, of domination and authority? On one hand, each of the three Yura kuraqkuna posts retains a real civil component—the jilaqatas collect the tasa; the alcaldes fill police functions; and the kurakas are called upon to mobilize the labor of the ayllus and to represent the Andean peasants before the vecino authorities. I would argue, however, that the form of power or domination (in Weber's terms) exercised by the occupants of the authority roles has changed. Their power today is a cohesive, rather than a coercive, force, designed to bring people together in the context of group ritual. The kuraqkuna serve primarily as agents to create consensus when public disputes or demands threaten group unity. They enunciate the sense of the ayllu in public contexts; most important, they sponsor, through ritual, the ongoing re-creation of the particular symbolic world in which Yura identity—and the claims on the state that accompany that identity—are validated.

I argued in chapter 7 that a major element of what the kuraqkuna do today is to host festivals. The annual cycle of fiestas, even after the reductions of recent years, involves a monumental investment of time, resources, talent, and energy. In a festival such as Reyes, described in chapter 8, the ostensible celebration of the investiture of new alcaldes is only one aspect of a week-long performance which demonstrates, in symbolic fashion, the Yuras' concepts of social order. During Reyes, not only are the new alcaldes installed and the work of the old honored, but also, and just as important, the ayllus, in the course of the visits to patios in the central village, are made visible; the social units of the ethnic group are made manifest through the dance troupes associated with them.

The actions of the kurakuna during the festivals are, however, based on an understanding of the world that is only partially expressed in the festivals themselves. In chapter 9 we examined some aspects of the Yura symbolic universe which underlie festival ritual. Here the layers of meaning uncovered through an analysis of the staff of authority, the kinsa rey, reveal many aspects of the larger context of thought of the kuraqkuna. The symbolic complexity of the kinsa rey links it to fundamental cosmological and supernatural forces, as was seen in chapter 10, in which there is an identification of the person in the authority role with the kinsa rey, and both of these with Pacha Mama and the gods of the mountain peaks. These conceptual relationships become most fully socialized in the festival of Carnaval, when the authorities and their staffs visit each house of the ayllu while on their way to the peaks marking the edge of Yura territory. Finally, we have argued that the ayllus are not only brought into play at the festivals in the central village, but are also systematically created anew. The kuraqkuna and the staffs confront the gods at the periphery and then, upon returning to the center, express in ritual action the Yuras' conception of their ambiguous relationship with the state.

It is clear that the kuraqkuna's role in ritual is today at the core of their activities and their identity. They serve to create, and to re-create, a model of Yura social organization and ethnicity. They ground that model in statements of how the world, in essence, is constructed. The Yuras' ties to their fields and other productive resources, to each other, to the state, and to the gods are all "imaged" and mediated by the kuraqkuna: the jilaqata, the alcalde, and the kuraka.

I do not mean to imply that by having lost the coercive power of their predecessors the kuraqkuna are reduced to nothing but their ritual role. That is not the case; the kuraqkuna participate in the activities of everyday life, and it falls to them to articulate the sense of the ayllu to outside authorities and to attempt to respond to, or to resist, impositions from above as they mediate between peasant and vecino, or between peasant and officials of the central government.

More fundamentally, however, I am arguing that the symbolic communication that occurs in the performance of ritual is central to the Yuras' continuity as a group. As Berger and Luckmann recognized (1967), social institutions and the cultural precepts associated with them are precarious constructions, created in history by particular social entities. Principles of organization, values, and worldview exist only as they are socially reproduced in interaction and, we might add, in a particular context of power and property relations. Nor is this cultural construction a one-time thing; it must be enunciated again and again, to the current members of society and to future generations. For their part, the Yura have chosen to discuss many of their most basic principles of organization and many of their underlying values and concepts in the rituals of the kuraqkuna. That is, these rituals serve not only to legitimate one set of social roles—the kuraqkuna—they also play a similar role in legitimating the broader institutional framework of the Yura ethnic group and its relations to the encompassing society. It is here in the kuraqkuna ritual that we find what Berger and Luckmann (1967) have termed the overarching legitimations of the symbolic universe.

The inherent difficulty of the Yuras' structural situation, faced as they are with a national society which denigrates them and refuses to acknowledge the validity of their own self-definition, puts a heavy burden on this process of legitimation. It is perhaps for this reason that so much ritual emphasis is placed on boundaries, both geographic and social. Nevertheless, if reality is socially constructed, it must also be socially maintained. That is the special task of the kuraqkuna.

Since symbol systems are human creations built up in social interactions, they also change as a result of such interactions: every definition of reality must be articulated in social life for it to continue to exist, and a group's definition must serve usefully to orient their actions and to illuminate its real social situation, or it will not long endure. It can be argued that the legitimations that the kuraqkuna communicate today provide a sense of solidarity and common purpose which helps to define the Yura in relation to surrounding social groups and which creates a basis for the expression of mutual interests. However, as that situation changes, the need to express the shared definition can diminish. Today the kuraqkuna continue as a central Yura institution which involves a large proportion of the population in its activities. On the other hand, pressures for change in the Bolivian countryside are stronger than ever, and there are indications of a diminishing investment of time and effort in festival sponsorship by the authorities. What are the prospects that the kuraqkuna will endure past the end of this decade?

It is, of course, not in the nature of the historical sciences to attempt to make rigid predictions concerning the course of future events. To paraphrase Geertz, cultural interpretations are valid to the degree they can survive events, not necessarily predict them; and this "depends on the degree to which they are well grounded socio-logically, not on their inner coherence, their rhetorical plausibility, or their aesthetic appeal" (1973:325). In the case of the kuraqkuna of Yura, a simple affirmation that the roles will be abandoned seems foolhardy given the centuries the Yura have maintained them, while a similar affirmation that they will be retained indefinitely seems equally difficult given the great obstacles the Yura face.

I have argued throughout that the kuraqkuna, in addition to their task of mobilizing resources for the state, have also served to pro-vide a focus for the continued integrity of the group, an integrity reinforced through the manipulation of powerful shared social sym-bols in ritual. What trends exist against this reproduction of group identity?

The change in the symbolism of personal identity, most notably in the style of dress, is one such trend. In a period of just five years almost all the males of Yura switched from homespun, hand-woven traditional clothing to factory-made Western clothes. There has been a gradual evolution of styles in the homemade Yura clothing through time. The everyday shifts of the women's traditional dress are not produced by the Yura themselves, but are rather made from *bayeta,* a rough woolen cloth woven by Bolivian craftsmen hun-dreds of miles to the north, who come to sell their wares at certain festivals. Nevertheless, the clothing was always distinctively that of the indigenous folk. It is true that the costume was not always worn completely by choice; both vecino and Yura informants agree that in the early part of this century the vecinos would insult or threaten indigenous men who wore Western-style pants rather than their knee-length *calzón*. If a Yura insisted on wearing "city" clothes, he might be punished, even beaten. This sanction no longer exists. The active vecino population has dwindled; the younger generation lives mostly in the cities and has no intention of returning to live in Yura. The older vecinos who reside in the central village now believe Yura men should wear Western clothing so they can "become civilized." This new sentiment is probably reinforced by the vecinos' hope of selling a pair of pants or a shirt from their tiendas. Some Yura women are now adopting the pleated skirt called the *pollera*. A few younger women who have worked outside the area are even starting to wear slacks. The trend seems to be away from the old dress styles. What does this mean for Yura ethnicity? Only time will tell whether the shared style of dress, now being abandoned, is a determining factor in the overall vision of the group's identity.

Another factor working against the continued integrity of the ethnic group is the desire on the part of some Yuras to divide the territory into separate cantons. So far this effort has not been successful; however, residents of both Thatuka and Wisijsa (perhaps recalling an animosity from the eighteenth century?) speak of attempts to establish themselves as separate canton capitals. Their plan would presumably lead to the multiplication of the administrative posts now found only in the central village of Yura. This is not a new idea; talk of Thatuka's separation apparently goes back several decades, with no positive resolution yet. Nor are there calls for the kind of extreme fragmentation of local governmental units that Albó (1972) has reported for the Altiplano community of Jesús de Machaca. Nevertheless, the idea is abroad. Would the administrative breakup of the canton lead to a dissolution of the kuraqkuna? The impact that this move might have is unclear.

A third element which may weaken the overall legitimacy of the kuraqkuna is the continued reduction in the round of festivals. The abolition, since 1977, of the octavas of both Encarnación (known as the "Festival of the Alcaldes"), and of Corpus Christi, as well as the abandonment of Navidad and the simplification of San Juan, may be seen as reducing the ritual opportunities of the kuraqkuna. On the other hand, it is also a streamlining of the festival cycle and could be a response to the decrease in "person power" resulting from the greater involvement of the Yura in migrant labor. So far the festivals that have been abolished for the kuraqkuna have been considered secondary ones. It remains to be seen if the festival cycle will be reduced further.

Yet another recent development at the local level since 1983 is the emergence of *sindicatos campesinos,* peasant unions, in some thirty settlements. While the stimulus for the creation of these groupings came partly from the administrative requirements of urban agencies which provided food relief during the critical drought year of 1982–83, these new organizations had considerable vitality when I visited Yura in mid-1984. The ground was prepared for this new form of association by the Spanish priest assigned to the area and by young associates of his who, through workshops and courses in Yura and Potosí, argued in favor of the sindicato as means of group cooperation and decisionmaking. In the sindicato movement, which had bypassed Yura in its first florescence after 1952, we see the creation of a new mechanism for action which could challenge the kuraqkuna in a profound way, since the peasant union provides alternative models for leadership and group mobilization. The potential for conflict between the generations also exists, since most of those who have become involved in the administrative roles of the new sindicatos are younger than those who serve as kuraqkuna. Nevertheless, it is difficult at this juncture to assess the viability of these new forms of organization. According to several informants, the economic pressures created by the last several years of extreme inflation and the more restrictive environment existing at the local level since the installation of the conservative government of Víctor Paz Estenssoro in 1985 have apparently discouraged many of the new union leaders. During visits to Yura in 1987 I found the peasant unions to be inactive.

In the long run, labor migration from the area will perhaps have the greatest impact on the continued relevance of the kuraqkuna.

This is true not only because a large number of young adults (both male and female) have left the canton, but also because of their consequent exposure to the outside world and all that this implies. In recent years many have traveled seeking work to agricultural regions around lowland Santa Cruz. This city, through which the seasonal workers pass on their way to the zones where they work, is strikingly different from Potosí. Santa Cruz is by Bolivian standards perhaps the most middle class of the department capitals; it enjoys, in general, a much higher standard of living than the rest of the country. The frigid temperatures of Potosí are replaced by the benign warmth of a sunny climate; instead of crowded open-air street markets, highlanders encounter discotheques and boutiques. These are images the Yuras bring home with them.

This movement to other areas is reinforced by the central government's changed vision of the role of the peasant majority in national society. Corresponding policy decisions have deeply affected the Yura and other highland groups. As we have seen, the central government, and later the departmental treasuries, relied on the kuraqkuna for the collection of tribute. Although the ayllus continue to pay their contribución to the Potosí treasury, the course of national economic development in the last decade indicates that government planners now view the peasants not as a source of direct tax payments but as a pool of cheap labor for the new industrial agriculture enterprises in Santa Cruz and elsewhere. The push for direct, individual land taxation is further evidence that the government is no longer concerned with the ayllus' integrity for tax purposes. Peasant producers are seen both as future small farmers and as a potential rural proletariat.

However, not all the factors leading to change today necessarily weaken the ayllu structure and the kuraqkuna. The economy of Bolivia continues to suffer the steep decline of recent years; few are predicting an early escape from the current depression. The reasons for this economic crisis are many and go beyond the scope of this study. Some aspects of the crisis are linked to Bolivia's traditional heavy reliance on the export of raw materials in the world market. Tin, the major export, has recently suffered a price collapse. Coupled with this have been such factors as the gradual decapitalization of the mining industry; a large international debt contracted principally by a series of military dictatorships; the criminalization of political and economic activity associated with the growth in the international demand for cocaine; the devastating weather conditions earlier in this decade; and the reaction on the part of Western leaders and governments to events in Bolivia after the military coup of 1980. The causes of the crisis, then, are multiple, but the overall result has been a serious contraction of the money economy and of production rivaling the impact of a major internal revolution or of losing a war. To add to these problems, in 1984–85 Bolivia had the highest rate of inflation in the world.[2] There are no simple cures in sight.

The economic crisis led some Yuras to curtail their work outside the canton, simply because the relative security of agricultural production is more attractive than reliance on the money economy, where the fluctuating (or, more recently, stagnant) wages and rising prices make the value of wage labor more dubious. Yuras are aware that those who can support themselves with their own agricultural production can weather the worst to come, regardless of the deterioration of the urban economy. From the point of view of capitalist agriculture, areas such as Yura provide a cushion in the labor force that agribusiness owners need in good times and which they are not obliged to support in bad (Wallerstein 1979). This, however, does not diminish the fact that conditions not conducive to market participation may also lead to an increased emphasis on traditional agriculture in Yura. This strengthening of the Yura subsistence economy could bring with it renewal of traditional cultural forms and practices.

The Yura situation can be defined in negative terms, that is, their economic marginality prevents them from participating fully in the market economy and has only some ambiguous benefits for the group. On the other hand, one can take a positive perspective and adopt a vision of Bolivia as a multicultural society in which ethnic realities can also shape class relationships. In this case, the Yuras' relative nonparticipation in the money economy and their focus on small-scale production lead to a reinforcement of the group's self-definition and cohesion.

A major theme of this study has been that the symbolism expressed in the rituals surrounding the kuraqkuna is a concerted imposition of meaning—a particular set of meanings—on the flux of social life. In general terms this set of shared orientations provides the Yura with fundamental definitions at an existential level: who they are; what they are; and what the predicaments of life mean. While Yura authorities have seen their leadership roles diminished from the time of the hereditary lords (in terms of their ability to coerce or to impose decisions), their power now lies in their ability and indeed their duty to define and redefine the nature of the group, the internal structures of the ayllu, and their relationship to the state. Thus the kuraqkuna provide the mechanism for the enunciation of Yura ethnic identity. This strategy has had its successes through the centuries, allowing the Yura to preserve control of their most valued economic resources. It has given them the means of presenting a united front toward attempts at hegemony by the dominant classes. To forgo this anchor in favor of a risky, unproven individuality drawn from the poor urban classes, one which must be learned and practiced, is not, for many, a very attractive alternative. The fact that Andean people like the Yura must confront discrimination and prejudice as a result of the racist ideology of the urban sectors only reinforces their reluctance to make this transformation.

The theme of ethnic identity and cohesion becomes a major element of the symbolic language of the last kuraqkuna festival we discussed, Carnaval. This celebration is, as we have seen, an exciting affair for the Yura, full of the joys and perplexities of a life close to the soil and lived on the edge. Carnaval is the keystone of Yura ethnicity, of their sense of being a separate people. Yet it, too, is not a static, unreflective tradition. Several youths, speaking from their own experience, told me that Carnaval had undergone something of a renaissance in the early 1970s after a period of decline. The renewed interest in the fiesta was led by a group of young men who had worked for years in Buenos Aires and who then returned to live permanently in Yura. I heard these young men, as they sat in their hamlet houseyards high above the valley floor watching an older Yura in traditional dress herd his llamas along the path below, joke about the "subway" between their own hamlet and neighboring Yura ranchos. These men and their wives have lived in a modern city the size of New York, they have traveled on the Buenos Aires subway, and they have worked on the construction of fashionable apartment buildings for the rich. Yet they now participate each year, with enthusiasm and deep conviction, in a ritual which re-creates Yura by means of a great pilgrimage. Each year they devise ways to surpass the celebratory efforts of dance troupes of other ayllus. Each year they give all the energy they can muster to the kuraqkuna they accompany. This ritual defines them, and gives them a place in the world, in the center of the world. Will they easily throw that away?

NOTES

Introduction

1 For an introduction to the prehistory of the Andes, several classic studies are good places to begin; among these are Bennet and Bird's *Andean Culture History* (1960), Lanning's *Peru before the Incas* (1967), and Lumbreras's *De los pueblos, las culturas, y las artes del antiquo Perú* (1969), all of which detail the developments in the Andean archeological record alluded to below. For a recent synthesis of modern archeology, ethnohistory, and ethnology of the Andes, see Masuda, Shimada, and Morris (1985).

1 The Cultural Traditionalism of the Andean World

1 A brief sketch of this history is provided in chapters 5 and 6.
2 Here the names that stand out are, of course, Pedro Cieza de León ([1553] 1947; [1553] 1967), Juan Polo de Ondegardo ([1554] 1916a; [1571] 1916b; [1567] 1916c), Domingo de Santo Tomás ([1560] 1951a; [1560] 1951b), and later, Father Bernabé de Cobo ([1653] 1956). Many more early Spanish writers who came to understand the complexities of Andean society could be added to this list.
3 All translations of sources originally in Spanish are mine. The clarifications of Spanish and Quechua phrases (usually in parentheses immediately following the phrase) are also mine.
4 As will be seen in the discussions in chapters 8–10, it is possible to say much more about the staff of authority in the case of Yura.
5 Thus, such continuities are real but not random, a point to which we shall return. In that vein Hobsbawn and Ranger (1984), along with their

contributors, describe various cases in which "traditions," often newly created, have been important tools in the struggles and strategies of social groups.

2 Yura: Environment and People

1 The doctoral dissertation of Inge Harman (1987:172–83) discusses in some detail the Yura system of irrigation as well as the forms of communal organization employed to maintain the canals. She analyzes other forms of collective labor, such as those utilized in agriculture and in festival sponsorship, in the course of her study.
2 A similar case of the familial ownership of pasture lands is described by Casaverde (1985) for the Peruvian herding community of Chalhuanca, Arequipa.
3 This is the *mink'a*. Here, too, Harman's study (1987) provides a detailed accounting of this practice of communal planting in Yura.
4 Quechua is still spoken today by some eight to ten million people in the Andean countries, from southern Colombia to northern Argentina. Originally spread by Inka expansion and then Spanish missionary work, the language continues to grow today due to the increase in rural populations. Yet now more than ever Quechua (and Aymara, with at least a million speakers in southern Peru and Bolivia) face the strong challenge of Spanish as the language of the schools, the written word, the dominant classes, and the media.
5 Crandon (1986) discusses the relative fluidity of social identities in rural Bolivia, citing cases of movement into and out of the category she terms "Indian." For Ecuador, the Belotes (1984) provide abundant documentation which demonstrates that there, too, these categories are not defined phenotypically or racially, but socially.
6 They apparently borrowed the concept from Pitt-Rivers (1971).
7 Van den Berghe and Primov's use of "cholo" is especially unfortunate for, as they recognize, this term is nearly always pejorative (1977:128–29, 134–35). There are no social groups which voluntarily, under normal circumstances, identify themselves as "cholos," which can be translated as "half-civilized Indian."

3 Social Organization and the Ayllu

1 Yet seventy-five years before, Saavedra knew enough to distinguish *estancia*, a single hamlet or village, and *ayllu*, a larger social unit (1903:105).
2 The evidence for this comes from the nineteenth-century censuses now

housed in the Archivo Nacional de Bolivia, Sucre. For 1831 the census is to be found in Revisitas, book 237a; for 1844, Revisitas, book 241a. For a parallel discussion of this phenomenon, see Platt 1982.

3 See chapters 5 and 6 for a more complete discussion of the evolution of the ayllus.

4 The 1980 rates were in effect when twenty Bolivian pesos could be exchanged for one U.S. dollar. By 1986 the hyperinflation of recent years had taken the exchange rate to two million pesos per dollar, and the tasa was adjusted accordingly. In 1987 a new currency, the *boliviano*, replaced the peso at a conversion ratio of one million to one.

4 The Kuraqkuna of Yura Today

1 Nawrar (Navidad, or Christmas), one of the festivals marking the change-over of the postillones, was sponsored by the jilaqatas after the postillón office was abolished in the early 1970s. In 1979 Christmas was not observed. Renewed for a few more times, the kuraqkuna festival of Nawrar is no longer celebrated in Yura. In 1978 another kuraqkuna-sponsored festival, the "fiesta of the alcaldes" was discontinued and has not been revived. This was carried out the octava, or second week of the patron saint festival of Our Lady of the Incarnation.

2 In other areas of the southern Andes these horns are called *pututus,* not pululus.

3 While the jilaqata role is closely linked to lands, neither the jilaqata nor any of the other kuraqkuna have responsibilities in terms of the management of irrigation water for agriculture. This contrasts sharply with Gelles's study (1985) of Huarochirí, Peru, where the local native authorities were primarily responsible for water control and the maintenance of the canal system. I suspect that his conclusion that political power is closely linked to water management cannot be generalized to the entire southern Andes.

4 Yura possess titles to their lands dating from colonial and early republican times, but these are no longer in themselves considered fully adequate deeds. The individual titles of the catastro lands in Yura have all been "regularized" according to new procedures established after the National Council of the Agrarian Reform was founded in 1953. Interestingly, the Yura are currently being granted joint titles, ayllu by ayllu or valley by valley, in a procedure undertaken by the agrarian reform office.

5 The 1986 Reforma Tributaria (tax reform) promulgated by the Paz Estenssoro government requires the same thing. These new regulations are no more likely to be enforced (or enforceable) than the 1979 order described here.

6 While the tasa continued to be paid in 1987, the Upper Moiety decided

not to renew the six jilaqataships of Qullana and Wisijsa. Those who supported discontinuing the posts argued that local comunario officials within the hamlets could collect the tasa and turn it over to the major ayllu's kuraka. The four jilaqatas of Urinsaya, in the major ayllus of Chiquchi and Qhurqa, continue to serve as before. As this goes to press, a move to reinstitute the six posts in Qullana and Wisijsa is under way; but the outcome of this effort is uncertain.

7 Even before alcalde service to the corregidor became rotational, it is said that the Qullana alcalde was still termed the "originario." What this seems to have meant was that he stood as a primus inter pares and enjoyed some precedence of respect or prestige. This is consistent with the higher position granted Qullana as the head of the Upper Moiety and is reinforced by the historical records which show that Qullana ayllu once provided hereditary leadership to the Yuras and their ancestors (a topic considered in chapters 5 and 6).

8 The comisionado is a person appointed by the ayllu kuraka in some twenty hamlets throughout the valleys of Yura. He has no festival obligations and works only within the hamlet; he may help to resolve minor disputes among settlement members. The comisionado is given the task of relaying an alcalde's message to his own and nearby villages.

9 This is a topic that is also analyzed in detail for Yura by Inge Harman (1987) in her study of the organization of obligation.

10 One informant claimed that those who continue to resist the post are sent by the corregidor to Uyuni to be convinced by someone in the office of the subprefect. I was never able to confirm that, however.

11 Izko (1986a:156) describes a similar concept in communities of the province of Charcas in the north of Potosí; in another article, the same author cites Albó making the same observation for an Aymara-speaking community on the Bolivian Altiplano (Izko 1986b:73).

12 Not surprisingly, I was never given an example of Yuras pushing the boundary into someone else's territory!

13 Palacios Ríos (1978) describes this special herding environment in southern Peru. However, while the bofedal supports several thousand camelids, the great majority are not alpacas, as one would expect from Palacios's description, but rather llamas. This of course reflects the reversal of proportions between the two species that we find in Bolivia as compared with Peru (Casaverde 1985).

5 Invasion and Adaptation to the Colonial System

1 The basis of this affirmation comes in the first place from a document detailing litigation on a small herding hacienda named Corincho (Qhurinchu

in modern spelling), located at the southern tip of Yura territory. In this 1905 court record the plaintiffs, who were the handful of Andean peasants resident there, submitted documents dating back to 1571 in an effort to convince the court that their lands should not be held by the hacienda owner. Their suit ultimately failed, but the existence of this record (hereafter referred to as "Corincho 1905") has enabled us to place Yura in the larger framework of Andean ethnic groups in Charcas. Inge Harman and I thank don Aurelio Choquevilca of Yura for permission to copy "Corincho 1905."

2 A volume of source documents and short essays is being prepared under the editorship of Tristan Platt, Thierry Saignes, Thérèse Bouysse, and Olivia Harris.

3 This was not always true, however. Spalding (1974:61–87) has shown how, in the area of Huarochirí, many who were formerly of commoner status were able to join, over time, the provincial elites through the cabildo posts.

4 In the following pages those archival sources cited as AGN 13.18.6.4, item 4, and segments from AGN 13.18.4.1 were both kindly provided me by Tom Abercrombie, whom I thank. A complete version of the latter document, the Wisijsa census of 1592, and all other extracts from archival sources in the Archivo General de la Nación in Buenos Aires (cited here as AGN) were obtained through the untiring assistance of Marilyn Cole and Jeff Cole, to whom I am also grateful.

5 Espinoza, in his introduction to the *Memorial de Charcas de 1582* (1969:6), mistakenly identifies the two original reducciones of the Wisijsa repartimiento as Caiza and Wisijsa. We now know that they were Yura and Toropalca (AGN 13.18.6.4, it. 4: fols. 2v–5v). The contemporary village named Wisijsa was never a reducción.

6 Repartimiento can be translated as a "territorial and ethnic administrative division implanted by Spanish rule." It derives, of course, from Spanish *repartir,* "to distribute," which is what the Spaniards did with native populations after the Spanish invasion. Some repartimientos were, as we have seen, given in encomienda to individuals. Others were retained, or, more often, reclaimed, by the Spanish Crown after the encomenderos' deaths. In the southern Andes the repartimientos frequently, but not always, adopted the lines of former ethnic groupings or even of larger units, such as the "Macha y Chaqui" repartimiento which included almost all of the groups of the Cara Caras, the Lower Moiety of the Charcas. As time passed, the repartimientos became smaller, and in the so-called repartimiento of "Bissisa y Caiza" we have most, but not all, of the ethnic Wisijsa.

7 A detailed discussion of the mita is beyond the scope of this work. Fortunately, the studies by Bakewell (1984) and Cole (1985) add greatly to our knowledge of the impact on Andean groups—both in terms of increased

burdens and new opportunities—of the creation of the state-organized mining mita and, in general, of the astounding growth of mining at Potosí.

8 Saignes (1985a:153–86) describes how the Lupaqa ethnic group, subject to the Potosí mita, lost three-quarters of its tributary population in the highlands and control of many of its eastern outliers in Larecaja in the century between 1574 and 1684. The number of forasteros from other groups in Larecaja increased by 61.7 percent in the same period, however.

9 The doctrina of Yura, which had 402 tribute payers in 1575 (AHP Cajas Reales 18:fol. 217v), did not reach that number again until 1830 (ANB Revisitas, Porco, book 237a).

10 But it is almost certain that they did not. Zavala reports (1979:72) that by 1620 many of the reducciones close to Potosí, among them Yura, had not fulfilled their mita obligation in persons for years; and Saignes (1985b) has detailed some of the alternatives to turning over direct laborers. Soon after the Toledan mita was established a system evolved whereby replacements could be hired in the stead of workers from the communities (see the discussion below).

11 "[D]on Alonso Choquebilca, who afterwards through his confirmation was called don Juan Baptista Choquebilca" (AGN 13.18.4.1., it. 2:fol. 3r).

12 When Murra (1978) examined the business undertakings in Potosí of a kuraka from Pomaata in the rich Lupaqa kingdom, he found that this native lord mobilized a wide range of products—wine, peppers, chuño, meat—to market in the mining center. Yet even his considerable wealth was severely strained by the task of organizing the mining mita from his area.

13 The three other examples of this kind of intellectual undertaking that Salomon analyzes, beyond Guaman Poma, are the writings of Tito Cusi Yupanqui Inca ([1568] 1917) and Santa Cruz Pachacuti Yamqui ([1613] 1968) as well as the collection of tales in Quechua collected, supposedly, in Huarochirí (Urioste 1983).

14 It may be, however, that many of those who became most assimilated were not the kurakas who retained their leadership roles within the ayllus, but rather Andeans, both of the kuraka class and of commoner status, who abandoned their communities and were able to use commercial successes, privatized lands, or newly acquired skills to gain entrance to Spanish colonial society. In the two best studies of early colonial society to appear in recent years (Stern 1982 and Spalding 1984), it appears that the majority of those discussed who were most fully accepted into regional elites were not kurakas at the time they appear in various archival records. Their ancestors may have been lords and even Inkas; but the successful native artisans, or incipient hacendados, or merchants and lenders that are described for Huamanga and Huarochirí have for the most part broken their ties to the

native communities and fully entered into the Spanish colonial economy. They are a higher-stratum version of the more humble forasteros and colonial yanaconas who left their native areas in order to break the bonds of obligation to their ayllus and to seek protection from those obligations through subservience to Spaniards.

15 In this figure there may have been some underreporting of male children; in all, there were 326 males counted and 360 females (AGN 13.18.7.3). Boys were perhaps hidden by their parents in order to help them avoid entering the tributario category as they grew older.

16 My thanks to Prof. Nicolás Sánchez-Albornoz, who provided me with the forastero figure for Yura in 1686, taken from AGN 13.25.5.4. AHP CGI 95 provides further information on the forastero population. There are slight discrepancies among the three sets of figures.

17 Yauricoya and Corincho are the only haciendas in Yura for which there are records. Corincho, still in existence, was discussed above in the first note of this chapter. Yauricoya was apparently a small hacienda, its valley lands located downriver from the present village of Yura. The ruins of the hacienda house stand today in a dry river valley off the road to the Taru River. Obviously in existence by 1679, it was in the hands of the Bega family until at least 1792 (AGN 13.19.1.2.:fol. 170r), when it was the home of twenty-two tributarios. Although their ancestors (judging by the surnames recorded in 1792) had lived there for more than a century, they were classified as "yanaconas without lands." The term yanacona is complex indeed, but meant by this time a category of persons who were either servants or had no capital resources of their own.

18 Recall the *yanasi mink'as* described in chapter 4, which are still provided to the Yura and vecino authorities.

19 Colonial taxation account books, known as "Cajas Reales," record the tax payments made by Andean peoples throughout the colonial period. Those for Charcas are found in the archives of the Casa de la Moneda in Potosí. They suggest that the Wisijsa, originally part of the "repartimiento de Macha Chaqui," paid their tasa regularly, even if they were often somewhat behind and paid only part of the amount due. Beyond examining the original assignation of tax rates made by Toledo (AHP Cajas Reales 18), tax records consulted with reference to Wisijsa groups were from 1623 (Cajas Reales 200), 1651 (Cajas Reales 328), 1661 (Cajas Reales 389), 1681 (Cajas Reales 466), 1700 (Cajas Reales 528), the period 1714–75 (Cajas Reales 607), and, within that, 1732–33 (Cajas Reales 705).

20 Around the time in question, the ethnic name "Wisijsa" appears in tax records from 1661, 1681, and 1728 (AHP Cajas Reales 389:fols. 5r, 35r; AHP Cajas Reales 466:fol. 20v; AHP Cajas Reales 607:fol. 91v). The three Wisijsa reducción units of Yura, Caiza, and Toropalca are grouped

together (but without the Wisijsa label attached) in records from 1700 and 1732 (AHP Cajas Reales 528:fol. 118r; AHP Cajas Reales 705:fol. 94v). After 1732 there is no longer any connection noted among these three groups (AHP Cajas Reales 607:passim).

6 Transformation of the Kurakaship:
From Kurakas to Kuraqkuna

1 This summary of events is taken from seven contemporary documents published in Daniel Valcárcel's *La Rebelión de Túpac Amaru*, vol. 2 (Lima, 1971). One report was authored by the archbishop of La Paz, dated September 1780 (ibid.:235–42). Two were dictated by Tomás Catari himself (ibid.:242–47, 259–65). The collection also includes the bureaucratic report of Catari's death (ibid.:443) and of his brothers' confessions (ibid.:540–46, 596–619). A report from the Viceroy Vertíz in Buenos Aires places most of the blame for the Catari insurrection on the Spanish corregidor (ibid.:248–52).

2 This document is the record of the military tribunal that investigated the "crimes" committed in early 1781 in Yura as a result of the rebellion. The document is in the collections of the National Archives of Bolivia in Sucre, and was located and transcribed by Inge Maria Harman. The following description of events is derived from it.

3 The state-derived pressures on indigenous kurakas after the defeat of Túpac Amaru described by O'Phelan Godoy (1978) may account for this.

4 That Yuras desired to keep members of their own group in governing positions is demonstrated by the fact that in 1797 several serving as kuraqkuna undertook the suit in Juan Choquevilca's behalf, although he himself was not interested in the post.

5 His statement is corroborated by a reading of a sample of titles held by Yura comunarios today, many of which date from late colonial and early republican times and which are phrased in terms of individual ownership of specific maize fields. Our thanks to Tristan Platt, who provided copies of ANB PD 1798, no. 38 and PD 2071, no. 6.

6 The forasteros in Andean communities (that is, those of that fiscal category not living on haciendas) who were so generously removed from the tax rolls in 1882 were redefined as agregados by 1890, however, and were once again expected to contribute (Platt 1982:137).

7 Corincho also had a kuraka, though no other authority (ANB, Revisitas, book 248:fol. 183v). Since its members have always remained marginal to the broader Yura organization and never moved through the process of status inflation that occurred in other ayllus, I am not including it in this description. Today, ties with Corincho are very tenuous indeed.

III The Kuraqkuna and the Construction
of the Yura Symbolic World

1 Adorno (1986:33–35) discusses the latter two terms in relation to Guaman Poma de Ayala's understanding of the past. While Guaman Poma, who was of a lineage of local lords of Chinchaysuyu, accepted the validity of Christianity and used such loaded terms as *infiel* and *bárbaro* when describing the Andean past, he also defuses the negative connotations of the terms by showing the parallels in Andean and Christian thought and by stressing the "spiritual purity and innocence" of the descendants.

2 Spalding (1984) recounts the case of don Sebastián Quispe Ninavilca of Huarochirí, who was buried in a Franciscan habit but who was also said to have protected participants in Andean rituals.

3 Two examples will give some indication of possible further research. Salomon (1983) tells of a highland lord of Otavalo in the Ecuador of 1703 who employed a shaman residing in the tropical forest zone within his domain to use his magical spells against a Spaniard with whom he was engaged in a power struggle. And Millones (1978) analyzes a litigation record from another place called Yura—this one in southern Peru—in which the local kurakas and other indigenous authorities were accused of participation in shamanic rites. These were said to be linked to festivals and to such communal rituals as cleaning the irrigation canals, as well as to more malevolent acts such as the casting of spells and murder by bewitchment.

4 This symbolic world is the subject of the rest of the study.

7 Festivals of the Kuraqkuna

1 The phrase is Durkheim's, from *Elementary Forms of the Religious Life* ([1912] 1947).

2 Ortner (1973:1339) suggests how such distinctions can be made.

3 Using the English cognate here yields a rather unfelicitous translation, so I have generally adopted various circumlocutions.

4 For an analysis of tales told by the Yura about Amunchis or Dyusninchis, the sun, see Rasnake (1988).

8 The Festival of Reyes

1 "Reyes" will thus have two principal referents here; first, it is the name of the festival, the kings deriving from the three kings of Epiphany. The civil significance of the date, January 6, may also be due to its proximity

to January 1, when by Toledan edict the alcaldes should take office ([1575] 1925:305–6). But the names *rey, rey tata, kinsa rey,* and *kinsa reyes* are also given to the staff of authority that all the kuraqkuna maintain in their possession while in office, as we shall see when we discuss the kinsa rey in chapter 9.

2 The names of individuals and ranchos have been changed.

3 Of course, one's ranchos are often also relatives. But ranchos who are not relatives are perhaps the most important participants.

4 *Pusay* means to "lead or take [a person] somewhere." The *-rqu* suffix has been called the "hortative" by Solá (1972:7–25) and suggests an attitude of encouragement or, in Yura, respect.

5 A *mallku* is a male condor (the female is known as *wallpa,* a word also applied to the European hen). *T'alla* refers to extreme age or body size, in spite of the Yuras' typical slightness of build. These terms are used for the kuraka couple only on ritual occasions.

6 When the body of a deceased comunario is being carried to the cemetery in the central village for burial, it will be set down there and a libation poured. There are many such places on the trails of Yura; as the last two alma samanas before entering the town, these two points at each end of the street take on a wider significance as moiety chapels.

7 This interpretation was proposed by R. T. Zuidema in a personal communication.

8 In the past the corregidor, it is said, would invite all the vecinos of Yura and they would proceed to sit and drink as long as the ten pitchers of *coctel* and the ten containers of corn beer lasted. Several vecinos complained to me that recent corregidores were not generous in this way. My own observations suggest that the corregidores' reputed avarice was exaggerated; almost all the vecinos partook in the drinking that followed these presentations.

9 I am calling "vecino Quechua" a version which shows a much greater influence from Spanish; not only is there considerably more borrowing from Spanish lexicon, but there is also a shift away from Quechua to Spanish grammatical forms in prepositions, the structuring of dependent clauses, and word order.

10 From this derived the decisions to drop the octava (eighth-day) celebrations from two festivals, Encarnación and Corpus Christi, as well as Christmas for 1979. Observing the octavas in the two festivals meant that they both lasted some twelve days in Yura, not counting preliminaries and post-fiesta activities—up to twenty days in all; and this was in the case of two festivals which are only two months apart. A consensus had grown that it was too much. Navidad, on the other hand, was similar in structure to Reyes.

11 *Enteray,* borrowed from the Spanish *enterar,* has the sense of "to pay,"

"to complete," or "to turn over [something]." In colonial times, "enterar la mita" came to mean "to mobilize the required labor for the mita."

12 From the Spanish *delantero*, "front" or "foremost"; this is a ritual term also applied to the first llama in a traveling troupe of animals or to a llama about to be sacrificed.

13 For the Yuras this is a kind of ritual battle, a widespread phenomenon in the Andes. The competition and fights can occur between members of the same moiety, as when, for example, the tropas of the lluqsiqkuna of Chiquchi and Qhurqa fight. It does not seem to occur within a major ayllu, however.

14 The classification by ayllu is the common way in everyday conversation to refer to each of the corners of the central plaza: "doña So-and-so's house on Qullana corner." On certain festive occasions—in 1987 at both Encarnación and Corpus Christi—the ayllu identification of the corners is emphasized by the fleeting erection of an elaborate altar; this is not done at Reyes, and the practice at other festivals has been declining in recent years.

15 I use the phrase "tend to" here. Along the "eastern street," the passage-way parallel to the north-south street that passes through the Qhurqa and Qullana corners, there are two Wisijsa patios interspersed among what are mostly Qhurqa ayllu patios. Interestingly (perhaps coincidentally), this replicated the seemingly anomalous segment of Wisijsa in Thullta, something of an island in a Qhurqa area.

16 This idea of concentric squares was proposed for the ayllu of Macha by Platt (1976).

17 The order of visits is not completely inflexible, for structural rules vie with the practicalities of sheer proximity between the patios of the town. Deviations in the prescribed order are made for convenience and to fit the particularities of the layout of ayllu patios. Yet the very clustering by ayllu of the patios within the village assures a certain congruence between "ideal" and "real."

18 The issue of male-female complementarity in Andean thought has been addressed most cogently by Harris (1978b), Isbell (1979), and Harman (1984).

19 The women pour their ch'allay at the men's sink'a llijlla, of course, but also at their own. The men do not ch'allay the women's sink'a llijlla.

20 Another interpretation is possible. In Macha, for example, the tower of the church is seen as a powerful symbol—the "torre mayku"—in a context of thought that is clearly Andean, not European (Platt 1976:17). In Yura, the church tower does not seem to have been assigned this role, and I never saw any ritual involving it or heard any such reference to it. This could be because of the location of the church, which is set back from the plaza with its own interior courtyard.

9 The Symbolic World of the Kuraqkuna:
The Staff of Authority

1 This is not the only function of ritual, however; another is to communicate changed circumstances and new arrangements to participants. Public ritual does not always support the status quo.

2 While this is not the place for a review of this work, a short list of important advances would probably include Douglas (1966, 1973); Geertz (1973, 1983); Lévi-Strauss (1963 and his later mythological studies); Ortner (1973, 1978); and Turner (1967, 1969, 1979).

3 This flexibility also accounts for the wide range of meanings assigned by individuals to symbols; but the individual invention and manipulation of symbols is a topic beyond us here.

4 Worsley's (1984:22–41) recent critique of the overly deterministic nature of many formulations of the superstructure-base relationship is relevant in this context.

5 Personal communication from José Ramón Merino.

6 *Wiraqucha* is a very complex term which has engaged the interest of Andeanists for decades. For a recent study of the debate concerning the nature of the concept of the Inka deity known by that name, see Demarest (1981). The term has traditionally been applied in Quechua to Europeans; one early explanation for this has it that the Inkas and other Andeans confused the invading Spaniards with the returning culture hero Wiraqucha. The two morphemes of the title mean, literally, "lake of fat." This imagery of referring to an honored personage by looking to material abundance (of which obesity and fat are the result) is not so foreign to our own metaphors, such as in the expression "to kill the fatted calf."

7 The awkis of Yura have recently suffered a high mortality, coincidentally of course, but with a large impact on their small numbers. Three of the four awkis I knew best died between 1979 and June 1981.

8 In American sociological usage subculture usually refers to a component group of the larger society, and not to the symbolic system in terms of which they orient their actions. They might better be called subsocieties or simply subgroupings.

9 I hope it is obvious that I am not speaking here of ability, but of a kind of cultural emphasis. The unalloyed tilt toward the "language alone" pole in the Western academic tradition might lead some to conclude that the opposite emphasis is deficient (or that I believe it to be deficient). That is not true.

10 Ritual can also be primarily verbal. However, I am putting the spotlight on ritual action in this context.

11 Awkis do not communicate directly with the spirit world as do the more versatile *aysiris* of other zones, but rely on divination through coca leaves

and playing cards to help them bring about their cures. For a description of the use of coca in divination, see Carter et al. (1980, chap. 7).

12 Most varieties of non-Catholic missionaries in the department of Potosí tend to be of a very fundamentalist stripe, from sects generally centered in the United States. Protestant missionaries, however, have not yet set their sights on Yura, except for a few limited areas. Some families have, since 1980, converted to various versions of the Assemblies of God, though no outside missionaries currently reside in Yura. Many converts have subsequently abandoned their new faith. The main effect of the new religion on its adherents is that they forgo alcohol, which is, of course, a major change.

13 To avoid repetition of this latter proviso, I shall refer to the people who have the kinsa rey in their power, whether they inherited it or borrowed it, as owners. It should be kept in mind, however, that this includes those who only possess it temporarily.

14 *Kuntur mamani* is the ritual name applied to one's house and refers to the house deity to which ch'allays are poured on certain occasions. I was unable to clarify whether or not the kinsa rey and the kuntur mamani are conceived to unite when the staff is hanging on the wall, or whether both deities were simply being addressed in the same invocation. Phrasing the question in those terms seems confusing or ridiculous to the Yuras, a sure indication of the need for further investigation.

15 Solá has termed what others have commonly (and inadequately) called the present tense in Quechua the potential aspect (1972:6.34.1). Therefore the phrase "mana kastiganchu" could perhaps be better translated in this context as "it does not have the power, or the potential, to punish."

16 I was told that most went to the church of San Martín in Potosí, where the misa would be done correctly for a low fee.

17 Although I attended several sacrifices, I have not yet been able to take part in a yawarchay for a kinsa rey.

10 A Symbolic Dialogue: The Spirit World, Carnaval, and the State

1 The sun is also paired with Mama Killa, the moon (also, as the name indicates, conceived to be feminine). This suggests an association between the moon and the earth. In Yura mythical history there was a day before the present stage of time when the earth was in darkness, illuminated only by the moon. The arrival of the sun, Dyusninchis, destroyed the beings of that time. In this context Dyusninchis is described as a kind of culture hero. For further analysis, see Rasnake (1988).

2 "Jach'a" is an Aymara term meaning "large," "great," or "tall" (Bertonio

[1612] 1956:107). Given the identification of the mountain peaks with the ancestors, who are called the Jach'a Tatas or Great Parents, this sense of the term seems to be primary. In the second version we see the form sach'a, which means "bush" or "small plant" in Yura. No one would volunteer an etymology of the term, however.

3 The wisk'acha is a large wild rodent inhabiting rocky areas. It is hunted for its meat.

4 Although in peninsular Spanish "cerro" does not normally mean "mountain," Bolivians apply the word to formations that fall unambiguously in that category.

5 She may take a person's life as a yawarchay; but the Yura do not sacrifice animals to her.

6 Given the Yura usage of these terms, it is intriguing that Izko (1986b:73) quotes Gil Rivière, who studied the Aymara speakers of Carangas on the Bolivian Altiplano, as identifying the mallku and the t'alla with mythical ancestors, "localized and materialized," of "different lineages" within the residential estancia.

7 Qhariwarmi is the Quechua phrase for married couple; it means literally "man-woman." This compound form seems to stress the essential unity of the couple that ritual and social life in Yura also demonstrate to be an indigenous value.

8 Inge Harman (1987) has dealt in detail with the varieties of obligational relationships in Yura.

9 Pujllay is a Quechua term meaning "to play" or "to frolic." The word is associated with Carnaval everywhere Quechua is spoken in rural Bolivia.

10 Postillones were the service roles charged with carrying the mails from Potosí in the east to as far away as Tomave in the west, a distance of some 200 miles round trip. The men and their wives who took on the post served for six-month periods, those of the Upper Moiety from Christmas to San Juan (June 24), and those of the Lower Moiety the other six months. Those of the Upper Moiety were therefore serving during Carnaval, and participated with their own supporters; those of the Lower were not in office.

11 There are two exceptions to this statement. The ayllus of Wisijsa and Qhapaqa are so dispersed that there are alternate routes that their authorities follow. This means that a limited set of households are only visited every other year.

12 Sullk'a means "lesser" or "younger," contrasting with jatun, "greater" or "big." The sullk'a ayllus apparently derive from categories of persons who were in past centuries not full members of the ayllus, but were rather in such fiscal categories as yanacona and forastero (loosely translated, servant, and stranger or outsider, respectively).

13 While there are four kurakas, one for each major ayllu, there are five

alcaldes. Qullana ayllu has two, one designated the "Qullana alcalde" and the other the "Phajcha alcalde." The latter is always someone who resides in the southern area of the same name where two minor ayllus, Agregado and Qhapaqa, have most (but not all) of their households. As mentioned above, the alcalde's civil duties are to act as an assistant to the canton corregidor, which, until the last few years, is a post that has always been filled by mestizos of the central village.

14 The best source of evidence for the age of the boundaries comes from a document in the hands of one of the descendants of an early Yura indigenous lord, the land litigation record to which we have referred in previous chapters relating to the small hacienda of Corincho. While the document dates largely from the early twentieth century, it incorporates into its pages earlier sources no longer available. One such section is a copy of the Yura boundaries established before a Crown-mandated land sale in 1592. As we have seen, the canton capitals were established by 1575 as reducciones. The territories associated with them, called doctrinas from the first years of the colonial period, were established for administrative purposes at that time or soon afterward.

15 It is neither a cactus, as Mario Montaño once suggested in an article in the La Paz newspaper *Presencia*, nor the head of a llama, as Gisbert (1982) has reported.

16 This sequential movement through ritualized space along a predetermined route is reminiscent of other lineal patterns in the sacralization of space in the Andes, most notably the ceque system of Cuzco described by Zuidema (1964). While Inka influence in this area of today's Bolivia was apparently not profound, the commonality of symbolic principles and practices probably indicates widespread contact throughout the Andean culture area.

17 Yuras state that all libations are in a sense offered to Pacha Mama. I now understand that to mean that even if another spiritual entity is highlighted in the libation and Pacha Mama is not the primary recipient, her powers are not forgotten.

18 Right after the "going out" from Yura on Thursday, most households who own llamas carry out a small, family-level ritual called a *t'ikanchay* (to adorn or to put flowers on). After the llamas are penned up in their corral, corn beer is sprinkled over them and corn paste is smeared on their backs, *miranankupaq* (so that they multiply). The same beer and paste, as a joke, are always applied to the human participants as well.

19 Again, as the vicuña is the jach'arana's llama, the puma is his cat. That is, the creatures of the wild belong to the jach'aranas as domesticated animals do to humans.

20 This is a theme that Platt (1982) has developed for the ayllus of the Norte de Potosí in Bolivia.

21 The willingness to take on the kuraqkuna roles derives from the same

motivation: Yuras respond almost universally to the question of why they are willing to assume the state-mediating ayllu authority posts by pointing out that they own land within the ayllu.

22 Ironically, the vecinos, through their recent refusal to offer hospitality to the dancers, define themselves out of a symbolic nexus which in the long term serves at least to explain, if not fully legitimate, their superior status over ayllu members. This apparent shortsightedness actually points to a realignment in rural power structures, where such vecinos are withdrawing to the cities.

23 The term *cabildo,* commonly used in other areas of Bolivia to mean the lowest level of ayllu organization (such as hamlets or groups of hamlets), does not retain that meaning in Yura. The term is only applied to the Rollo, or occasionally to the town of Yura itself.

II Conclusion: Symbolic Power and Cultural Resistance

1 This characteristic of symbolism is what Cohen (1974) highlighted in his examination of the relationship between the sets of meanings associated with ethnic identity and power.

2 An indication of this is revealed by the fact that from August 1981 to April 1986 the currency exchange rate on the free market rose from twenty-five pesos to the dollar to more than two million.

REFERENCES

Manuscript Sources

Archivo General de Indias (AGI), Sevilla, Spain

Excerpts from Charcas 56 provided by Prof. John V. Murra.

Archivo General de la Nación (AGN), Buenos Aires, Argentina

The following censuses and reports, consulted on microfilm, were cited in the text:

9.17.1.4. Padrones-Alto Perú 1645–1686. Revisita of Yura carried out in 1645. "En el pueblo de la Anunciación de Nuestra Señora de Yura del corregimiento de Porco . . . la lista de los indios naturales y forasteros que hay en este dicho pueblo."

13.8.4.1. Padrones-Potosí, 1589–1683. Revisita of Yura of 1609–1610 carried out by Francisco de Balderrama.

13.18.6.4, it. 1. Padrones-Potosí, 1575–1612. "Visita del pueblo de la Anunciación de Nuestra Señora de Yura . . ." made in 1592 by Pedro de Heredia.

13.18.6.4, it. 2. Padrones-Potosí, 1575–1612. "Los indios tributarios que parece tener el repartimiento de Visisa conforme al último padrón que del dicho repartimiento hizo el capitán Pablo Alonso de Villagra" in 1599.

13.18.6.4, it. 3. Padrones-Potosí, 1575–1612. "Revisita de los indios deste pueblo de la Anunciación de Nuestra Señora de Yura," made by Villagra in 1601.

13.18.6.4, it. 4. Padrones-Potosí, 1575–1612. "Relación que hace el capitán Francisco de Balderrama . . . del repartimiento de los Vissisas . . ." in 1610.

13.18.7.3. Padrones-Potosí, 1612–1686. "Revisita del repartimiento de Vissisas, pueblo de Yura . . ." carried out in 1686.

13.18.8.3. Padrones-Potosí, 1723–1726. Revisita made "en el pueblo de Nuestra Señora de la Encarnación de Yura" in 1724 by Francisco Urticaín Yriarte.

13.18.9.5. Padrones-Potosí, 1764–1766. "Padrón original de revisitas de los indios del curato y repartimiento de Nuestra Señora de la Encarnación de Yura, actuado por . . . Gral don Luis Francisco de Echeverria, Provincia de Porco, Año de 1764."

13.19.1.2. Padrones-Potosí, 1792–1793. "Padron de la revisita actuada por el subdelegado Dn Juan Antonio Segovia" in 1792.

Archivo Histórico de Postosí (AHP), Potosí, Bolivia.

The following account books and taxation records were cited:

Cajas Reales 18. "Libro donde se asientan las tasas de los indios que están en la Corona Real," 1575.

Cajas Reales 200. "Libro real común del cargo y data de la real hacienda," 1623.

Cajas Reales 328. "Libro real manual general de cargo y data de la Hacienda de Su Magestad," 1651.

Cajas Reales 389. "Libro real manual general de cargo, etc.," 1661.

Cajas Reales 466. "Libro real, manual general de cargo y data de la Hacienda de su Magestad," 1681.

Cajas Reales 528. "Libro real común de cargo y data, etc.," 1700.

Cajas Reales 607. "Libro donde se asientan las cantidades que se pagan de la caja general de censos de Indios," 1714–75.

Cajas Reales 705. "Libro real común general de la Hacienda de Su Magestad," 1732–33.

Cabildo-Gobierno-Intendencia 95. "Revisita del Duque de la Palata. Pueblo de Yura," 1688.

Archivo Nacional de Bolivia (ANB), Sucre, Bolivia

The following expedientes have been cited in the text:

ALP, Minas, vol. 125, no. 1118. "Don Bartolomé Gonsales, indio, capitán enterador de la mita de los pueblos de Toropalca, Yura, Potobamba, y Chaqui . . . sobre que le permita usar daga y espada . . ." in 1669.

EC 1679, no. 22. "Expediente del juicio criminal iniciado por el Fiscal, contra los caciques de Yura . . ." in 1679.

EC 1701, no. 3. "Sobre que el corregidor de Porco se arregle en su cobranza de tributos de los indios originarios y forasteros, a lo dispuesto y señalado por el Superior Gobierno," 1701.

ALP, Minas, t. 46, no. 164. "El capitán Francisco Gómez de Cabrera sobre que se le confirme el título de teniente de los asientos de Yura y Porco," 1724.

ALP, Minas, t. 126, no. 12. "Los indios de la provincia de Porco pidiendo se cumplan las reales cédulas . . ." in 1728.

EC 1731, no. 4. "Recurso de Lucas Copacava, indio cobrador de la tasa del pueblo de Yura . . . para que se le haga rebaja por los muertos y ausentes," 1731.

EC 1772, no. 105. "Diligencias practicadas por el corregidor de Porco, para que se diese razón de los repartimientos que ha hecho en su provincia," 1772.

EC 1781, no. 61. "Causa criminal contra Ramón Paca, Bentura Pinto, Pedro Copacava, y demás indios principales, comprehendidos en la sublevación, muertos, y robos perpetrados en este pueblo de Yura y sus inmedaciones," 1781.

EC 1797, no. 14. "Expediente seguido por los indios del pueblo de Yura sobre que dn Marcos Mariaca se ha introducido en el cacicazgo de Anansaya," 1797.

Mano de Obra catalog. SG 1339. Dispositions concerning the mita; SG 2186a. Dispositions concerning the mita.

Revisitas of Porco Province: Book 235, 1818; Book 237, 1820; Book 237a, 1831; Book 241, 1841; Book 241a, 1845; Book 243, 1855; Book 246, 1867; Book 247, 1872; Book 248, 1877.

PD 1798, no. 39. "Las operaciones de la insinuada revisita . . . ," 1882.

PD 2071, no. 6. "Las varias reclamaciones que los indígenas de este cantón de Yura en revisita han elevado a los altos poderes del Estado . . . ," 1886.

Corincho 1905. Land litigation record over the lands of Corincho, Yura canton. Private archive of Aurelio Choquevilca, Yura.

Published Sources

Adorno, Rolena
1986. *Guaman Poma: Writing and Resistance in Colonial Peru.* Austin: University of Texas Press.

Albó, Javier, et al.
1972. "Dinámica en la estructura inter-comunitaria de Jesús de Machaca." *América Indígena* 32:773–816.

Allen, Catherine

1981. "To Be Quechua: The Symbolism of Coca Chewing in Highland Perú." *American Ethnologist* 8(1):157–71.

1984. "Patterned Time: The Mythic History of a Peruvian Community." *Journal of Latin American Lore* 10(2):151–73.

1986. "Coca and Cultural Identity in Andean Communities." In *Coca and Cocaine: Effects on People and Policy in Latin America.* D. Pacini and C. Franquemont, eds., pp. 35–48. Cambridge, Mass.: Cultural Survival, Inc., and the Latin American Studies Program, Cornell University.

Althusser, Louis

1971. "Ideology and Ideological State Apparatuses." In *Lenin and Philosophy.* New York: Monthly Review Press.

Anonymous

[1603] 1965. "Descripción de la villa y minas de Potosí." In *Relaciones Geográficas de Indias,* vol. 1. Marcos Jiménez de la Espada, ed. *Biblioteca de Autores Españoles,* vol. 183. Madrid: Ediciones Atlas.

Arguedas, José María

1956. "Puquio: una cultura en proceso de cambio." *Revista del Museo Nacional* (Lima) 25:184–232.

Assadourian, Carlos S.

1983. "Dominio colonial y señores étnicos en el espacio andino." *HISLA (Revista Latinoamericana de Historia Económica y Social)* 1:7–20.

Bakewell, Peter

1984. *Miners of the Red Mountain: Indian Labor in Potosí, 1545–1650.* Albuquerque: University of New Mexico Press.

Barnadas, Josep

1973. *Charcas: orígines históricos de una sociedad colonial.* La Paz: Centro de Investigación y Promoción del Campesinado.

Barth, Fredrik

1969. "Introduction." In *Ethnic Groups and Boundaries.* F. Barth, ed. Boston: Little, Brown.

Bastien, Joseph W.

1978. *Mountain of the Condor.* St. Paul, Minn.: West Publishing.

Bauman, Richard

1974. "Speaking in the Light: The Role of the Quaker Minister." In *Explorations in the Ethnography of Speaking.* Richard Bauman and Joel Sherzer, eds. New York: Cambridge University Press.

Belote, Jim, and Linda Belote

1977. "The Limitation of Obligation in Saraguro Kinship." In *Andean Kinship and Marriage.* Ralph Bolton and Enrique Mayer, eds. Washington: American Anthropological Association.

1984. "Drain from the Bottom: Individual Ethnic Identity Change in Southern Ecuador." *Social Forces* 63(1):24–50.

Bendix, Reinhard
1977. *Max Weber: An Intellectual Portrait*. Berkeley: University of California Press.
Bennett, Wendell C., and Junius Bird
1960. *Andean Culture History*. New York: American Museum of Natural History.
Berger, Peter, and Thomas Luckmann
1967. *The Social Construction of Reality*. Garden City, N.Y.: Anchor Books.
Bertonio, Ludovico
[1612] 1956. *Vocabulario de la lengua aymara*. La Paz.
Bills, Garland; Bernardo Vallejo; and Rudolph Troike
1969. *An Introduction to Spoken Bolivian Quechua*. Austin: University of Texas Press.
Bolivia
1955. *Censo demográfico, 1950*. La Paz: Ministerio de Hacienda y Estadística.
1973. *Censo general de la población de la República de Bolivia en 1900*. 2d ed. Cochabamba: Editorial Canelas, S.A.
Bolivia, Departamento de Meterología
1973. *Anuario meteorológico 1973*. La Paz: Ministerio de Transportes y Comunicaciones.
Bolivia, Dirección General de Economía Rural
1956. *Resúmen general de medidas*. La Paz: Ministerio de Agricultura, Ganadería y Colonización.
Bolivia, Instituto Nacional de Estadística
1977. *Resultados provisionales: Departamento de Potosí. Censo Nacional de Población y Vivienda*. La Paz: Instituto Nacional de Estadística.
Bolivia, Ministerio de Asuntos Campesinos y Agropecuarios
1975. *Mapa ecológico de Bolivia: Memoria explicativa*. La Paz: Ministerio de Asuntos Campesinos y Agropecuarios.
Bolton, Ralph, and Douglas Sharon
1976. "Andean Ritual Lore: An Introduction." *Journal of Latin American Lore* 2(1):63–69.
Bonilla, Heraclio
1978. "Notas en torno a la historia económica y social de Bolivia (1821–1879)." *Históricas* 2(2):159–82.
1980. *Un siglo a la deriva: ensayos sobre el Perú, Bolivia y la guerra*. Lima: Instituto de Estudios Peruanos.
Borricaud, François
1967. *Cambios en Puno: estudios de sociología andina*. Mexico: Instituto Interamericano Indigenista.

Bourdieu, Pierre
  1977. *Outline of a Theory of Practice*. R. Nice, trans. Cambridge: Cambridge University Press.
Brush, Stephen
  1977. *Mountain, Field, and Family: The Economy and Human Ecology of an Andean Valley*. Philadelphia: University of Pennsylvania Press.
Brush, Stephen, and David W. Guillet
  1985. "Small-scale Agro-pastoral Production in the Central Andes." *Mountain Research and Development* 5(1):19–30.
Buechler, Hans C., and Judith Maria Buechler
  1971. *The Bolivian Aymara*. New York: Holt, Rinehart and Winston.
Burke, Kenneth
  1973. *The Philosophy of Literary Form*. 3d ed. Berkeley: University of California Press.
Butler, Barbara
  1985. "Ideological Traditionalism and Pragmatic Flexibility in the Internal Politics of an Otavalo Indian Community." In *Political Anthropology in Ecuador: Perspectives from Indigenous Cultures*. J. Ehrenreich, ed., pp. 191–216. Albany, N.Y.: Society for Latin American Anthropology and the Center for the Caribbean and Latin America, State University of New York at Albany.
Caballero, José María
  1983. "Agricultura peruana: Economía política y campesinado. Balance de la investigación reciente y patrón de evolución." In *La cuestión rural en el Perú*. Javier Iguiñiz, ed., pp. 261–332. Lima: Fondo Editorial de la Pontificia Universidad Católica del Perú.
Cajías, Fernando
  1983. "Los objetivos de la revolución indígena de 1781: el caso de Oruro." *Revista Andina* 1(2):407–28.
Campbell, Leon G.
  1976. "The Army of Peru and the Tupac Amaru Revolt." *Hispanic American Historical Review* 56:31–57.
  1979. "Recent Research on Andean Peasant Revolts, 1750–1820." *Latin American Research Review* 14:3–49.
Cancian, Frank
  1965. *Economics and Prestige in a Maya Community: The Religious Cargo System in Zinacantan*. Stanford: Stanford University Press.
Cañete, Pedro Vicente de
  [1797] 1952. *Historia física y política de la provincia de Potosí*. Gunnar Mendoza, ed. La Paz: Fundación Universitaria "Simon T. Patiño."
Capoche, Luis
  [1585] 1959. *Relación general de la Villa Imperial de Potosí*. Biblioteca de Autores Españoles. Vol. 122, pp. 9–221. Madrid: Ediciones Atlas.

Carrasco, Pedro
1961. "The Civil-Religious Hierarchy in Meso-American Communities: Pre-Spanish Background and Colonial Development." *American Anthropologist* 63:484–97.

Carter, William, et al.
1980. *Coca in Bolivia*. La Paz: UFLA/NIDA–Tutapi.

Casaverde, Juvenal
1985. "Sistema de propiedad y tenencia de pastos naturales altoandinos." *Allpanchis* 24:271–88.

Castelli, Amalia; Marcia Koth de Paredes; and Mariana Mould de Pease
1981. *Ethnohistoria y antropología andina*. Lima: Museo Nacional de Historia.

Castro Pozo, Hildebrando
1924. *Nuestra comunidad indígena*. Lima: Editorial "El Lucero."

Choque Canqui, Roberto
1978. "Pedro Chipana: cacique comerciante de Calamarca." *Avances* 1:28–32.

Christian, William
1972. *Person and God in a Spanish Valley*. New York: Seminar Press.

Cieza de León, Pedro
[1553] 1947. *Primera parte de la crónica del Perú*. Biblioteca de Autores Españoles. Vol. 16. Madrid: Ediciones Atlas.
[1553] 1967. *El señorío de los incas: Segunda parte de la crónica del Perú*. Lima: Instituto de Estudios Peruanos.

Cobo, Bernabé
[1653] 1956. *Historia del nuevo mundo*. Biblioteca de Autores Españoles. Vols. 91–92. Madrid: Editorial Atlas.

Cohen, Abner
1969. *Custom and Politics in Urban Africa*. Berkeley: University of California Press.
1971. "The Politics of Ritual Secrecy." *Man* 6:427–48.
1976. *Two-dimensional Man*. Berkeley: University of California Press.
1981. *The Politics of Elite Culture*. Berkeley: University of California Press.

Cohen, Abner, ed.
1974. *Urban Ethnicity*. London: Tavistock.

Cole, Jeffrey
1985. *The Potosí Mita, 1575–1700*. Stanford: Stanford University Press.

Comaroff, Jean
1985. *Body of Power, Spirit of Resistance*. Chicago: University of Chicago Press.

Cook, Noble David
1981. *Demographic Collapse: Indian Peru, 1520–1620*. Cambridge: Cambridge University Press.

Cornblit, Oscar

1976. "Levantamientos de masas en Perú y Bolivia durante el siglo XVIII." In *Tupac Amaru II—1780*. A. Flores Galindo, ed., pp. 129–98. Lima: Retablo de Papel.

Cotari, Daniel, et al.

1978. *Diccionario aymara-castellano, castellano-aymara*. Cochabamba: Instituto de Idiomas de los Padres de Maryknoll.

Crandon, Libbet

1986. "Medical Dialogue and the Political Economy of Medical Pluralism: A Case from Rural Highland Bolivia." *American Ethnologist* 13(3):463–76.

Demarest, Arthur A.

1981. *Viracocha: The Nature and Antiquity of the Andean High God*. Cambridge: Peabody Museum of Archeology and Ethnology.

Dobyns, Henry F.

1963. "An Outline of Andean Epidemic History to 1720." *Bulletin of the History of Medicine* 37:493–515.

1966. "Estimating Aboriginal American Populations: An Appraisal of Techniques with a New Hemispheric Estimate." *Current Anthropology* 78: 395–449.

Douglas, Mary

1966. *Purity and Danger*. Baltimore: Penguin Books.

1973. *Natural Symbols*. New York: Vintage Books.

Durkheim, Emile

[1912] 1947. *The Elementary Forms of the Religious Life*. Glencoe, Ill.: Free Press.

Duviols, Pierre

1972. *La lutte contre les religions autochtones dans le Pérou colonial*. Lima: Institut Français d'Etudes Andines.

Escobar, Gabriel

1961. *La estructura política rural del departamento de Puno*. Cuzco: Editorial H. G. Rozas, S.A.

1967. *Organización social y cultural del sur del Perú*. Mexico: Instituto Indigenista Interamericano.

Espinoza, Waldemar

1969. *El memorial de Charcas: crónica inédita de 1582*. Chosica, Perú: Cantuta, Revista de la Universidad Nacional de Educación.

1980. "El curaca de los cayambes y su sometimiento al imperio español." *Bulletin de l'Institut Français d'Etudes Andines* 9(1–2):89–119.

1981. "El fundamento territorial del ayllu serrano: siglos XV y XVI." In *Ethnohistoria y antropología andina*. A. Castelli et al., eds., pp. 93–130. Lima: Museo Nacional de Historia.

Evans, Brian

1986. "Migration Process in Upper Peru in the Seventeenth Century." Unpublished manuscript.

Favre, Henri

1967. "Tayta Wamani: Le culte des montagnes dans le centre sud des Andes péruviennes." *Annales de la Faculte de Lettres et Sciences Humaines* (Aix-en-Provence) 3:121–40.

Fernández de Santillán, Felipe

[1601] 1868. "Memorial sobre las minas de Potosí." *Colección de Documentos Inéditos para la Historia de España* 52:445–55.

Figueroa, Alberto

1983. "Mito y realidad de la economía campesina en el Perú." In *La cuestión rural en el Perú.* J. Iguíñiz, ed., pp. 197–209. Lima: Fondo Editorial de la Pontificia Universidad Católica del Perú.

Fisher, John

1976. "La rebelión de Tupac Amaru y el programa imperial de Carlos III." In *Tupac Amaru II—1780.* A. Flores Galindo, ed., pp. 106–28. Lima: Retablo de Papel.

Flores Galindo, Alberto, ed.

1976. *Tupac Amaru II—1780.* Lima: Retablo de Papel.

Fuenzalida, Fernando

1980. "Santiago y el wamani: aspectos de un culto pagano en Moya." *Debates en Antropología* 5:155–88.

Gade, Daniel, and María Escobar

1982. "Village Settlement and the Colonial Legacy in Southern Peru." *Geographical Review* 27(4):430–49.

García, José María

1983. *Con las comunidades andinas del Ausangate.* Lima: Centro de Proyección Cristiana.

Garcilaso de la Vega, el Inca

[1609] 1960. *Segunda parte de los comentario reales de los Incas. Biblioteca de Autores Españoles.* Vol. 134. Madrid: Ediciones Atlas.

Geertz, Clifford

1973. *The Interpretation of Cultures.* New York: Basic Books.

1983. *Local Knowledge.* New York: Basic Books.

Gelles, Peter

1985. "Sociedades hidraulicas en los Andes: Algunas perspectivas desde Huarochirí." *Allpanchis* 26:99–147.

Gisbert, Teresa, et al.

1981. "Los Yuras y el arte textil contemporáneo en Bolivia." *Historia y Cultura* (La Paz) 4:155–71.

Godoy, Ricardo

1983. "From Indian to Miner and Back Again: Small Scale Mining in the

Jukumani Ayllu, Northern Potosí, Bolivia." Ph.D. diss., Columbia University.

1985. "State, Ayllu, and Ethnicity in Northern Potosí, Bolivia." *Anthropos* 80:53–65.

Golte, Jürgen

1980a. *Repartos y rebeliones: Tupac Amaru y las contradicciones de la economía colonial*. Lima: Instituto de Estudios Peruanos.

1980b. *La racionalidad de la organización andina*. Lima: Instituto de Estudios Peruanos.

Gonçalez Holguín, Diego

[1608] 1952. *Vocabulario de la lengua general . . . llamada la lengua Qquichua*. Lima: Imprenta Santa Maria.

Gose, Peter

1986. "Sacrifice and the Commodity Form in the Andes." *Man* 21(2):296–310.

Gow, David

1976. "The Gods and Social Change in the High Andes." Ph.D. diss., University of Wisconsin-Madison.

Grieshaber, Erwin

1980. "Survival of Indian Communities in Nineteenth-century Bolivia: A Regional Comparison." *Journal of Latin American Studies* 12(2):223–69.

Grimes, Ronald

1976. "Ritual Studies: Two Models." *Religious Studies Review* 2(4):13–25.

Grondín, Marcelo

1975. *Tupac Katari y la rebelión campesina*. Oruro: INDICEP.

Gross, Daniel

1983. "Fetishism and Functionalism: The Political Economy of Capitalist Development in Latin America: A Review Article." *Comparative Studies in Society and History* 25(4):694–702.

Guaman Poma de Ayala, Felipe

[1613?] 1980. *El primer nueva corónica y buen gobierno*, J. V. Murra, R. Adorno, and J. Urioste (eds.) 3 vols. Mexico: Siglo XXI.

Hanke, Lewis

1959. *Prólogo de la relación general de la Villa Imperial de Potosí. Biblioteca de Autores Españoles*. Vol. 122. Madrid: Ediciones Atlas.

Harman, Inge Maria

1984. "Women and Cooperative Labor in the Southern Bolivian Andes." *Women in International Development Working Papers*, no. 65. Lansing: Michigan State University.

1986. "Land Tenure and Ayllu Transformations in the Southern Bolivian Andes." Paper presented at the American Anthropological Association meeting, Philadelphia, Pennsylvania.

1987. "Collective Labor and Rituals of Reciprocity in the Southern Bolivian Andes." Ph.D. diss., Cornell University.

Harris, Marvin

1964. *Patterns of Race in the Americas*. New York: W. W. Norton.

Harris, Olivia

1978a. "El parentesco y la economía vertical en el Ayllu Laymi (Norte de Potosí)." *Avances* (La Paz) 1:51–64.

1978b. "Complementarity and Conflict: An Andean View of Male and Female." In *Sex and Age as Principles of Social Differentiation*. J. La Fontaine, ed. London: Tavistock.

1982a. "Labour and Produce in an Ethnic Economy, Northern Potosí, Bolivia." In *Ecology and Exchange in the Andes*. David Lehmann, ed., pp. 70–98. Cambridge: Cambridge University Press.

1982b. "The Dead and the Devils among the Bolivian Laymi." In *Death and the Regeneration of Life*. M. Bloch and J. Parry, eds. Cambridge: Cambridge University Press.

1985. "Ecological Duality and the Role of the Center: Northern Potosí." In *Andean Ecology and Civilization*. S. Masuda, I. Shimada, and C. Morris, eds., pp. 311–35. Tokyo: University of Tokyo Press.

Hemming, John

1970. *The Conquest of the Incas*. New York: Harcourt Brace Jovanovich.

Hidalgo Lehuede, Jorge

1982. "Fases de la rebelión indígena en 1781 en el Corregimiento de Atacama y esquema de la inestabilidad política que la precede, 1749–1781." *Chungara* (Arica, Chile) 9:192–246.

Hobsbawn, Eric, and Terence Ranger, eds.

1984. *The Invention of Tradition*. Cambridge: Cambridge University Press.

Isbell, Billie Jean

1978. *To Defend Ourselves: Ecology and Ritual in an Andean Village*. Austin: Institute of Latin American Studies.

1979. "La otra mitad esencial: un estudio de complementaridad sexual andina." *Estudios Andinos* 12:37–56.

Izko, Javier

1986a. "Condores y mast'akus: Vida y muerte en los valles norpotosinos." In *Tiempo de vida y muerte*. J. Izko, R. Molina, and R. Pereira, eds., pp. 11–168. La Paz: Consejo Nacional de Población, Ministerio de Planeamiento.

1986b. "Comunidad andina: Persistencia y cambio." *Revista Andina* 4(1): 59–99.

Joralemon, Donald

1985. "Altar Symbolism in Peruvian Ritual Healing." *Journal of Latin American Lore* 11:3–29.

Kahn, Joel S.
1985. "Peasant Ideologies in the Third World." *Annual Review of Anthropology* 14:49–75.

Kleymeyer, Charles
1982. *Poder y dependencia entre quechuas y criollos.* Lima: Universidad Nacional Agraria.

Konetzke, Richard
1965. *Süd- und Mittelamerika.* Vol. 1. Frankfurt: Fishers Weltgeschichte.

Kubler, George
1946. "The Quechua in the Colonial World." In *Handbook of South American Indians.* Vol. 2. Julian Steward, ed., pp. 331–410. Washington: Smithsonian Institution.

Lanning, Edward
1967. *Peru before the Incas.* Englewood Cliffs, N.J.: Prentice-Hall.

Lara, Jesus
1971. *Diccionario qheshwa-castellano, castellano-qheshwa.* La Paz: Los Amigos del Libro.

Larson, Brooke
1979. "Caciques, Class Structure, and the Colonial State in Bolivia." *Nova Americana* 2:197–235.

1984. *Explotación agraria y resistencia campesina en Cochabamba.* Cochabamba: CERES.

Larson, Brooke, and Robert Wasserstrom
1983. "Coerced Consumption in Colonial Bolivia and Guatemala." *Radical History Review* 27:49–78.

Levillier, Roberto
1935. *Don Francisco de Toledo, supremo organizador del Perú.* Vol. 1. Buenos Aires: Biblioteca del Congreso Argentino.

Lévi-Strauss, Claude
1963. *Structural Anthropology.* New York: Basic Books.

Lewin, Boleslao
1973. *Vida de Tupac Amaru.* Havana: Instituto Cubano del Libro.

Lira, Jorge A.
1944. *Diccionario kkechuwa-espanol.* Tucumán: Instituto de Historia, Lingüística y Folklore.

Lohmann Villena, Guillermo
1949. *Las minas de Huancavelica (s. XVI–XVII).* Sevilla: Escuela de Estudios Hispanoamericanos.

Lumbreras, Luis
1969. *De los pueblos, las culturas, y las artes del antiguo Perú.* Lima: Moncloa-Campodonico.

Málaga Medina, Alejandro
1972. "El virrey don Francisco de Toledo y la reglamentación del tributo

en el virreinato del Perú." *Anuario de Estudios Americanos* 29:597–623.

1974. "Las reducciones en el Perú durante el gobierno del virrey Francisco de Toledo." *Anuario de Estudios Americanos* 31:819–42.

Mangin, William

1954. "The Cultural Significance of the Fiesta Complex in an Indian Hacienda in Peru." Ph.D. diss., Yale University.

Mannheim, Bruce

1979. "Semantic Coupling in Quechua Verse." Unpublished manuscript.

Mariscotti de Görlitz, Ana María

1978. *Pachamama Santa Tierra*. *Indiana*, Beiheft 8. Berlin: Gebr. Mann Verlag.

Marzal, Manuel

1971. *El mundo religioso de Urcos*. Cusco: Instituto de Pastoral Andina.

Masuda, Shozo; Izumi Shimada; and Craig Morris, eds.

1985. *Andean Ecology and Civilization*. Tokyo: University of Tokyo Press.

Mathews, Holly

1985. " 'We are Mayorodomo': A Reinterpretation of Women's Roles in the Mexican Cargo System." *American Ethnologist* 12(2):285–301.

Matienzo, Juan de

[1567] 1967. *Gobierno del Perú*. Lima: Institut Français d'Etudes Andines.

Millones Santa Gadea, Luis

1978. *Los ganados del señor: mecanismos de poder en las comunidades andinas. Arequipa, siglos XVIII–XIX*. Lima: Pontificia Universidad Católica del Perú, Programa Académico de Ciencias Sociales.

Mishkin, Bernard

1946. "The Contemporary Quechua." In *Handbook of South American Indians*. Vol. 2. Julian H. Steward, ed., pp. 411–70. Washington: Smithsonian Institution.

Mitchell, William P.

1972. "The System of Power in Quinua, a Community of the Central Peruvian Highlands." Ph.D. diss., University of Pittsburgh.

Moreno Cebrián, Alfredo

1977. *El corregidor de indios y la economía peruana del siglo XVIII: los repartos forzosos de mercancías*. Madrid: Consejo Superior de Investigaciones Científicas.

Mujía, Ricardo

1914. *Bolivia-Paraguay*. Vol. 2. La Paz: Empresa Editorial "El Tiempo."

Murra, John V.

1960. "Rite and Crop in the Inca State." In *Culture in History*. Stanley Diamond, ed. New York: Columbia University Press.

1962. "Cloth and Its Functions in the Inca State." *American Anthropologist* 64:710–28.

1972. "El 'control vertical' de un máximo de pisos ecológicos en la economía de las sociedades andinas." In *Visita de la provincia de León de Huánuco (1562) por Iñigo Ortiz de Zúñiga*. Vol. 1, pp. 426–68. Huánuco, Perú: Universidad Hermilio Valdizán.

1975. *Formaciones económicas y políticas del mundo andino*. Lima: Instituto de Estudios Peruanos.

1978. "Aymara Lords and Their European Agents in Potosí." *Nova Americana* 1:231–43.

1980. *The Economic Organization of the Inka State*. Greenwich, Conn.: JAI Press.

1984. "Andean Societies." *Annual Review of Anthropology* 13:119–41.

Murra, John V., ed.

1964. *Visita hecha a la provincia de Chucuito por Garci Diez de San Miguel en el año 1567*. Lima: Ediciones de la Casa de Cultura del Perú.

Núñez del Prado B., Juan Víctor

1985. "The Supernatural World of the Quechua of Southern Perú as Seen from the Community of Qotobamba." In *Native South Americans*. P. J. Lyon, ed. Prospect Heights, Ill.: Waveland Press.

Núñez del Prado, Oscar

1973. *Kuyo Chico*. Chicago: University of Chicago Press.

O'Phelan Godoy, Scarlett

1976. "Túpac Amaru y las sublevaciones del s. XVIII." In *Tupac Amaru II —1780*. A. Flores Galindo, ed., pp. 67–81. Lima: Retablo de Papel.

1978. "El sur andino a fines del siglo XVIII: cacique o corregidor?" *Allpanchis* 11-12:17–32.

1979. "La rebelión de Tupac Amaru: su organización interna, dirigencia y alianzas." *Historia* 3(2):89–122.

Ordóñez, Pastor

1919–1920. "Los varayocc." *Revista Universitaria de la Universidad del Cuzco*, no. 27 (March 1919); no. 28 (September 1919); no. 31 (March 1920).

Orlove, Benjamin

1985. "The History of the Andes: A Brief Overview." *Mountain Research and Development* 5(1):45–60.

Orlove, Benjamin, and Glynn Custred

1980. "The Alternative Model of Agrarian Society in the Andes: Households, Networks, and Corporate Groups." In *Land and Power in Latin America: Agrarian Economies and Social Process in the Andes*. Benjamin Orlove and Glynn Custred, eds. New York: Holmes and Meier.

Ortner, Sherry

1973. "On Key Symbols." *American Anthropologist* 75(5):1338–45.

1978. *Sherpas through Their Rituals*. Cambridge: Cambridge University Press.

1984. "Theory in Anthropology since the Sixties." *Comparative Studies in Society and History* 26(1):126–66.

Ossio, Juan

1981. "Expresiones simbólicas y sociales de los ayllus andinos: el caso de los ayllus de la comunidad de Cabana y del antiguo repartimiento de los Rucanas-Antamarcas." In *Etnohistoria y antropología andina*. A. Castelli et al., eds., pp. 189–214. Lima: Museo Nacional de Historia.

Palacios Ríos, Félix

1977. "Pastizales de regadío para alpacas." In *Pastores de puna: Uywamichiq punarunakuna*. J. Flores Ochoa, ed., pp. 155–70. Lima: Instituto de Estudios Andinos.

Palomino, Salvador

1972. "Dualidad en la organización socio-cultural de algunas poblaciones andinas." *Revista del Museo Nacional* (Lima) 37:231–60.

Pease, Franklin

1978. *De Tawantinsuyu a la historia del Perú*. Lima: Instituto de Estudios Peruanos.

1980. "Historia andina: hacia una historia del Perú." *Revista Histórica* 32:197–212.

Pitt-Rivers, Julian

1971. "Race, Color, and Class in Central America and the Andes." In *Majority and Minority*. N. Yetman and C. H. Steele, eds., pp. 90–97. Boston: Allyn and Bacon.

Platt, Tristan

n.d. "La confederación Charcas." Unpublished manuscript.

1976. *Espejos y maiz*. La Paz: CIPCA.

1978. "Acerca del sistema tributario pre-toledano en el Alto Perú." *Avances* (La Paz) 1:33–46.

1981. "El papel del ayllu andino en la reproducción del regimen mercantil simple en el Norte de Potosí." *America Indigena* 41:665–728.

1982. *Estado boliviano y ayllu andino*. Lima: Instituto de Estudios Peruanos.

1984. "Liberalism and Ethnocide in the Southern Andes." *History Workshop Journal* 17:3–18.

Polo de Ondegardo, Juan

[1554] 1916a. "Errores y supersticiones." *Colección de libros y documentos referentes a la Historia del Perú*. Series 1, vol. 3. Lima.

[1571] 1916b. "Relación de los fundamentos acerca del notable daño que resulta de no guardar a los indios sus fueros." *Colección de libros y documentos referentes a la Historia del Perú*. 1a serie, T. 3. Lima.

[1567] 1916c. "Institución contra las ceremonias y ritos." *Colección de libros y documentos referentes a la Historia del Perú*. 1a serie, T. 3. Lima.

[1561] 1940. "Informe . . . al licenciado Briviesca de Munatones." *Revista Histórica* (Lima) 13:125–96.

Rappaport, Joanne

1985. "History, Myth, and the Dynamics of Territorial Maintenance in Tierradentro, Colombia." *American Ethnologist* 12(1):27–45.

Rasnake, Roger

1988. "Myths of Resistance to Colonial Domination." In *From History to Myth in South America*. J. Hill, ed. Urbana: University of Illinois Press.

Ricardo, Antonio

[1586] 1951. *Vocabulario y phrasis en la lengua general . . . llamada Quichua*. Lima: Instituto de Historia de la Facultad de Letras, Universidad Nacional Mayor de San Marcos.

Rivera, Silvia

1978. "El mallku y la sociedad colonial en el siglo XVII: el caso de Jesús de Machaca." *Avances* (La Paz) 1:7–27.

1984. *Oprimidos pero no vencidos: luchas del campesinado aymara y qhechwa 1900–1980*. La Paz: Hisbol-CSUTCB.

Rostworowski de Diez Canseco, María

1977. *Etnia y sociedad: costa peruana prehispánica*. Lima: Instituto de Estudios Peruanos.

1978. *Señoríos indígenas de Lima y Canta*. Lima: Instituto de Estudios Peruanos.

1983. *Estructuras andinas del poder*. Lima: Instituto de Estudios Peruanos.

Rowe, John H.

1946. "Inca Culture at the Time of the Spanish Conquest." In *Handbook of South American Indians*. Vol. 2. Julian H. Steward, ed., pp. 183–330. Washington: Bureau of American Ethnology.

[1954] 1976. "El movimiento nacional inca del siglo XVIII." In *Túpac Amaru II—1780*. A. Flores Galindo, ed., pp. 11–66. Lima: Retablo de Papel.

1982. "Genealogía y rebelión en el siglo XVIII: algunos antecedentes de la sublevación de José Gabriel Thupa Amaru." *Histórica* 6:65–86.

Saavedra, Bautista

1903. *El ayllu*. La Paz: Imprenta Artística Velarde, Aldazosa y Cia.

Saignes, Thierry

1983. "Políticas étnicas en Bolivia colonial, siglos XVI–XIX." *Historia Boliviana* 3(1):1–30.

1984. "Las etnias de Charcas frente al sistema colonial (siglo XVII)." *Jahrbuch für Geschichte von Staat, Wirtschaft, und Gesellschaft Lateinamerikas* 21:27–76.

1985a. *Los andes orientales: historia de un olvido*. La Paz: CERES and IFEA.

1985b. "Notes on the Regional Contribution to the *Mita* in Potosí in the

Early Seventeenth Century." *Bulletin of Latin American Research* 4(1): 65–76.

1985c. "From Drunkenness to Portrait: The South Andean Caciques between Two Legitimacies (XVII Century)." Unpublished manuscript.

Salomon, Frank

1980. *Los señores étnicos de Quito en la época de los incas.* Otavalo: Instituto Otavaleño de Antropología.

1982. "Chronicles of the Impossible: Notes on Three Peruvian Indigenous Historians." In *From Oral to Written Expression: Native Andean Chronicles of the Early Colonial Period.* R. Adorno, ed. pp. 9–39. Syracuse, N.Y.: Maxwell School of Citizenship and Public Affairs, Foreign and Comparative Studies Program, Latin American Series, no. 4.

1983. "Shamanism and Politics in Late-colonial Ecuador." *American Ethnologist* 19(3):413–28.

Sánchez-Albornoz, Nicolás

1978. *Indios y tributos en el Alto Perú.* Lima: Instituto de Estudios Peruanos.

Santa Cruz Pachacuti Yamqui [1613] 1968. "Relación de antigüedades deste reyno del Peru." In Biblioteca de Autores Españoles, vol. 209. Madrid.

Santo Tomás, Domingo de

[1560] 1951a. *Gramática o arte de la lengua general de los indios de los reynos del Perú.* Lima: Instituto de Historia, Universidad Nacional Mayor de San Marcos.

[1560] 1951b. *Lexicon o vocabulario de la lengua general de los indios de los reynos del Perú.* Lima: Instituto de Historia, Universidad Nacional Mayor de San Marcos.

Service, Elman R.

1955. "Indian-European Relations in Latin America." *American Anthropologist* 57:411–25.

Sherzer, Joel

1974. "Namakke, Sunmakke, Kormakke: Three Types of Cuna Speech Event." In *Explorations in the Ethnography of Speaking.* Richard Bauman and Joel Sherzer, eds. New York: Cambridge University Press.

Silverblatt, Irene

1987. *Moon, Sun, and Witches: Gender Ideologies and Class in Inca and Colonial Peru.* Princeton: Princeton University Press.

Singer, Milton

1955. "Cultural Patterns of Indigenous Civilizations." *Far Eastern Quarterly* 15:23–36.

Skar, Harald O.

1982. *The Warm Valley People.* Oslo: Universitetsforlaget.

Smith, Waldemar

1977. *The Fiesta System and Economic Change.* New York: Columbia University Press.

Solá, Donald F.

1972. "Quechua Language Handbook." Unpublished manuscript.

Solá, Donald F., and Antonio Cusihuamán

1975. *Quechua hablado del Cuzco, primero libro.* Ithaca, N.Y.: Cornell University, Latin American Studies Program.

Spalding, Karen

1973. "Kurakas and Commerce." *Hispanic American Historical Review* 53:581–99.

1974. *De indio a campesino.* Lima: Instituto de Estudios Peruanos.

1984. *Huarochirí: An Andean Society under Inca and Spanish Rule.* Stanford: Stanford University Press.

Stein, William W.

1961. *Hualcan: Life in the Highlands of Peru.* Ithaca, N.Y.: Cornell University Press.

Stern, Steve

1982. *Peru's Indian People and the Challenge of the Spanish Conquest.* Madison: University of Wisconsin Press.

1983. "Struggle for Solidarity: Class, Culture, and Community in Highland Indian America." *Radical History Review* 27:21–45.

Szeminski, Jan

1983. *La utopía tupamarista.* Lima: Pontifica Universidad Catolica del Perú.

Thompson, E. P.

1967. "Time, Work-Discipline, and Industrial Capitalism." *Past and Present* 38:56–97.

Tito Cusi Yupanqui Inca

[1568] 1917. "Relación de la conquista del Perú y hechos del Manco II." *Libros y documentos referentes a la historia del Perú.* Vol. 2. H. Oreteaga, ed. Lima.

Toledo, Francisco

[1575] 1925. "Ordenanzas . . . para los indios de Charcas." In *Gobernantes del Perú.* Vol. 8. Roberto Levillier, ed., pp. 304–82. Madrid: Juan Pueyo.

Tschopik, Harry

1951. "The Aymara of Chucuito, Peru. I. Magic." *Anthropological Papers of the American Museum of Natural History* 44(2):137–308.

Turner, Victor

1967. *The Forest of Symbols.* Ithaca, N.Y.: Cornell University Press.

1968. *The Drums of Affliction.* Oxford: Clarendon Press.

1969. *The Ritual Process.* Chicago: Aldine.

1974. *Dramas, Fields, and Metaphor.* Ithaca, N.Y.: Cornell University Press.

1979. *Process, Performance, and Pilgrimage.* New Delhi: Concept Publishing.

Turner, Victor, and Edith Turner

1978. *Image and Pilgrimage in Christian Culture.* New York: Columbia University Press.

Urioste, George

1983. *Hijos de Pariya Qaqa: La tradición oral de Waru Chiri.* 2 vols. Syracuse, N.Y.: Syracuse University, Maxwell School of Citizenship and Public Affairs.

Urioste de Aguirre, Marta

1978. "Los caciques guarache." In *Estudios bolivianos en homenaje a Gunnar Mendoza.* M. Urioste de Aguirre et al., eds., pp. 131–40. La Paz.

Urton, Gary

1984. "Chuta: el espacio de la práctica social en Pacariqtambo, Perú." *Revista Andina* 2(1):7–56.

1985. "Animal Metaphors and the Life Cycle in an Andean Community." In *Animal Myths and Metaphors in South America.* Gary Urton, ed., pp. 251–84. Salt Lake City: University of Utah Press.

Valcárcel Esparza, Carlos Daniel

1970. *Tupac Amaru.* Lima: Moncloa-Campodonico.

1971. *La rebelión de Tupac Amaru.* Vol. 2, *La rebelión.* Lima: Comisión Nacional del Sesquicentario de la Independencia del Perú.

Van den Berghe, Pierre, and George Primov

1977. *Inequality in the Peruvian Andes: Class and Ethnicity in Cuzco.* Columbia: University of Missouri Press.

Varese, Stéfano

1967. "La rebelión de Juan Santos Atahualpa: un movimiento mesiánico del siglo XVIII en la selva peruana." *Cuadernos de Antropología* 5(10):1–9.

Vargas Ugarte, Ruben, S.J.

1966. *Historia del Perú, Virreinato: 1596–1689.* Vol. 3, pp. 359–84. Lima: Editor Carlos Milla Batres.

Verlinden, Charles

1960. "L'état el l'administration des communautés indigénes dan l'empire espagnol d'Amérique." *Resumés des Communications,* International Congress of Historical Sciences. Goteborg: Almquist and Wiksell.

Wachtel, Nathan

1973. *Sociedad e ideología.* Lima: Instituto de Estudios Peruanos.

1977. *The Vision of the Vanquished.* Ben Reynolds and Sian Reynolds, trans. New York: Barnes and Noble.

Wagley, Charles

1965. "On the Concept of Social Race in the Americas." In *Contemporary Cultures and Societies of Latin America.* D. Heath and R. N. Adams, eds., pp. 531–45. New York: Random House.

Wagley, Charles, and Marvin Harris
 1955. "A Typology of Latin American Subcultures." *American Anthropologist* 57:428–51.
Wallerstein, Emmanuel
 1979. *The Capitalist World-Economy*. Cambridge: Cambridge University Press.
Weber, Max
 1978. *Economy and Society*. Guenther Roth and Claus Wittich, eds. Berkeley: University of California Press.
Webster, Steven
 1974. "Factores de la jerarquía social en una comunidad nativa quechua." *Estudios Andinos* 4(2):131–60.
Wilson, Monica
 1954. "Nyakyusa Ritual and Symbolism." *American Anthropologist* 58: 228–41.
Wolf, Eric R.
 1957. "Closed Corporate Communities of Mesoamerica and Central Java." *Southwest Journal of Anthropology* 13:1–18.
 1986. "The Vicissitudes of the Closed Corporate Peasant Community." *American Ethnologist* 13(2):325–29.
Worsley, Peter
 1984. *The Three Worlds*. Chicago: University of Chicago Press.
Zavala, Silvio
 1978. *El servicio personal de los indios en el Perú (extractos del siglo XVI)*. Vol. 1. Mexico: El Colegio de Mexico.
 1979. *El servicio personal de los indios en el Perú (extractos del siglo XVII)*. Vol. 2. Mexico: El Colegio de Mexico.
Zimmerman, Arthur Franklin
 1938. *Francisco de Toledo*. Caldwell, Idaho: Caxton Printers.
Zuidema, R. Tom
 1964. *The Ceque System of Cuzco*. Leiden: Brill.
 1977. "The Inka Kinship System: A New Theoretical View." In *Andean Kinship and Marriage*. Ralph Bolton and Enrique Mayer, eds. Washington: American Anthropological Association.
 1978. "Lieux sacrés et irrigation: Tradition historique, mythes et rituels au Cuzco." *Annales ESC* 33(5–6):1037–56.

Author Index

Subject Index

Agregado (ayllu), 54, 60, 71, 204, 245, 291 n.13

Agregado (fiscal category), 6, 124, 143, 152, 156, 157, 158, 159, 162, 163, 164, 284 n.6

Alcalde, 9, 38, 65, 66, 67, 68, 76–80, 87, 91, 151, 152, 162, 256, 262, 267, 291 n.13; in colonial period, 100; festival role, 80, 176, 180, 182–209 passim, 242, 245, 279 n.1

Alférez. *See* Festival sponsorship

Alférez festival, 38, 68, 175–77, 179

Alma samana, 186, 286 n.6

Anansaya. *See* Upper Moiety

Aqha. *See* Corn beer

Araya Chacti, 104, 117, 124, 125, 133, 146, 150, 152, 264

Authorities, indigenous, 7–8, 9–12, 15, 21, 52, 63, 95; evolution, 96, 150; of the historical Wisijsa and Yura, 104–5, 118–20, 141–43, 150, 151–53, 154, 162, 163. *See also* Ethnic lords; Kuraqkuna

Authority: defined, 265–66

Awki, 219, 221, 288 n.7

Ayllu, 12, 13–14, 15, 18, 23–24, 74, 87, 273, 287 n.14; in contemporary Yura, 38, 40, 44, 48, 51–64 passim, 193, 203–5, 251, 257, 258, 276, 290 n.11; defined, 49–51; major ayllu, 51, 53, 55, 56, 57, 65, 70, 142, 153, 203, 204, 207, 208, 230, 246, 248, 249, 251, 261; maximal or unitary ayllu, 53, 56, 64, 208, 234, 249, 251, 254, 261; minor ayllu, 56, 62, 65, 70, 72, 74, 142, 153, 204, 207, 208, 251, 261; obligations of membership, 60–63, 83, 84–85, 291 n.21; and territory, 56, 58; in Yura's past, 94, 104–5, 115, 117, 118, 119, 124–25, 133, 141–43, 146–47, 150, 151–53, 156–57, 158, 162

Aymara, 50, 57, 93, 104, 147, 298 n.2, 290 n.6

Boundary marker, 88–89, 245, 250–51, 252, 253, 254, 257–58, 259, 280 n.12

Cabildo, 100, 258, 292 n.23

Canton, 20, 21, 26, 42, 57, 59, 76, 86, 155, 248, 271. *See also* Yura (location)

Roger Neil Rasnake received his Ph.D. in anthropology from Cornell University in 1982. He has been an assistant professor of anthropology at Goucher College and spent a year on a Fulbright research fellowship in Bolivia. He is currently an advisor in anthropology at the Program for Alternative Development in Cochabamba, Bolivia.